Romantic and Victorian English Literature

ABOUT THE BOOK

In a strict sense, Victorian Literature is the literature produced during the reign of Queen Victoria (1837-1901) and corresponds to the Victorian era. It forms a link and transition between the writers of the romantic period and the very different literature of the 20 century. The Romantic period was one of major social change in England, because of the depopulation of the countryside and the rapid development of overcrowded industrial cities, that took place in the period roughly between 1798 and 1832. The movement of so many people in England was the result of two forces: the Agricultural Revolution, that involved the enclosure of the land, drove workers off the land, and the Industrial Revolution which provided them employment, "in the factories and mills, operated by machines driven by steam-power". Indeed, Romanticism may be seen in part as a reaction to the Industrial Revolution, though it was also a revolt against aristocratic social and political norms of the Age of Enlightenment, as well as a reaction against the scientific rationalization of nature. The French Revolution was an especially important influence on the political thinking of many at this time. The Victorian Age was essentially a period of peace and prosperity for England. The few colonial wars that broke out during this period exercised little adverse effects on the national life. The Crimean War, of course, caused a stir in England, but its effect were soon forgotten and the people "regained the normal tenor of their lives without feeling the aftermaths of war in their round of daily activities". This will be equally useful to undergraduate and postgraduate students besides researchers and the teachers of English.

ABOUT THE AUTHOR

Dr. Aprajita Sharma (b. 1964) is a professor of English at Govt. Hamidia Arts and Commerce P.G. College Bhopal. She obtained her doctorate in English from Barkatullah University Bhopal. She has presented a number of articles and research papers at international and national conferences and seminars in India. She has been teaching for the last 26 years. She has produced 22 research scholars who are working in India and abroad. She has published books namely 'A Semiotic Approach to H.D. Thoreau's Walden; [A book on American literature], 'Unspoken feelings' [A collection of short stories], 'Feelings of the Heart' [A collection of poems] and 'Introduction to linguistics' which provides a brief introduction to the subject.

Romantic and Victorian English Literature

Dr. Aprajita Sharma

AMIGA PRESS. INC
Delhi -110051

AMIGA PRESS INC.

H.O :- 28-A, Indra Park,

Chander Nagar, Delhi :- 110051 (India)

Tel :- 011-22504028, +91-98736-57000

Email :- amigapress@gmail.com
amigaeditorial@gmail.com
amigapub@gmail.com

Website :- www.amigapress.co.in

This edition is published by Amiga Press Inc.

ISBN : 978-93-84533-47-2

First Published 2019

Printed and bound by Replika Press Pvt. Ltd.

Preface

The early Romantic Poets brought a new emotionalism and introspection, and their emergence is marked by the first romantic manifesto in English literature, the "Preface" to Lyrical Ballads (1798). In it Wordsworth discusses what he sees as the elements of a new type of poetry, one based on the "real language of men", and which avoids the poetic diction of much 18th-century poetry. Here, Wordsworth gives his famous definition of poetry, as "the spontaneous overflow of powerful feelings" which "takes its origin from emotion recollected in tranquility."

The Romantic movement in English literature of the early 19th century has its roots in 18th-century poetry, the Gothic novel and the novel of sensibility. This includes the graveyard poets, who were a number of pre-Romantic English poets, writing in the 1740s and later, whose works are characterised by their gloomy meditations on mortality, "skulls and coffins, epitaphs and worms" in the context of the graveyard. To this was added, by later practitioners, a feeling for the 'sublime' and uncanny, and an interest in ancient English poetic forms and folk poetry.

The European Romantic movement reached America in the early 19th century. American Romanticism was just as multifaceted and individualistic as it was in Europe. Like the Europeans, the American Romantics demonstrated a high level of moral enthusiasm, commitment to individualism and the unfolding of the self, an emphasis on intuitive perception, and the assumption that the natural world was inherently good, while human society was filled with corruption. Romanticism became popular in American politics, philosophy and art. The movement appealed to the revolutionary spirit of America as well as to those longing to break free of the strict religious traditions of early settlement. The Romantics rejected rationalism and religious intellect. It appealed to those in opposition of Calvinism, which includes the belief that the destiny of each individual is preordained.

The Victorian Age was essentially a period of peace and prosperity for England. The few colonial wars that broke out during this period exercised little adverse effects on the national life. The Crimean War, of course, caused a stir in England, but its effect were soon forgotten and the people "regained the normal tenor of their lives without feeling the aftermaths of war in their round of daily activities".

It was in the Victorian era (1837-1901) that the novel became the leading form of literature in English. Most writers were now more concerned to meet the tastes of a large middle class reading public than to please aristocratic patrons. The best known works of the era include the emotionally powerful works of the Brontë sisters; the satire Vanity Fair by William Makepeace Thackeray; the realist novels of George Eliot; and Anthony Trollope's insightful portrayals of the lives of the landowning and professional classes.

Charles Dickens emerged on the literary scene in the 1830s, confirming the trend for serial publication. Dickens wrote vividly about London life and the struggles of the poor, but in a good-humoured fashion which was acceptable to readers of all classes. His early works such as the Pickwick Papers are masterpieces of comedy. Later his works became darker, without losing his genius for caricature. An interest in rural matters and the changing social and economic situation of the countryside may be seen in the novels of Thomas Hardy, Elizabeth Cleghorn Gaskell, and others. Leading poetic figures of the Victorian era included Alfred Tennyson, Robert Browning and his wife, Elizabeth Barrett Browning, Matthew Arnold and Dante Gabriel Rossetti and his sister, Christina Rossetti. Literature for children was published during the Victorian period, some of which has become globally well-known, such as the work of Lewis Carroll who was a proponent of nonsense verse, as was Edward Lear.

This is a reference book. All the matter is just compiled and edited in nature, taken from the various sources which are in public domain.

This will be equally useful to undergraduate and postgraduate students besides researchers and the teachers of English.

—*Editor*

Contents

1

Romantic English Literature

Romanticism was an artistic, literary, and intellectual movement that originated in Europe toward the end of the 18th century. Various dates are given for the Romantic period but here the publishing of William Wordsworth's *Lyrical Ballads* in 1798 is taken as the beginning, and the crowning of Queen Victoria in 1837 as its end. Romanticism arrived later in other parts of the English-speaking world, such as America.

The Romantic period was one of major social change in England, because of the depopulation of the countryside and the rapid development of overcrowded industrial cities, that took place in the period roughly between 1798 and 1832. The movement of so many people in England was the result of two forces: the Agricultural Revolution, that involved the enclosure of the land, drove workers off the land, and the Industrial Revolution which provided them employment, "in the factories and mills, operated by machines driven by steam-power". Indeed, Romanticism may be seen in part as a reaction to the Industrial Revolution, though it was also a revolt against aristocratic social and political norms of the Age of Enlightenment, as well as a reaction against the scientific rationalization of nature. The French Revolution was an especially important influence on the political thinking of many at this time.

ROMANTIC POETRY

The physical landscape is prominent in the poetry of this period—the Romantics, and especially Wordsworth, are often described as 'nature poets'. However, these 'nature poems' have wider concerns in that they are often meditations on "an emotional problem or personal crisis".

The poet, painter, and printmaker William Blake (1757–1827) was an early writer of this kind. Largely disconnected from the major streams of the literature of the time, Blake was generally unrecognised during his lifetime, but is now considered a seminal figure in the history of both the poetry and visual arts of the Romantic Age. Considered mad by contemporaries for his idiosyncratic views, Blake is held in high regard by later critics for his expressiveness and creativity, and for the philosophical and mystical undercurrents within his work. Among his most important works are *Songs of Innocence* (1789) and *Songs of Experience* (1794) "and profound and difficult 'prophecies' " such as *Visions of the Daughters of Albion* (1793), *The First Book of Urizen* (1794), *Milton* (1804–?11), and "Jerusalem: the Emanation of the Giant Albion" (1804–?20).

After Blake, among the earliest Romantics were the Lake Poets, a small group of friends, including William Wordsworth (1770–1850), Samuel Taylor Coleridge (1772–1834), Robert Southey (1774–1843) and journalist Thomas de Quincey (1785–1859). However, at the time Walter Scott (1771–1832) was the most famous poet. Scott achieved immediate success with his long narrative poem *The Lay of the Last Minstrel* in 1805, followed by the full epic poem *Marmion* in 1808. Both were set in the distant Scottish past.

The early Romantic Poets brought a new emotionalism and introspection, and their emergence is marked by the first romantic manifesto in English literature, the "Preface" to *Lyrical Ballads* (1798). In it Wordsworth discusses what he sees as the elements of a new type of poetry, one based on the "real language of men", and which avoids the poetic diction of much 18th-century poetry. Here, Wordsworth gives his famous definition of poetry, as "the spontaneous overflow of powerful feelings" which "takes its origin from emotion recollected in tranquility." The poems in *Lyrical Ballads* were mostly by Wordsworth, though Coleridge contributed, one of the great poems of English literature, the long "Rime of the Ancient Mariner", a tragic ballad about the survival of one sailor through a series of supernatural events on his voyage through the South Seas, and which involves the symbolically significant slaying of an albatross. Coleridge is also especially remembered for "Kubla Khan", "Frost at Midnight", "Dejection: an Ode", "Christabel", as well as the major prose work *Biographia Literaria*. His critical work, especially on Shakespeare, was highly influential, and he helped introduce German idealist philosophy to English-speaking culture. Coleridge and Wordsworth, along with Carlyle, were a major influence, through Emerson, on American transcendentalism. Among Wordsworth's most important poems, are "Michael", "Lines Composed a Few Miles Above Tintern Abbey", "Resolution and Independence", "Ode: Intimations of Immortality from Recollections of Early Childhood" and the long, autobiographical, epic *The Prelude*. *The Prelude* was begun in 1799 but published posthumously in 1850. Wordsworth's poetry is noteworthy for how he "inverted the traditional hierarchy of poetic genres, subjects, and style by elevating humble and rustic life and the plain [...] into the main subject and medium of poetry in general", and how, in Coleridge's words, he awakens in the reader "freshness of sensation" in his depiction of familiar, commonplace objects.

Robert Southey (1774–1843) was another of the so-called "Lake Poets", and Poet Laureate for 30 years from 1813 to his death in 1843. Although his fame has been long eclipsed by that of his contemporaries and friends William Wordsworth and Samuel Taylor Coleridge. Thomas De Quincey (1785–1859) was an English essayist, best known for his *Confessions of an English Opium-Eater* (1821), an autobiographical account of his laudanum use and its effect on his life. William Hazlitt (1778–1830), friend of both Coleridge and Wordsworth, is another important essayist at this time, though today he is best known for his literary criticism, especially *Characters of Shakespeare's Plays* (1817–18).

Second generation

The second generation of Romantic poets includes Lord Byron (1788–1824), Percy Bysshe Shelley (1792–1822) and John Keats (1795–1821). Byron, however, was still influenced by 18th-century satirists and was, perhaps the least 'romantic' of the three, preferring "the brilliant wit of Pope to what he called the 'wrong poetical system' of his Romantic contemporaries". Byron achieved enormous fame and influence throughout Europe with works exploiting the violence and drama of their exotic and historical settings.

Goethe called Byron "undoubtedly the greatest genius of our century". A trip to Europe resulted in the first two cantos of Childe Harold's Pilgrimage (1812), a mock-heroic epic of a young man's adventures in Europe, but also a sharp satire against London society.

The poem contains elements thought to be autobiographical, as Byron generated some of the storyline from experience gained during his travels between 1809 and 1811. However, despite the success of *Childe Harold* and other works, Byron was forced to leave England for good in 1816 and seek asylum on the Continent, because, among other things, of his alleged incestuous affair with his half-sister Augusta Leigh. Here he joined Percy Bysshe and Mary Shelley, with his secretary John William Polidori on the shores of Lake Geneva, during the 'year without a summer'. Polidori's *The Vampyre* was published in 1819, creating the literary vampire genre. This short story was inspired by the life of Lord Byron and his poem *The Giaour* (1813). Between 1819 and 1824 Byron published his unfinished epic satire *Don Juan*, which, though initially condemned by the critics, "was much admired by Goethe who translated part of it".

Shelley is perhaps best known for poems such as *Ozymandias, Ode to the West Wind, To a Skylark, Music, When Soft Voices Die, The Cloud, The Masque of Anarchy* and *Adonaïs,* an elegy written on the death of Keats. Shelley's early profession of atheism, in the tract "The Necessity of Atheism", led to his expulsion from Oxford, and branded him as a radical agitator and thinker, setting an early pattern of marginalization and ostracism from the intellectual and political circles of his time. Similarly, Shelley's 1851 essay "A Defense of Poetry" displayed a radical view of poetry, in which the poet acts as "the unacknowledged legislators of the world," because, of all of artists, they best perceive the undergirding structure of society. His close circle of admirers, however, included the most progressive thinkers of the day, including his future father-in-law, philosopher William Godwin. A work like *Queen Mab* (1813) reveal Shelley, "as the direct heir to the French and British revolutionary intellectuals of the 1790s. Shelley became an idol of the next three or four generations of poets, including important Victorian and Pre-Raphaelite poets such as Robert Browning, and Dante Gabriel Rossetti, as well as later W. B. Yeats. Shelley's influential poem *The Masque of Anarchy* (1819) calls for nonviolence in protest and political action. It is perhaps the first modern statement of the principle of nonviolent protest.Mahatma Gandhi's passive resistance was influenced and inspired by Shelley's verse, and Gandhi would often quote the poem to vast audiences.

Though John Keats shared Byron and Shelley's radical politics, "his best poetry is not political", but is especially noted for its sensuous music and imagery, along with a concern with material beauty and the transience of life. Among his most famous works are: "The Eve of St Agnes", "Ode to Psyche", "La Belle Dame sans Merci", "Ode to a Nightingale", "Ode on a Grecian Urn", "Ode on Melancholy", "To Autumn" and the incomplete *Hyperion,* a 'philosophical' poem in blank verse, which was "conceived on the model of Milton's *Paradise Lost* ". Keats' letters "are among the finest in English" and important "for their discussion of his aesthetic ideas", including 'negative capability' ". Keats has always been regarded as a major Romantic, "and his stature as a poet has grown steadily through all changes of fashion".

Other poets

Another important poet in this period was John Clare (1793–1864), Clare was the son of a farm labourer, who came to be known for his celebratory representations of the English countryside and his lamentation for the changes taking place in rural England. His poetry underwent a major re-evaluation in the late 20th century and he is often now considered to be among the most important 19th-century poets. His biographer Jonathan Bate states that Clare was "the greatest labouring-class poet that England has ever produced. No one has ever written more powerfully of nature, of a rural childhood, and of the alienated and unstable self".

George Crabbe (1754–1832) was an English poet who, during the Romantic period, wrote "closely observed, realistic portraits of rural life [...] in the heroic couplets of the Augustan age". Lord Byron who was an admirer of Crabbe's poetry, described him as "nature's sternest painter, yet the best". Modern critic Frank Whitehead has said that "Crabbe, in his verse tales in particular, is an important–indeed, a major–poet whose work has been and still is seriously undervalued." Crabbe's works include *The Village* (1783), *Poems* (1807), *The Borough* (1810), and his poetry collections *Tales* (1812) and *Tales of the Hall* (1819).

Women poets

Women writers were increasingly active in all genres throughout the 18th century, and by the 1790s women's poetry was flourishing. Notable poets later in the period include Anna Laetitia Barbauld, Joanna Baillie, Susanna Blamire, Hannah More. Other women poets include Mary Alcock (c. 1742-1798) and Mary Robinson (1758-1800) both of whom "highlighted the enormous discrepancy between life for the rich and the poor", and Felicia Hemans (1793-1835) author of nineteen individual books during her lifetime, and who continued to republished widely after her death in 1835.

More interest has been shown in recent years in Dorothy Wordsworth (1771-1855), William's sister, who "was modest about her writing abilities, [but] she produced poems of her own; and her journals and travel narratives certainly provided inspiration for her brother."

In the past decades there has been substantial scholarly and critical work done on women poets of this period, both by make them available in print or online, and second, to assess them and position them within the literary tradition.

THE ROMANTIC MOVEMENT

The reaction which was bound to accompany the triumph of Pseudo-classicism, as a reassertion of those instincts in human nature which Pseudo-classicism disregarded, took the form of a distinct Romantic Revival. Beginning just about as Pope's reputation was reaching its climax, and gathering momentum throughout the greater part of the eighteenth century, this movement eventually gained a predominance as complete as that which Pseudo-classicism had enjoyed, and became the chief force, not only in England but in all Western Europe, in the literature of the whole nineteenth century. The impulse was not confined to literature, but permeated all the life of the time. In the sphere of religion, especially, the second decade of the eighteenth century saw the awakening of the English church from lethargy by the great revival of John and Charles Wesley, whence, quite contrary to their original intention, sprang the Methodist denomination. In political life the French Revolution was a result of the same set of influences. Romanticism showed itself partly in the supremacy of the Sentimental Comedy and in the great share taken by Sentimentalism in the development of the novel, of both of which we shall speak hereafter; but its fullest and most steadily progressive manifestation was in non-dramatic poetry. Its main traits as they appear in the eighteenth century are as clearly marked as the contrasting ones of Pseudo-classicism, and we can enumerate them distinctly, though it must of course be understood that they appear in different authors in very different degrees and combinations.

1. There is, among the Romanticists, a general breaking away not only from the definite pseudo-classical principles, but from the whole idea of submission to fixed authority. Instead there is a spirit of independence and revolt, an insistence on the value of originality and the right of the individual to express himself in his own fashion.
2. There is a strong reassertion of the value of emotion, imagination, and enthusiasm. This naturally involves some reaction against the pseudo-classic, and also the true classic, regard for finished form.
3. There is a renewal of genuine appreciation and love for external Nature, not least for her large and great aspects, such as mountains and the sea. The contrast between the pseudo-classical and the romantic attitude in this respect is clearly illustrated, as has often been pointed out, by the difference between the impressions recorded by Addison and by the poet Gray in the presence of the Alps. Addison, discussing what he saw in Switzerland, gives most of his attention to the people and politics. One journey he describes as 'very troublesome,' adding: 'You can't imagine how I am pleased with the sight of a plain.' In the mountains he is conscious chiefly of difficulty and danger, and the nearest approach to admiration which he indicates is 'an agreeable kind of horror.' Gray, on the other hand, speaks of the Grande Chartreuse

as 'one of the most solemn, the most romantic, and the most astonishing scenes.... I do not remember to have gone ten paces without an exclamation that there was no restraining. Not a precipice, not a torrent, nor a cliff, but is pregnant with religion and poetry.'

4. The same passionate appreciation extends with the Romanticists to all full and rich beauty and everything grand and heroic.
5. This is naturally connected also with a love for the remote, the strange, and the unusual, for mystery, the supernatural, and everything that creates wonder. Especially, there is a great revival of interest in the Middle Ages, whose life seemed to the men of the eighteenth century, and indeed to a large extent really was, picturesque and by comparison varied and adventurous. In the eighteenth century this particular revival was called 'Gothic,' a name which the Pseudo-classicists, using it as a synonym for 'barbarous,' had applied to the Middle Ages and all their works, on the mistaken supposition that all the barbarians who overthrew the Roman Empire and founded the medieval states were Goths.
6. In contrast to the pseudo-classical preference for abstractions, there is, among the Romanticists, a devotion to concrete things, the details of Nature and of life. In expression, of course, this brings about a return to specific words and phraseology, in the desire to picture objects clearly and fully.
7. There is an increasing democratic feeling, a breaking away from the interest in artificial social life and a conviction that every human being is worthy of respect. Hence sprang the sentiment of universal brotherhood and the interest in universal freedom, which finally extended even to the Negroes and resulted in the abolition of slavery. But from the beginning there was a reawakening of interest in the life of the common people—an impulse which is not inconsistent with the love of the remote and unusual, but rather means the discovery of a neglected world of novelty at the very door of the educated and literary classes.
8. There is a strong tendency to melancholy, which is often carried to the point of morbidness and often expresses itself in meditation and moralizing on the tragedies of life and the mystery of death. This inclination is common enough in many romantic-spirited persons of all times, and it is always a symptom of immaturity or lack of perfect balance. Among the earlier eighteenth century Romanticists there was a very nourishing crop of doleful verse, since known from the place

where most of it was located, as the 'Graveyard poetry.' Even Gray's 'Elegy in a Country Churchyard' is only the finest representative of this form, just as Shakspere's 'Hamlet' is the culmination of the crude Elizabethan tragedy of blood. So far as the mere tendency to moralize is concerned, the eighteenth century Romanticists continue with scarcely any perceptible change the practice of the Pseudo-classicists.

9. In poetic form, though the Romanticists did not completely abandon the pentameter couplet for a hundred years, they did energetically renounce any exclusive allegiance to it and returned to many other meters. Milton was one of their chief masters, and his example led to the revival of blank verse and of the octo-syllabic couplet. There was considerable use also of the Spenserian stanza, and development of a great variety of lyric stanza forms, though not in the prodigal profusion of the Elizabethan and Jacobean period.

James Thomson

The first author in whom the new impulse found really definite expression was the Scotsman James Thomson. At the age of twenty-five, Thomson, like many of his countrymen during his century and the previous one, came fortune-hunting to London, and the next year, 1726, while Pope was issuing his translation of 'The Odyssey,' he published a blank-verse poem of several hundred lines on 'Winter.' Its genuine though imperfect appreciation and description of Nature as she appears on the broad sweeps of the Scottish moors, combined with its novelty, gave it great success, and Thomson went on to write also of Summer, Spring and Autumn, publishing the whole work as 'The Seasons' in 1730.

He was rewarded by the gift of sinecure offices from the government and did some further writing, including, probably, the patriotic lyric, 'Rule, Britannia,' and also pseudo-classical tragedies; but his only other poem of much importance is 'The Castle of Indolence' (a subject appropriate to his own good-natured, easy-going disposition), which appeared just before his death, in 1748. In it he employs Spenser's stanza, with real skill, but in a half-jesting fashion which the later eighteenth-century Romanticists also seem to have thought necessary when they adopted it, apparently as a sort of apology for reviving so old-fashioned a form.

'The Seasons' was received with enthusiasm not only in England but in France and Germany, and it gave an impulse for the writing of descriptive poetry which lasted for a generation; but Thomson's romantic achievement, though important, is tentative and incomplete, like that of all beginners. He described Nature from full and sympathetic first-hand observation, but there is still a certain stiffness about his manner, very different from the intimate and confident familiarity and power of spiritual interpretation which characterizes the great poets of three generations later. Indeed, the attempt to write several thousand lines of pure descriptive poetry was in itself ill-judged, since as the German critic Lessing later pointed out, poetry is the natural medium not for description but for narration; and Thomson himself virtually admitted this in part by resorting to long dedications and narrative episodes to fill out his scheme. Further, romantic as he was in spirit, he was not able to free himself from the pseudo-classical mannerisms; every page of his poem abounds with the old lifeless phraseology—'the finny tribes' for 'the fishes,' 'the vapoury whiteness' for 'the snow' or 'the hard-won treasures of the year' for 'the crops.' His blank verse, too, is comparatively clumsy—padded with unnecessary words and the lines largely end-stopped.

William Collins

There is marked progress in romantic feeling and power of expression as we pass from Thomson to his disciple, the frail lyric poet, William Collins. Collins, born at Chichester, was an undergraduate at Oxford when he published 'Persian Eclogues' in rimed couplets to which the warm feeling and free metrical treatment give much of romantic effect. In London three years later (1746) Collins put forth his significant work in a little volume of 'Odes.' Discouraged by lack of appreciation, always abnormally high-strung and neurasthenic, he gradually lapsed into insanity, and died at the age of thirty-seven. Collins' poems show most of the romantic traits and their impetuous emotion often expresses itself in the form of the false Pindaric ode which Cowley had introduced. His 'Ode on the Popular Superstitions of the Highlands,' further, was one of the earliest pieces of modern literature to return for inspiration to the store of medieval supernaturalism, in this case to Celtic supernaturalism. But Collins has also an exquisiteness of feeling which makes others of his pieces perfect examples of the true classical style.

The two poems in 'Horatian' ode forms, that is in regular short stanzas, the 'Ode Written in the Year 1746' and the 'Ode to Evening' (unrimed), are particularly fine. With all this, Collins too was not able to escape altogether from pseudo-classicism. His subjects are often abstract—'The Passions,' 'Liberty,' and the like; his characters, too, in almost all his poems, are merely the old abstract personifications, Fear, Fancy, Spring, and many others; and his phraseology is often largely in the pseudo-classical fashion. His work illustrates, therefore, in an interesting way the conflict of poetic forces in his time and the influence of environment on a poet's mind. The true classic instinct and the romanticism are both his own; the pseudo-classicism belongs to the period.

Thomas Gray

Precisely the same conflict of impulses appears in the lyrics of a greater though still minor poet of the same generation, a man of perhaps still more delicate sensibilities than Collins, namely Thomas Gray. Gray, the only survivor of many sons of a widow who provided for him by keeping a millinery shop, was born in 1716. At Eton he became intimate with Horace Walpole, the son of the Prime Minister, who was destined to become an amateur leader in the Romantic Movement, and after some years at Cambridge the two traveled together on the Continent. Lacking the money for the large expenditure required in the study of law, Gray took up his residence in the college buildings at Cambridge, where he lived as a recluse, much annoyed by the noisy undergraduates. During his last three years he held the appointment and salary of professor of modern history, but his timidity prevented him from delivering any lectures. He died in

1771. He was primarily a scholar and perhaps the most learned man of his time. He was familiar with the literature and history not only of the ancient world but of all the important modern nations of western Europe, with philosophy, the sciences of painting, architecture, botany, zoology, gardening, entomology (he had a large collection of insects), and even heraldry. He was himself an excellent musician. Indeed almost the only subject of contemporary knowledge in which he was not proficient was mathematics, for which he had an aversion, and which prevented him from taking a college degree.

The bulk of Gray's poetry is very small, no larger, in fact, than that of Collins. Matthew Arnold argued in a famous essay that his productivity was checked by the uncongenial pseudo-classic spirit of the age, which, says Arnold, was like a chill north wind benumbing his inspiration, so that 'he never spoke out.' The main reason, however, is really to be found in Gray's own over-painstaking and diffident disposition. In him, as in Hamlet, anxious and scrupulous striving for perfection went far to paralyze the power of creation; he was unwilling to write except at his best, or to publish until he had subjected his work to repeated revisions, which sometimes, as in the case of his 'Elegy Written in a Country Churchyard,' extended over many years. He is the extreme type of the academic poet.

His work shows, however, considerable variety, including real appreciation for Nature, as in the 'Ode on the Spring,' delightful quiet humor, as in the

'Ode on a Favorite Cat,' rather conventional moralizing, as in the 'Ode on a Distant Prospect of Eton College,' magnificent expression of the fundamental human emotions, as in the 'Elegy,' and warlike vigor in the 'Norse Ode' translated from the 'Poetic Edda' in his later years. In the latter he manifests his interest in Scandinavian antiquity, which had then become a minor object of romantic enthusiasm. The student should consider for himself the mingling of the true classic, pseudo-classic, and romantic elements in the poems, not least in the 'Elegy,' and the precise sources of their appeal and power. In form most of them are regular 'Horatian' odes, but 'The Bard' and 'The Progress of Poesy' are the best English examples of the genuine Pindaric ode.

Oliver Goldsmith

Next in order among the romantic poets after Gray, and more thoroughly romantic than Gray, was Oliver Goldsmith, though, with characteristic lack of the power of self-criticism, he supposed himself to be a loyal follower of Johnson and therefore a member of the opposite camp. Goldsmith, as every one knows, is one of the most attractive and lovable figures in English literature. Like Burke, of mixed English and Irish ancestry, the son of a poor country curate of the English Church in Ireland, he was born in 1728. Awkward, sensitive, and tender-hearted, he suffered greatly in childhood from the unkindness of his fellows. As a poor student at the University of Dublin he was not more happy, and his lack of application delayed the gaining of his degree until two years after the regular time.

The same Celtic desultoriness characterized all the rest of his life, though it could not thwart his genius. Rejected as a candidate for the ministry, he devoted three years to the nominal study of medicine at the Universities of Edinburgh and Leyden (in Holland). Next he spent a year on a tramping trip through Europe, making his way by playing the flute and begging. Then, gravitating naturally to London, he earned his living by working successively for a druggist, for the novelist-printer Samuel Richardson, as a teacher in a boys' school, and as a hack writer. At last at the age of thirty-two he achieved success with a series of periodical essays later entitled 'The Citizen of the World,' in which he criticized European politics and society with skill and insight. Bishop Percy now introduced him to Johnson, who from this time watched over him and saved him from the worst results of his irresponsibility.

He was one of the original members of 'The Club.' In 1764 occurred the well-known and characteristic incident of the sale of 'The Vicar of Wakefield.' Arrested for debt at his landlady's instance, Goldsmith sent for Johnson and showed him the manuscript of the book. Johnson took it to a publisher, and though without much expectation of success asked and received L60 for it. It was published two years later. Meanwhile in 1764 appeared Goldsmith's descriptive poem, 'The Traveler,' based on his own experiences in Europe. Six years later it was followed by 'The Deserted Village,' which was received with the great enthusiasm that it merited.

Such high achievement in two of the main divisions of literature was in itself remarkable, especially as Goldsmith was obliged to the end of his life to spend much of his time in hack writing, but in the later years of his short life he turned also with almost as good results to the drama (comedy). We must stop here for the few words of general summary which are all that the eighteenth century drama need receive in a brief survey like the present one. During the first half of the century, as we have seen, an occasional pseudo-classical tragedy was written, none of them of any greater excellence than Addison's 'Cato' and Johnson's 'Irene.'

The second quarter of the century was largely given over to farces and burlesques, which absorbed the early literary activity of the novelist Henry Fielding, until their attacks on Walpole's government led to a severe licensing act, which suppressed them. But the most distinctive and predominant forms of the middle and latter half of the century were, first, the Sentimental Comedy, whose origin may be roughly assigned to Steele, and, second, the domestic melodrama, which grew out of it. In the Sentimental Comedy the elements of mirth and romance which are the legitimate bases of comedy were largely subordinated to exaggerated pathos, and in the domestic melodrama the experiences of insignificant persons of the middle class were presented for sympathetic consideration in the same falsetto fashion. Both forms (indeed, they were one in spirit) were extreme products of the romantic return to sentiment and democratic feeling. Both were enormously popular and, crossing the Channel, like Thomson's poetic innovation, exerted a great influence on the drama of France and Germany (especially in the work of Lessing), and in general on the German Romantic Movement. Goldsmith was inferior to no one in genuine sentiment, but he was disgusted at the sentimental excesses of these plays.

His 'Good Natured Man,' written with the express purpose of opposing them, and brought out in 1768, was reasonably successful, and in 1771 his far superior 'She Stoops to Conquer' virtually put an end to Sentimental Comedy. This is one of the very few English comedies of a former generation which are still occasionally revived on the stage today. Goldsmith's comedies, we may add here for completeness, were shortly followed by the more brilliant ones of another Irish-Englishman, Richard Brinsley Sheridan, who displayed Congreve's wit without his cynicism. These were 'The Rivals,' produced in 1775, when Sheridan was only twenty-four, and 'The School for Scandal,' 1777.

Sheridan, a reckless man of fashion, continued most of his life to be owner of Drury Lane Theater, but he soon abandoned playwriting to become one of the leaders of the Whig party. With Burke and Fox, as we have seen, he conducted the impeachment of Hastings.

'She Stoops to Conquer' was Goldsmith's last triumph. A few months later, in 1774, he died at the age of only forty-five, half submerged, as usual, in foolish debts, but passionately mourned not only by his acquaintances in the literary and social worlds, but by a great army of the poor and needy to whom he had been a benefactor. In the face of this testimony to his human worth his childish vanities and other weaknesses may well be pardoned. All Goldsmith's literary work is characterized by one main quality, a charming atmosphere of optimistic happiness which is the expression of the best side of his own nature.

The scene of all his most important productions, very appropriately, is the country—the idealized English country. Very much, to be sure, in all his works has to be conceded to the spirit of romance. Both in 'The Vicar of Wakefield' and in 'She Stoops to Conquer' characterization is mostly conventional, and events are very arbitrarily manipulated for the sake of the effects in rather free-and-easy disregard of all principles of motivation. But the kindly knowledge of the main forces in human nature, the unfailing sympathy, and the irrepressible conviction that happiness depends in the last analysis on the individual will and character make Goldsmith's writings, especially 'The Vicar,' delightful and refreshing. All in all, however, 'The Deserted Village' is his masterpiece, with its romantic regret, verging on tragedy but softened away from it, and its charming type characterizations, as incisive as those of Chaucer and Dryden, but without any of Dryden's biting satire. In the choice of the rimed couplet for 'The Traveler' and 'The Deserted Village' the influence of pseudo-classicism and of Johnson appears; but Goldsmith's treatment of the form, with his variety in pauses and his simple but fervid eloquence, make it a very different thing from the rimed couplet of either Johnson or Pope.

'The Deserted Village,' it should be added, is not a description of any actual village, but a generalized picture of existing conditions. Men of wealth in England and Ireland were enlarging their sheep pastures and their hunting grounds by buying up land and removing villages, and Goldsmith, like Sir

Thomas More, two hundred years earlier, and likewise patriots of all times, deeply regretted the tendency.

Percy, Macpherson and Chatterton

The appearance of Thomson's 'Winter' in 1726 is commonly taken as conveniently marking the beginning of the Romantic Movement. Another of its conspicuous dates is 1765, the year of the publication of the 'Reliques [pronounced Relics] of Ancient English Poetry' of the enthusiastic antiquarian Thomas (later Bishop) Percy. Percy drew from many sources, of which the most important was a manuscript volume, in which an anonymous seventeenth century collector had copied a large number of old poems and which Percy rescued just in the nick of time, as the maids in the house of one of his friends were beginning to use it as kindling for the fires. His own book consisted of something less than two hundred very miscellaneous poems, ranging in date from the fourteenth century to his own day. Its real importance, however, lies in the fact that it contained a number of the old popular ballads. Neither Percy himself nor any one else in his time understood the real nature of these ballads and their essential difference from other poetry, and Percy sometimes tampered with the text and even filled out gaps with stanzas of his own, whose sentimental style is ludicrously inconsistent with the primitive vigor of the originals. But his book, which attained great popularity, marks the beginning of the special study of the ballads and played an important part in the revival of interest in medieval life.

Still greater interest was aroused at the time by the Ossianic poems of James Macpherson. From 1760 to 1763 Macpherson, then a young Highland Scots schoolmaster, published in rapid succession certain fragments of Gaelic verse and certain more extended works in poetical English prose which, he asserted, were part of the originals, discovered by himself, and translations, of the poems of the legendary Scottish bard Ossian, of the third Christian century. These productions won him substantial material rewards in the shape of high political offices throughout the rest of his long life. About the genuineness of the compositions, however, a violent controversy at once arose, and Dr. Johnson was one of the skeptics who vigorously denounced Macpherson as a shameless impostor. The general conviction of scholars of the present day is that while Macpherson may have found some fragments of very ancient Gaelic verse in circulation among the Highlanders, he fabricated most of what he published. These works, however, 'Fingal' and the rest, certainly contributed to the Romantic Movement; and they are not only unique productions, but, in small quantities, still interesting. They can best be described as reflections of the misty scenes of Macpherson's native Highlands—vague impressionistic glimpses, succeeding one another in purposeless repetition, of bands of marching warriors whose weapons intermittently flash and clang through the fog, and of heroic women, white-armed and with flowing hair, exhorting the heroes to the combat or lamenting their fall.

A very minor figure, but one of the most pathetic in the history of English literature, is that of Thomas Chatterton. While he was a boy in Bristol, Chatterton's imagination was possessed by the medieval buildings of the city, and when some old documents fell into his hands he formed the idea of composing similar works in both verse and prose and passing them off as medieval productions which he had discovered. To his imaginary author he gave the name of Thomas Rowley. Entirely successful in deceiving his fellow-townsmen, and filled with a great ambition, Chatterton went to London, where, failing to secure patronage, he committed suicide as the only resource against the begging to which his proud spirit could not submit. This was in 1770, and he was still only eighteen years old. Chatterton's work must be viewed under several aspects. His imitation of the medieval language was necessarily very imperfect and could mislead no one today; from this point of view the poems have no permanent significance. The moral side of his action need not be seriously weighed, as Chatterton never reached the age of responsibility and if he had lived would soon have passed from forgery to genuine work. That he might have achieved much is suggested by the evidences of real genius in his boyish output, which probably justify Wordsworth's description, of him as 'the marvelous boy.' That he would have become one of the great English poets, however, is much more open to question.

William Cowper

Equally pathetic is the figure of William Cowper (pronounced either Cowper or Cooper), whose much longer life (1731-1800) and far larger literary production give him a more important actual place than can be claimed for Chatterton, though his natural ability was far less and his significance today is chiefly historical. Cowper's career, also, was largely frustrated by the same physical weaknesses which had ruined Collins, present in the later poet in still more distressing degree. Cowper is clearly a transition poet, sharing largely, in a very mild fashion, in some of the main romantic impulses, but largely pseudo-classical in his manner of thought and expression. His life may be briefly summarized. Morbid timidity and equally morbid religious introspection, aggravated by disappointments in love, prevented him as a young man from accepting a very comfortable clerkship in the House of Lords and drove him into intermittent insanity, which closed more darkly about him in his later years. He lived the greater part of his mature life in the household of a Mrs. Unwin, a widow for whom he had a deep affection and whom only his mental affliction prevented him from marrying.

A long residence in the wretched village of Olney, where he forced himself to cooperate in all phases of religious work with the village clergyman, the stern enthusiast John Newton, produced their joint collection of 'Olney Hymns,' many of which deservedly remain among the most popular in our church song-books; but it inevitably increased Cowper's disorder. After this he resigned himself to a perfectly simple life, occupied with the writing of poetry, the care of pets, gardening, and carpentry. The bulk of his work consists of long moralizing poems, prosy, prolix, often trivial, and today largely unreadable. Same of them are in the rimed couplet and others in blank verse. His blank-verse translation of Homer, published in 1791, is more notable, and 'Alexander Selkirk' and the humorous doggerel 'John Gilpin' are famous; but his most significant poems are a few lyrics and descriptive pieces in which he speaks out his deepest feelings with the utmost pathetic or tragic power.

In the expression of different moods of almost intolerable sadness 'On the Receipt of My Mother's Picture' and 'To Mary' (Mrs. Unwin) can scarcely be surpassed, and 'The Castaway' is final as the restrained utterance of morbid religious despair. Even in his long poems, in his minutely loving treatment of Nature he is the most direct precursor of Wordsworth, and he is one of the earliest outspoken opponents of slavery and cruelty to animals. How unsuited in all respects his delicate and sensitive nature was to the harsh experiences of actual life is suggested by Mrs. Browning with vehement sympathy in her poem, 'Cowper's Grave.'

William Blake

Still another utterly unworldly and frankly abnormal poet, though of a still different temperament, was William Blake (1757-1827), who in many respects is one of the most extreme of all romanticists. Blake, the son of a London retail shopkeeper, received scarcely any book education, but at fourteen he was apprenticed to an engraver, who stimulated his imagination by setting him to work at making drawings in Westminster Abbey and other old churches. His training was completed by study at the Royal Academy of Arts, and for the rest of his life he supported himself, in poverty, with the aid of a devoted wife, by keeping a print-and-engraving shop. Among his own engravings the best known is the famous picture of Chaucer's Canterbury Pilgrims, which is not altogether free from the weird strangeness that distinguished most of his work in all lines.

For in spite of his commonplace exterior life Blake was a thorough mystic to whom the angels and spirits that he beheld in trances were at least as real as the material world. When his younger brother died he declared that he saw the released soul mount through the ceiling, clapping its hands in joy. The bulk of his writing consists of a series of 'prophetic books' in verse and prose, works, in part, of genius, but of unbalanced genius, and virtually unintelligible. His lyric poems, some of them composed when he was no more than thirteen years old, are unlike anything else anywhere, and some of them are of the highest quality. Their controlling trait is childlikeness; for Blake remained all his life one of those children of whom is the Kingdom of Heaven. One of their commonest notes is that of childlike delight in the mysterious joy and beauty of the world, a delight sometimes touched, it is true, as in 'The Tiger,' with a maturer consciousness of the wonderful and terrible power behind all the beauty. Blake has intense indignation also for all cruelty and everything which he takes for cruelty, including the shutting up of children in school away from the happy life of out-of-doors. These are the chief sentiments of 'Songs of Innocence.' In 'Songs of Experience' the shadow of relentless fact falls somewhat more perceptibly across the page, though the prevailing ideas are the same. Blake's significant product is very small, but it deserves much greater reputation than it has actually attained. One characteristic external fact should be added. Since Blake's poverty rendered him unable to pay for having his books printed, he himself performed the enormous labor of engraving them, page by page, often with an ornamental margin about the text.

Robert Burns

Blake, deeply romantic as he is by nature, virtually stands by himself, apart from any movement or group, and the same is equally true of the somewhat earlier lyrist in whom eighteenth century poetry culminates, namely Robert Burns. Burns, the oldest of the seven children of two sturdy Scotch peasants of the best type, was born in 1759 in Ayrshire, just beyond the northwest border of England.

In spite of extreme poverty, the father joined with some of his neighbors in securing the services of a teacher for their children, and the household possessed a few good books, including Shakspere and Pope, whose influence on the future poet was great. But the lot of the family was unusually hard. The father's health failed early and from childhood the boys were obliged to do men's work in the field. Robert later declared, probably with some bitter exaggeration, that his life had combined 'the cheerless gloom of a hermit with the unceasing moil of a galley slave.'

His genius, however, like his exuberant spirit, could not be crushed out. His mother had familiarized him from the beginning with the songs and ballads of which the country was full, and though he is said at first to have had so little ear for music that he could scarcely distinguish one tune from another, he soon began to compose songs (words) of his own as he followed the plough. In the greatness of his later success his debt to the current body of song and music should not be overlooked. He is only the last of a long succession of rural Scottish song-writers; he composed his own songs to accompany popular airs; and many of them are directly based on fragments of earlier songs. None the less his work rises immeasurably above all that had gone before it.

The story of Burns' mature life is the pathetic one of a very vigorous nature in which genius, essential manliness, and good impulses struggled against and were finally overcome by violent passions, aggravated by the bitterness of poverty and repeated disappointments. His first effort, at eighteen, to better his condition, by the study of surveying at a neighboring town, resulted chiefly in throwing him into contact with bad companions; a venture in the business of flax-dressing ended in disaster; and the same ill-fortune attended the several successive attempts which he made at general farming.

He became unfortunately embroiled also with the Church, which (the Presbyterian denomination) exercised a very strict control in Scotland. Compelled to do public penance for some of his offenses, his keen wit could not fail to be struck by the inconsistency between the rigid doctrines and the lives of some of the men who were proceeding against him; and he commemorated the feud in his series of overwhelming but painfully flippant satires.

His brief period of dazzling public success dawned suddenly out of the darkest moment of his fortunes. At the age of twenty-seven, abandoning the hope which he had already begun to cherish of becoming the national poet of Scotland, he had determined in despair to emigrate to Jamaica to become an overseer on a plantation. (That this chief poet of democracy, the author of 'A Man's a Man for a' That,' could have planned to become a slave-driver suggests how closely the most genuine human sympathies are limited by habit and circumstances.)

To secure the money for his voyage Burns had published his poems in a little volume. This won instantaneous and universal popularity, and Burns, turning back at the last moment, responded to the suggestion of some of the great people of Edinburgh that he should come to that city and see what could be done for him. At first the experiment seemed fortunate, for the natural good breeding with which this untrained countryman bore himself for a winter as the petted lion of the society of fashion and learning (the University) was remarkable. None the less the situation was unnatural and necessarily temporary, and unluckily Burns formed associations also with such boon companions of the lower sort as had hitherto been his undoing. After a year Edinburgh dropped him, thus supplying substantial fuel for his ingrained poor man's jealousy and rancor at the privileged classes. Too near his goal to resume the idea of emigrating, he returned to his native moors, rented another farm, and married Jean Armour, one of the several heroines of his love-poems.

The only material outcome of his period of public favor was an appointment as internal revenue collector, an unpopular and uncongenial office which he accepted with reluctance and exercised with leniency. It required him to occupy much of his time in riding about the country, and contributed to his final failure as a farmer. After the latter event he removed to the neighboring market-town of Dumfries, where he again renewed his companionship with unworthy associates. At last prospects for promotion in the revenue service began to open to him, but it was too late; his naturally robust constitution had given way to over-work and dissipation, and he died in 1796 at the age of thirty-seven.

Burns' place among poets is perfectly clear. It is chiefly that of a song-writer, perhaps the greatest songwriter of the world. At work in the fields or in his garret or kitchen after the long day's work was done, he composed songs because he could not help it, because his emotion was irresistibly stirred by the beauty and life of the birds and flowers, the snatch of a melody which kept running through his mind, or the memory of the girl with whom he had last talked. And his feelings expressed themselves with spontaneous simplicity, genuineness, and ease. He is a thoroughly romantic poet, though wholly by the grace of nature, not at all from any conscious intention—he wrote as the inspiration moved him, not in accordance with any theory of art.

The range of his subjects and emotions is nearly or quite complete—love; comradeship; married affection, as in 'John Anderson, My Jo'; reflective sentiment; feeling for nature; sympathy with animals; vigorous patriotism, as in 'Scots Wha Hae' (and Burns did much to revive the feeling of Scots for Scotland); deep tragedy and pathos; instinctive happiness; delightful humor; and the others. It should be clearly recognized, however, that this achievement, supreme as it is in its own way, does not suffice to place Burns among the greatest poets. The brief lyrical outbreaks of the song-writer are no more to be compared with the sustained creative power and knowledge of life and character which make the great dramatist or narrative poet than the bird's song is to be compared with an opera of Wagner. But such comparisons need not be pressed; and the song of bird or poet appeals instantly to every normal hearer, while the drama or narrative poem requires at least some special accessories and training.

Burns' significant production, also, is not altogether limited to songs. 'The Cotter's Saturday Night' (in Spenser's stanza) is one of the perfect descriptive poems of lyrical sentiment; and some of Burns' meditative poems and poetical epistles to acquaintances are delightful in a free-and-easy fashion. The exuberant power in the religious satires and the narrative 'Tam o' Shanter' is undeniable, but they belong to a lower order of work.

Many of Burns' poems are in the Lowland Scots dialect; a few are wholly in ordinary English; and some combine the two idioms. It is an interesting question whether Burns wins distinctly greater success in one than in the other. In spite of his prevailing literary honesty, it may be observed, his English shows some slight traces of the effort to imitate Pope and the feeling that the pseudo-classical style with its elegance was really the highest—a feeling which renders some of his letters painfully affected.

ROMANTIC NOVEL

Mary Shelley (1797–1851) is remembered as the author of *Frankenstein* (1818). The plot of this is said to have come from a waking dream she had, in the company of Percy Shelley, Lord Byron, and John Polidori, following a conversation about galvanism and the feasibility of returning a corpse or assembled body parts to life, and on the experiments of the 18th-century natural philosopher and poet Erasmus Darwin, who was said to have animated dead matter. Sitting around a log fire at Byron's villa, the company also amused themselves by reading German ghost stories, prompting Byron to suggest they each write their own supernatural tale.

Jane Austen's works critique the novels of sensibility of the second half of the 18th century and are part of the transition to 19th-century realism. Her plots, though fundamentally comic, highlight the dependence of women on marriage to secure social standing and economic security. Austen brings to light the hardships women faced, who usually did not inherit money, could not work and where their only chance in life depended on the man they married. She reveals not only the difficulties women faced in her day, but also what was expected of men and of the careers they had to follow. This she does with wit and humour and with endings where all characters, good or bad, receive exactly what they deserve. Her work brought her little personal fame and only a few positive reviews during her lifetime, but the publication in 1869 of her nephew's *A Memoir of Jane Austen* introduced her to a wider public, and by the 1940s she had become accepted as a major writer. The second half of the 20th century saw a proliferation of Austen scholarship and the emergence of a Janeite fan culture. Austen's works include *Sense and Sensibility* (1811), *Pride and Prejudice* (1813), *Mansfield Park* (1814), *Emma* (1815), *Northanger Abbey* (1817) and *Persuasion*(1817).

DRAMA

Byron, Keats and Shelley all wrote for the stage, but with little success in England, with Shelley's *The Cenci* perhaps the best work produced, though that was not played in a public theatre in England until a century after his death. Byron's plays, along with dramatizations of his poems and Scott's novels, were much more popular on the Continent, and especially in France, and through these versions several were turned into operas, many still performed today. If contemporary poets had little success on the stage, the period was a legendary one for performances of Shakespeare, and went some way to restoring his original texts and removing the Augustan "improvements" to them. The greatest actor of the period, Edmund Kean, restored the tragic ending to *King Lear*; Coleridge said that, "Seeing him act was like reading Shakespeare by flashes of lightning."

ENGLAND

18th-century precursors

The Romantic movement in English literature of the early 19th century has its roots in 18th-century poetry, the Gothic novel and the novel of sensibility. This includes the graveyard poets, who were a number of pre-Romantic English poets, writing in the 1740s and later, whose works are characterised by their gloomy meditations on mortality, "skulls and coffins, epitaphs and worms" in the context of the graveyard. To this was added, by later practitioners, a feeling for the 'sublime' and uncanny, and an interest in ancient English poetic forms and folk poetry. They are often considered precursors of the Gothic genre. The poets include Thomas Gray (1716–71), whose *Elegy Written in a Country Churchyard*(1751) is "the best known product of this kind of sensibility"; William Cowper (1731–1800); Christopher Smart (1722–71); Thomas Chatterton (1752–70); Robert Blair (1699–1746), author of *The Grave* (1743), "which celebrates the horror of death"; and Edward Young (1683–1765), whose *The Complaint, or Night Thoughts on Life, Death and Immortality* (1742–45) is another "noted example of the graveyard genre". Other precursors of Romanticism are the poets James Thomson (1700–48) and James Macpherson(1736–96).

The sentimental novel or "novel of sensibility" is a genre which developed during the second half of the 18th century. It celebrates the emotional and intellectual concepts of sentiment, sentimentalism, and sensibility. Sentimentalism, which is to be distinguished from sensibility, was a fashion in both poetry and prose fiction which began in the 18th century in reaction to the rationalism of the Augustan Age. Sentimental novels relied on emotional response, both from their readers and characters. They feature scenes of distress and tenderness, and the plot is arranged to advance emotions rather than action. The result is a valorization of "fine feeling", displaying the characters as a model for refined, sensitive emotional effect. The ability to display feelings was thought to show character and experience, and to shape social life and relations. Among the most famous sentimental novels in English are Samuel Richardson's *Pamela, or Virtue Rewarded* (1740), Oliver Goldsmith's *Vicar of Wakefield* (1766), Laurence Sterne's *Tristram Shandy* (1759–67), *Sentimental Journey* (1768), Henry Brooke's *The Fool of Quality* (1765–70), Henry Mackenzie's *The Man of Feeling* (1771) and Maria Edgeworth's *Castle Rackrent* (1800).

Significant foreign influences were the Germans Goethe, Schiller and August Wilhelm Schlegel and French philosopher and writer Jean-Jacques Rousseau (1712–78). Edmund Burke's *A Philosophical Enquiry into the Origin of Our Ideas of the Sublime and Beautiful* (1757) is another important influence. The changing landscape, brought about by the industrial and agricultural revolutions, with the expansion of the city and depopulation of the countryside, was another influence on the growth of the Romantic movement in Britain. The poor condition of workers, the new class conflicts and the pollution of the environment led to a reaction against urbanism and industrialization and a new emphasis on the beauty and value of nature.

In the late 18th century, Horace Walpole's 1764 novel *The Castle of Otranto* created the Gothic fiction genre, that combines elements of horror and romance. The pioneering gothic novelist Ann Radcliffe introduced the brooding figure of the gothic villain which developed into the Byronic hero. Her most popular and influential work *The Mysteries of Udolpho*(1795) is frequently cited as the archetypal Gothic novel. *Vathek* (1786) by William Beckford, and *The Monk*

(1796) by Matthew Lewis, were further notable early works in both the gothic and horror literary genres. The first short stories in the United Kingdom were gothic tales like Richard Cumberland's "remarkable narrative" *The Poisoner of Montremos*(1791).

WALES

Wales had its own Romantic movement, especially in Welsh literature (which was rarely translated or known outside Wales). The countryside and history of Wales exerted an influence on the Romantic imagination of Britons, especially in travel writings, and the poetry of Wordsworth.

The "poetry and bardic vision" of Edward Williams (1747-1826), better known by his bardic name Iolo Morganwg, bear the hallmarks of Romanticism. "His Romantic image of Wales and its past had a far-reaching effect on the way in which the Welsh envisaged their own national identity during the nineteenth century".

SCOTLAND

James Macpherson was the first Scottish poet to gain an international reputation. Claiming to have found poetry written by the ancient bard Ossian, he published "translations" that acquired international popularity, being proclaimed as a Celtic equivalent of the Classical epics. *Fingal*, written in 1762, was speedily translated into many European languages, and its appreciation of natural beauty and treatment of the ancient legend have been credited, more than any single work, with bringing about the Romantic movement in European, and especially in German literature, through its influence on Johann Gottfried von Herder and Johann Wolfgang von Goethe. It was also popularised in France by figures that included Napoleon. Eventually it became clear that the poems were not direct translations from the Gaelic, but flowery adaptations made to suit the aesthetic expectations of his audience. Both Robert Burns (1759–96) and Walter Scott (1771–1832) were highly influenced by the Ossian cycle. Robert Burns (1759–1796) was a pioneer of the Romantic movement, and after his death he became a cultural icon in Scotland. As well as writing poems, Burns also collected folk songs from across Scotland, often revising or adaptingthem. His *Poems, chiefly in the Scottish Dialect* was published in 1786. Among poems and songs of Burns that remain well known across the world are, "Auld Lang Syne"; "A Red, Red Rose"; "A Man's A Man for A' That"; "To a Louse"; "To a Mouse"; "The Battle of Sherramuir"; "Tam o' Shanter" and "Ae Fond Kiss".

The most important British novelist at the beginning of the early 19th century was Sir Walter Scott, who was not only a highly successful novelist, but "the greatest single influence on fiction in the 19th century [...] [and] a European figure". Scott's novel writing career was launched in 1814 with *Waverley*, often called the first historical novel, and was followed by *Ivanhoe*. The Waverley Novels, including *The Antiquary, Old Mortality, The Heart of Midlothian*, and whose subject is Scottish history, are now generally regarded as Scott's masterpieces. He was one of the most popular novelist of the era and his historical romances inspired a generation of painters, composers, and writers throughout Europe, including Franz Schubert, Felix Mendelssohn and J. M. W. Turner. His novels also inspired many operas, of which the most famous are *Lucia di Lammermoor* (1835) by Donizetti and Bizet's, *La jolie fille de Perth, The Fair Maid of Perth* (1867). However, today his contemporary, Jane Austen, is widely read and the source for films and television series, while Scott is neglected. He also inspired French authors such as Flaubert with Madame Bovary and Hugo in The Hunchback of Notre-Dame.

AMERICA

The European Romantic movement reached America in the early 19th century. American Romanticism was just as multifaceted and individualistic as it was in Europe. Like the Europeans, the American Romantics demonstrated a high level of moral enthusiasm, commitment to individualism and the unfolding of the self, an emphasis on intuitive perception, and the assumption that the natural world was inherently good, while human society was filled with corruption. Romanticism became popular in American politics, philosophy and art. The movement appealed to the revolutionary spirit of America as well as to those longing to break free of the strict religious traditions of early settlement. The Romantics rejected rationalism and religious intellect. It appealed to those in opposition of Calvinism, which includes the belief that the destiny of each individual is preordained.

Romantic Gothic literature made an early appearance with Washington Irving's *The Legend of Sleepy Hollow* (1820) and *Rip Van Winkle*(1819), There are picturesque "local color" elements in Washington Irving's essays and especially his travel books. From 1823 the prolific and popular novelist James Fenimore Cooper (1789–1851) began publishing his historical romances of frontier and Indian life, to create a unique form of American literature. Cooper is best remembered for his numerous sea-stories and the historical novels known as the *Leatherstocking Tales*, with their emphasis on heroic simplicity and their fervent landscape descriptions of an already-exotic mythicized frontier peopled by "noble savages", exemplified by Uncas, from *The Last of the Mohicans* (1826) show the influence of Rousseau's (1712–78) philosophy. Edgar Allan Poe's tales of the macabre that first appeared in the early 1830s, and his balladic poetry were more influential in France than at home.

By the mid-19th century, the pre-eminence of literature from the British Isles began to be challenged by writers from the former American colonies. This included one of the creators of the new genre of the short story, and inventor of the detective story Edgar Allan Poe (1809–49). A major influence on American writers at this time was Romanticism. The Romantic movement gave rise to New England Transcendentalism, which portrayed a less restrictive relationship between God and Universe. The publication of Ralph Waldo Emerson's 1836 essay *Nature* is usually considered the watershed moment at which transcendentalism became a major cultural movement. The new philosophy presented the individual with a more personal relationship with God. Transcendentalism and Romanticism appealed to Americans in a similar fashion, for both privileged feeling over reason, individual freedom of expression over the restraints of tradition and custom. It often involved a rapturous response to nature. It encouraged the rejection of harsh, rigid Calvinism, and promised a new blossoming of American culture.

The romantic American novel developed fully with Nathaniel Hawthorne's (1804–1864) *The Scarlet Letter* (1850), a stark drama of a woman cast out of her community for committing adultery. Hawthorne's fiction had a profound impact on his friend Herman Melville (1819–1891). In *Moby-Dick* (1851), an adventurous whaling voyage becomes the vehicle for examining such themes as obsession, the nature of evil, and human struggle against the elements. By the 1880s, however, psychological and social realism were competing with Romanticism in the novel.

WILLIAM WORDSWORTH

William Wordsworth was born in 1770 in Cumberland, in the 'Lake Region,' which, with its bold and varied mountains as well as its group of charming lakes, is the most picturesque part of England proper. He had the benefit of all the available formal education, partly at home, partly at a 'grammar' school a few miles away, but his genius was formed chiefly by the influence of Nature, and, in a qualified degree, by that of the simple peasant people of the region. Already as a boy, though normal and active, he began to be sensitive to the Divine Power in Nature which in his mature years he was to express with deeper sympathy than any poet before him. Early left an orphan, at seventeen he was sent by his uncles to Cambridge University.

Here also the things which most appealed to him were rather the new revelations of men and life than the formal studies, and indeed the torpid instruction of the time offered little to any thoughtful student.

On leaving Cambridge he was uncertain as to his lifework. He said that he did not feel himself 'good enough' for the Church, he was not drawn towards law, and though he fancied that he had capacity for a military career, he felt that 'if he were ordered to the West Indies his talents would not save him from the yellow fever.' At first, therefore, he spent nearly a year in London in apparent idleness, an intensely interested though detached spectator of the city life, but more especially absorbed in his mystical consciousness of its underlying current of spiritual being. After this he crossed to France to learn the language. The Revolution was then in its early stages, and in his 'Prelude' Wordsworth has left the finest existing statement of the exultant anticipations of a new world of social justice which the movement aroused in himself and other young English liberals. When the Revolution past into the period of violent bloodshed he determined, with more enthusiasm than judgment, to put himself forward as a leader of the moderate Girondins. From the wholesale slaughter of this party a few months later he was saved through the stopping of his allowance by his more cautious uncles, which compelled him, after a year's absence, to return to England.

For several years longer Wordsworth lived uncertainly. When, soon after his return, England, in horror at the execution of the French king, joined the coalition of European powers against France, Wordsworth experienced a great shock the first, he tells us, that his moral nature had ever suffered at seeing his own country arrayed with corrupt despotisms against what seemed to him the cause of humanity. The complete degeneration of the Revolution into anarchy and tyranny further served to plunge him into a chaos of moral bewilderment, from which he was gradually rescued partly by renewed communion with Nature and partly by the influence of his sister Dorothy, a woman of the most sensitive nature but of strong character and admirable good sense. From this time for the rest of her life she continued to live with him, and by her unstinted and unselfish devotion contributed very largely to his poetic success. He had now begun to write poetry, and the receipt of a small legacy from a friend enabled him to devote his life to the art. Six or seven years later his resources were several times multiplied by an honourable act of the new Lord Lonsdale, who voluntarily repaid a sum of money owed by his predecessor to Wordsworth's father.

In 1795 Wordsworth and his sister moved from the Lake Region to Dorsetshire, at the other end of England, likewise a country of great natural beauty. Two years later came their change to Alfoxden, the association with Coleridge, and 'Lyrical Ballads,' containing nineteen of Wordsworth's poems. After their winter in Germany the Wordsworths settled permanently in their native Lake Region, at first in 'Dove Cottage,' in the village of Grasmere. This simple little stone house, buried, like all the others in the Lake Region, in brilliant flowers, and opening from its second story onto the hillside garden where Wordsworth composed much of his greatest poetry, is now the annual center of pilgrimage for thousands of visitors, one of the chief literary shrines of England and the world. Here Wordsworth lived frugally for several years; then after intermediate changes he took up his final residence in a larger house, Rydal Mount, a few miles away. In 1802 he married Mary Hutchinson, who had been one of his childish schoolmates, a woman of a spirit as fine as that of his sister, whom she now joined without a thought of jealousy in a life of self-effacing devotion to the poet.

Wordsworth's poetic inspiration, less fickle than that of Coleridge, continued with little abatement for a dozen years; but about 1815, as he himself states in his fine but pathetic poem 'Composed upon an Evening of Extraordinary Splendor,' it for the most part abandoned him. He continued, however, to produce a great deal of verse, most of which his admirers would much prefer to have had unwritten. The plain Anglo-Saxon yeoman strain which was really the basis of his nature now asserted itself in the growing conservatism of ideas which marked the last forty years of his life. His early love of simplicity hardened into a rigid opposition not only to the materialistic modern industrial system but to all change the Reform Bill, the reform of education, and in general all progressive political and social movements. It was on this abandonment of his early liberal principles that Browning based his spirited lyric 'The Lost Leader.'

During the first half or more of his mature life, until long after he had ceased to be a significant creative force, Wordsworth's poetry, for reasons which will shortly appear, had been met chiefly with ridicule or indifference, and he had been obliged to wait in patience while the slighter work first of Scott and then of Byron took the public by storm. Little by little, however, he came to his own, and by about 1830 he enjoyed with discerning readers that enthusiastic appreciation of which he is certain for all the future.

The crowning mark of recognition came in 1843 when on the death of his friend Southey he was made Poet Laureate. The honour, however, had been so long delayed that it was largely barren. Ten years earlier his life had been darkened by the mental decay of his sister and the death of Coleridge; and other personal sorrows now came upon him. He died in 1850 at the age of eighty. Wordsworth, as we have said, is the chief representative of some of the most important principles in the Romantic Movement; but he is far more than a member of any movement; through his supreme poetic expression of some of the greatest spiritual ideals he belongs among the five or six greatest English poets. First, he is the profoundest interpreter of Nature in all poetry. His feeling for Nature has two aspects. He is keenly sensitive, and in a more delicately discriminating way than any of his predecessors, to all the external beauty and glory of Nature, especially inanimate Nature of mountains, woods and fields, streams and flowers, in all their infinitely varied aspects.

A wonderfully joyous and intimate sympathy with them is one of his controlling impulses. But his feeling goes beyond the mere physical and emotional delight of Chaucer and the Elizabethans; for him Nature is a direct manifestation of the Divine Power, which seems to him to be everywhere immanent in her; and communion with her, the communion into which he enters as he walks and meditates among the mountains and moors, is to him communion with God. He is literally in earnest even in his repeated assertion that from observation of Nature man may learn more of moral truth than from all the books and sages. To Wordsworth Nature is man's one great and sufficient teacher. It is for this reason that, unlike such poets as Keats and Tennyson, he so often views Nature in the large, giving us broad landscapes and sublime aspects. Of this mystical semi pantheistic Nature religion his 'Lines composed above Tintern Abbey' are the noblest expression in literature. All this explains why Wordsworth considered his function as a poet a sacred thing and how his intensely moral temperament found complete satisfaction in his art. It explains also, in part, the limitation of his poetic genius. Nature indeed did not continue to be to him, as he himself says that it was in his boyhood, absolutely 'all in all'; but he always remained largely absorbed in the contemplation and interpretation of it and never manifested, except in a few comparatively short and exceptional poems, real narrative or dramatic power.

In the second place, Wordsworth is the most consistent of all the great English poets of democracy, though here as elsewhere his interest is mainly not in the external but in the spiritual aspect of things. From his insistence that the meaning of the world for man lies not in the external events but in the development of character results his central doctrine of the simple life. Real character, he holds, the chief proper object of man's effort, is formed by quietly living, as did he and the dales men around him, in contact with Nature and communion with God rather than by participation in the feverish and sensational struggles of the great world. Simple country people, therefore, are nearer to the ideal than are most persons who fill a larger place in the activities of the world. This doctrine expresses itself in a striking though one-sided fashion in his famous theory of poetry its proper subjects, characters, and diction. He stated his theory definitely and at length in a preface to the second edition of 'Lyrical Ballads,' published in 1800, a discussion which includes incidentally some of the finest general critical interpretation ever made of the nature and meaning of poetry.

Wordsworth declared:

- Since the purpose of poetry is to present the essential emotions of men, persons in humble and rustic life are generally the fittest subjects for treatment in it, because their natures and manners are simple and more genuine than those of other men, and are kept so by constant contact with the beauty and serenity of Nature.
- Not only should artificial poetic diction be rejected, but the language of poetry should be a selection from that of ordinary people in real life, only purified of its vulgarities and heightened so as to appeal to the imagination.

There neither is nor can be any essential difference between the language of prose and that of poetry. This theory, founded on Wordsworth's disgust at eighteenth century poetic artificiality, contains a very important but greatly exaggerated element of truth. That the experiences of simple and common people, including children, may adequately illustrate the main spiritual aspects of life Wordsworth unquestionably demonstrated in such poems as 'The Reverie of Poor Susan,' 'Lucy Gray,' and 'Michael.' But to restrict poetry largely to such characters and subjects would be to eliminate not only most of the external interest of life, which certainly is often necessary in giving legitimate body to the spiritual meanings, but also a great range of significant experiences which by the nature of things can never come to lowly and simple persons. That the characters of simple country people are on the average inevitably finer and more genuine than those of others is a romantic theory rather than a fact, as Wordsworth would have discovered if his meditative nature had, allowed him to get into really direct and personal contact with the peasants about him. As to the proper language of poetry, no one today defends artificiality, but most of Wordsworth's own best work, as well as that of all other poets, proves clearly that there is an essential difference between the language of prose and that of poetry, that much of the meaning of poetry results from the use of unusual, suggestive, words and picturesque expressions, which create the essential poetic atmosphere and stir the imagination in ways distinctly different from those of prose. Wordsworth's obstinate adherence to his theory in its full extent, indeed, produced such trivial and absurd results as 'Goody Blake and Harry Gill,' 'The Idiot Boy,' and 'Peter Bell,' and great masses of hopeless prosiness in his long blank verse narratives.

This obstinacy and these poems are only the most conspicuous result of Wordsworth's chief temperamental defect, which was an almost total lack of the sense of humour. Regarding himself as the prophet of a supremely important new gospel, he never admitted the possibility of error in his own point of view and was never able to stand aside from his poetry and criticize it dispassionately. This somewhat irritating egotism, however, was perhaps a necessary element in his success; without it he might not have been able to live serenely through the years of misunderstanding and ridicule which would have silenced or embittered a more diffident spirit. The variety of Wordsworth's poetry deserves special mention; in addition to his short lyric and narrative poems of Nature and the spiritual life several kinds stand out distinctly.

A very few poems, the noble 'Ode to Duty,' 'Laodamía,' and 'Dion,' are classical in inspiration and show the finely severe repression and finish of classic style. Among his many hundreds of sonnets is a very notable group inspired by the struggle of England against Napoleon. Wordsworth was the first English poet after Milton who used the sonnet powerfully and he proves himself a worthy successor of Milton. The great bulk of his work, finally, is made up of his long poems in blank verse. 'The Prelude,' written during the years 1799-1805, though not published until after his death, is the record of the development of his poet's mind, not an outwardly stirring poem, but a unique and invaluable piece of spiritual autobiography. Wordsworth intended to make this only an introduction to another work of enormous length which was to have presented his views of Man, Nature, and Society. Of this plan he completed two detached parts, namely the fragmentary 'Recluse' and 'The Excursion,' which latter contains some fine passages, but for the most part is uninspired.

Wordsworth, more than any other great English poet, is a poet for mature and thoughtful appreciation; except for a very small part of his work many readers must gradually acquire the taste for him. But of his position among the half dozen English poets who have made the largest contribution to thought and life there can be no question; so that some acquaintance with him is a necessary part of any real education.

2

Romantic Literature of the Middle Ages

From the time of the first Crusade, A.D. 1093, to the end of the twelfth century, was the golden age of chivalry in Europe. Hence the poetry of this period partook of the spirit that was abroad in the world. Of this chivalrous poetry of the Middle Ages there are three classifications: The first, taken from old legends, shows a style of verse peopled with the Gothic, Frankish and Burgundian heroes who flourished in the time of the great Northern emigrations; and for these there is usually some historical foundation, while they are also closely knit to the traditions of the old heathenish mythology of the Gothic Nations. The second subject of chivalrous verse was Charlemagne, the Saracens and Roncesvalle. These were chiefly composed by the Normans, who, after the Crusades, gave a new direction to literature. Marked changes were introduced by them, not only into France, but throughout Europe. They were filled with the spirit of adventure and enthusiasm, and in their onward march conquered England and Sicily, and took the lead in the next Crusade. Essentially a poetic people, the wonderful was the object of all their admiration and desire. Hence they sang old war songs, especially of the battle of Roncesvalles in which Roland dies when the Franks are conquered by the Spaniards and Turks.

In the tale of a fabulous Crusade, invented in the ninth century, and which was embodied in poetry by the Normans, the true history of the Empire became so bewilderingly mixed up with magicians, genii, sultans, Oriental fables, and comical characters, who met with astonishing adventures, that it was difficult to distinguish the true from the false. There was nothing of the romantic and wonderful in the history of the East, which did not find its way into the poetry that treated of Charlemagne and Roland, until it lost all traces of the real wars and achievements of Charlemagne. The third subject of chivalric verse was Arthur of the Round Table; but this, at the time, was also invested with Oriental wonders and attachments. Other chivalric poetry of this epoch had to do with Godfrey of Bouillon, the Crusades, and old French tales and fabliaux which were brought into Europe by the oral narratives of the Crusaders.

The Northern mythology always abounded with mountain spirits, mermaids, giants, dwarfs, dragons, elves and mandrakes. These reappear in the songs of the Crusades, and are elements of the old Northern and Persian superstitions. All that the East contributed to the song of the chivalric period was a Southern magic, and a brilliance of Oriental fancy with which some of the poems were clothed.

A Persian poem that became very popular in Europe in the Middle Ages was Ferdusi's Book of Heroes. It has had a marked influence on the Arabian "Thousand and One Nights." In this poem of Ferdusi's we note the contest between light and darkness (an idea nowhere found in Greek poetry). It seemed to touch the poetical thought of the age of chivalry; for we find it reproduced in their songs, mingled with Scriptural and love scenes.

Next to Chivalric poetry, the age of the Crusaders was essentially a period of love songs. They attained their greatest perfection in Provence, whence they spread over the whole of France, and from there into Germany in the twelfth century.

Love poetry in Italy failed to attain any degree of perfection until the time of Petrarch in the fourteenth century; and its real era in Spain was not until a century later. Love poetry developed in different ways in Europe, and, as we have seen, at different times. Except among the Italians it was not so much borrowed from one nation to another as had been the case with other branches of literature.

It is different with Chivalric poetry, which was considered the common property of all. The form of poetical composition also varied in each country, and the only thing common to all the nations was rhyme. Almost all the love poems seem to have been written to be sung, and this was carried to such lengths that in the reign of Lewis the Pious of Germany, an edict had to be sent to the nuns of the German Cloisters by their Bishops, forbidding them to sing their love songs, or Mynelieder.

FRENCH

It is in the first ages of national existence that the foundations of national character and poetry are laid; and the farther back that history is studied, the more closely do we find the different peoples of the world united in their literature. Its first history in France is undoubtedly that of the Troubadours. Provence, where it originated, early became an independent kingdom, while in the north the literature of the Trouveres became the foundation of the national literature of France.

Latin was the language of the country after its conquest by Julius Caesar; then came the Northern hordes, when language became corrupted, until, in the time of Charlemagne, German was the Court language, Latin the written language, and the Romance dialect, still in its barbaric state, was the speech of the people. The Gauls in the North, who used the Romance, were also called the Roman-Wallons; they were distinguished from Charlemagne's German subjects, while in the South the natives were called the Romans-Provencaux.

In the tenth century the Normans invaded France, and infused another element in the language, which gradually became Norman-French; and from the twelfth century the two dialects were known as Provencal and French. The Provencal dialect, although much changed, is still spoken in Provence, Languedoc, Catalonia, Valencia, Majorca, and Minorca, while the French was brought, by gradual polish, to its present perfection.

The Troubadours who flourished for three centuries, from 950 to 1250, used the Romance language in their poems. The brilliance of this period of literature, its sudden rise, and as sudden disappearance, is not unlike the rise and fall of the Arabian literature.

Among the thousands of poets who flourished during this time, none ever wrote anything of any special note. The love, romance and imagination of these poems breathes that chivalry toward women, amounting almost to veneration, which was a feature of this class of poetry. It is therefore to be regretted that as actual tales, shorn of the poetical and chivalric setting, there was something left to be desired. The immorality of the incidents, and the coarseness of the language, makes this "Gay Science," as the Troubadours called it, unfit to be classed with the best literature. In 1092 the crown of Provence passing to the Count of Barcelona brought a more refined taste into the Provencal poetry; the arts and the sciences of the Arabians obtained a foothold in the country; rhyme—the method used in Arabian poetry, was adopted by the Troubadours, and from them has been handed down to the nations of modern Europe.

This period has been described as "one that shone out at once over Provence and all the south of Europe, like an electric flash in the midst of profound darkness, illuminating all things with the splendor of its flame."

During the Crusades many of the Troubadours departed for the Holy Land. In the history of the world there is no event that fired the poetry and imagination of the people like these holy wars, and religious enthusiasm began to influence the poetry of the time. When the Plantagenet kings of England assumed by right the sovereignty over Languedoc (as Provence was called), a new impetus was given to the Provencal poetry, as well as a wider scope, when it was introduced into England. Chaucer, the father of English literature, found in the Provencal literature all his first models.

With the decline of the Troubadours occurred the rise of the Trouveres in northern France.

In the tenth century Normandy was invaded by Rollo the Dane, who incorporated himself and his followers with the Normans. They adopted the Norman-French; but gave it a power and scope it had hitherto lacked. While the Romance-Provencal in the South was a language of sweetness and beauty, the Northern language after the advent of Rollo, was strong and warlike. Its poetry, which differed from the love chansons of the South, was the song of brave warriors, recounting the heroic deeds of their ancestors.

The Langue d'oui, as this Northern speech was called, became, in the twelfth century, the universal medium of literature. The poets and story writers called themselves Trouveres, and they invented the fabliaux, the dramatic mysteries and romances of ancient chivalry. The first great literary work of this class is a marvellous history of the early kings of England, commencing with Brutus, a grandson of Aeneas, who, sailing among many enchanted Isles, at length settles in England, where he meets Arthur of the Round Table, and the old wizard, Merlin, one of the most popular creations of the Middle Ages. Born of this legend were some of the best known of modern romances. The word romance, which in the early history of France was used to distinguish the common dialect from the Latin, was later applied to all imaginative and inventive tales. Of this class was "Tristam de Leonois," written in 1190; the "San Graal," and "Lancelot." In the same century appeared "Alexander," a poem which became so celebrated that poetry, written in the same measure, is to this day called Alexandrine verse.

A poetess known as Marie of France, wrote twelve lays to celebrate the glories of the Round Table. She addresses herself to a king supposed to be Henry VI, and has made extensive use of early British legends. Chaucer and other English poets, have drawn many inspirations from her poems.

The Trouveres not only originated the romances of chivalry; but they also invented allegorical poems. The most celebrated is the "Romance of the Rose," written in the thirteenth century. It consisted of 20,000 verses, and although tedious, because of its length, it was universally admired, and became the foundation of all subsequent allegory among the different nations. The poetry of the Trouveres was unlike anything in antiquity, and unlike, too, to what came after it. It dealt with high-minded love and honor, the devotion of the strong to the weak, and the supernatural in fiction. All this, which formed part of its composition, has been attributed to both the Arabians and the Germans; but it was in truth a peculiar production of the Normans, the most active and enterprising people in Europe, a nation who pushed into Russia, Constantinople, England, France, Sicily and Syria. A treasury of a later date, from which the Trouveres drew their fabliaux in the thirteenth century, was a collection of Indian tales that had been translated into Latin in the tenth century. These fabliaux show that inventiveness, gaiety, and simple, yet delightful esprit, which is found nowhere but among the French. The Arabian tales, which had found their way into France, were also turned into verse, while the anecdotes that were picked up in the castles and towns of France, furnished other material for the fabliaux. These tales were the common property of the country at large, and are the source from which Boccaccio, La Fontaine, and others drew their inspiration. Some of them became famous and have been passed down from one age to another.

The Renard of Goethe, and the Zaire of Voltaire were taken from the old fabliaux. In the fourteenth century the coming of the Popes and the Roman Court to Avignon introduced an Italian element, and the language of Tuscany took the place of the Provencal among the upper classes.

La Fontaine, called the "Prince of Fablists," appeared in the seventeenth century. Many of his fables were borrowed from ancient sources; but clothed in a new dress. He has been closely imitated by his Confreres and by the fablists of other nations; but has easily remained the most renowned of them all.

The philosophy of Descartes in the sixteenth century prepared the way for Locke, Newton and Leibnitz; and his system, although now little used, was really the foundation of what followed. He is said to have given new and fresher impulse to mathematical and philosophical study than any other student, either ancient or modern.

Pascal, a contemporary of Descartes, is renowned for his Provencal Letters, a book that has become a classic in France. It is full of wit, and of exquisite beauty of language; but its teaching is pure sophistry. Pascal first set the example of writing about religion in a tone of mock levity, especially when by so doing, he could abuse the Jesuits. In the end this weapon of keen and delicate satire was turned against Christianity itself, when Voltaire in the eighteenth century recognized its possibilities, and made use of it.

The older French literature in the sixteenth century had become so neglected, and was so lacking in cultivation; so little adapted to poetry, that the nation seemed in danger of losing all its earlier traditions. For a hundred years France was given over to profane and light literature. Montaigne, Charyon, Ronsard and de Balzac are some of the names of this period. The death of a cat or dog was made the subject of a poem that was no real poetry. It is due to the women of France—to Madame de Rambouillet and her confreres, and to the literary coteries that arose in the middle of the seventeenth century—that French literature acquired a deeper and more serious tone.

This period was followed by the founding of the French Academy, of which Cardinal Richelieu was the chief patron. The tragic dramatists, Corneille and Racine, now appeared on the literary horizon. Racine's language and versification was said to be far superior to either Milton in English or Virgil in Latin.

In tragedy the French stand pre-eminent; but it is matter for regret that their subjects are never taken from their own nation—they rarely represent French heroes; and it is a weakness of their literature that they make no direct appeal to the national feeling. There is a close connection between the classical dramas of Racine and Corneille, and such works as Pope's Iliad, Addison's Cato and Dryden's Alexander's Feast, showing the general interest in Greek and Roman subjects during their time.

The older poetry of the chivalric period was entirely discarded, though it would have been possible to unite the old chivalric spirit, the freedom and romance of mediaeval times, with the later renaissance, as was done by other nations. The French literature is more closely formed on the model of the earlier refined nations of antiquity, as the Roman was on the Greek.

The later French poetry of the seventeenth century came into opposition with the teaching of Rousseau, this gave birth to a taste for English poetry and the classic poetry of France was a copy of the descriptive poetry of England. In the eighteenth century prose writings superseded verse. At this time the English had taken the lead in literature, and modern French philosophy was built on that of Bacon and Locke. It was no part of the plan of the English philosophers, however, to inculcate such ideas as the French philosophers drew from their writings. Bacon, who was profoundly Christian, believed that man alone was the type of God, and nature the work of God's hands; but the

French leaders in philosophy went beyond this, they deified nature, and threw aside as mysticism whatever could not be proved by sense. Voltaire made use of all the wonderful greatness of science, as revealed by Bacon and Newton, not to exalt the Creator; but to lower man to the level of the brute. Like the old Greek sophists, who defended first one side of a question, and then the one diametrically opposed to it, Voltaire would write one book in favor of God, and another to deny Him; but it is not difficult to see which is his real belief. This perverted philosophy of Voltaire in turn reacted on the English mind, and particularly on history. We see its workings in both Gibbon and Hume. The "little philosophy" which "inclineth a man's mind to atheism," led the eighteenth century philosophers to fancy that Newton's discoveries meant that everything could be attained without religion, and that the only true and wide vision could be reached by the senses alone. They taught a pure materialism, to their own undoing; for it is not possible to thus lightly throw aside our great links with the past, in which both Christian and heathen, knowingly and unknowingly, in mediaeval poetry, in heroic ballad, and in Egyptian prose, testified to the existence of God.

The nineteenth century in France has been rich in dramatists, novelists, historians and poets, as well as in science and learning of all kinds; but it has had no especial power, or aim, and its opinions are constantly changing. The early novelists were strongly directed by the writings of Sir Walter Scott, while later ones have sought to imitate Victor Hugo and George Sand. The literature of this period has had no effect outside of France. Poetry has not risen any higher than Alfred de Musset; and any further greatness in French poetry must come from a revival of their own ancient poems and legends.

Poetry that deals only with the present becomes local, and in the end is influenced by the constant caprice and change of fashion instead of by the deep, heart-stirring beliefs of a strong and united people.

DUTCH

Erasmus said of Ghent at the end of the fifteenth century that there was no city in Europe that could compare with it in greatness, power, and the cultivation of its people. The lays of the minstrels and the chivalric romances of other nations were translated into Dutch. In the middle of the thirteenth century Reynard the Fox was rendered into the same language, while this era also saw a translation of the Bible made into Flemish rhyme.

The close of the fourteenth century saw the rise of some wandering poets called Sprekers, who visited the courts of Kings and Princes and became so popular that in the fifteenth century they were federated into different societies that became known as "Chambers of Rhetoric," somewhat similar to the German Guilds of the Meistersingers. These societies spread rapidly through the country, and from rhyme the members passed to the mystery plays, and to the beginnings of the drama.

The Court of Burgundy in the fifteenth century brought a strong French element into the literature of the Dutch nation, and the poets and chroniclers of that age are chiefly Flemish.

The taste for Greek and Latin was introduced into Holland in the fifteenth and sixteenth centuries by Erasmus and Grotius, the two most learned men among the Dutch literati of their age.

Hooft in the seventeenth century made an extensive study of Italian poetry, and succeeded in imparting to his tragic and lyric verse a certain quality of sweetness and volume which it has since retained. His style, which also embraces tragedy, has been extensively imitated by his own countrymen.

Nearly the whole of the eighteenth century passed without any advancement in Dutch literature. The country experienced the French influence, in common with the rest of Europe; and French works and translations abounded. Toward the close of this century German taste began to predominate, and a young Dutchman, Van Effen, founded a magazine in French, called the "Spectator," which was in imitation of, and on the same lines as the English magazine of the same name.

Many native writers arose at this time and gained distinction in poetry, prose and the drama; but the overthrow of the Dutch Republic, and the confusion attending it, for a time extinguished the national literature, and the beginning of the nineteenth century saw the country flooded with poor translations of foreign books, and all the noble national literature was forgotten. This evil was partly remedied in the latter part of the nineteenth century; but as a whole, the Dutch literature, while it has been influenced by foreign taste, has had little or no weight outside of its own nation, and has not in any way shaped the literature of other peoples.

GERMAN

Germany, like the other Northern nations, had primitive war songs sung by the bards. Her mythology is akin to the Scandinavian, and like the latter she assigns a high place to women. Tacitus says: "It is believed that there is something holy and prophetic about them, and therefore the warriors neither despise their counsels nor disregard their responses."

This German paganism was eminently fanciful—it peopled the earth, air and sea with supernatural beings—the rivers had their Undines, the caverns their Gnomes, the woods their Sprites, and the ocean its Nixes. Besides these, there were a host of mythological figures—the Walkyres or bridal maidens, the river maids; and the white women, Hertha and Frigga. These legends have formed a rich treasure house from which later German authors have freely drawn for song or story. Before the Christian age Germany had no literature and the first national work that can be dignified by the name is a translation of the Bible into Moeso-Gothic by Ulphilas, a bishop of the Goths, in the fourth century A.D. This is a Catholic work that antedated Luther by a thousand years.

Bishop Ulphilas invented an alphabet of Runic, Greek and Roman letters, and this translation of the Bible remained the only literary monument of the Germans for four hundred years. The minstrel lays of this period were later collected by Charlemagne, of which two specimens have come down to us. Like the Icelandic, Anglo-Saxon, Scandinavian, old English, and old Saxon, they are in a measure called alliteration, that is, a repetition of the sound without the regular rhyme at the end of lines, or such as we call rhyme. This circumstance made Klopstock, at a later period, try to banish rhyme as not being correct according to ancient usage. One of these poems, the Hildebrand-lied, belongs to the time of Theodoric the Great. The songs collected by Charlemagne, were later remodelled and have come down to us as the Heldenbuch and the Nibelungen-lied. The intellectual light in Germany went out with the death of Charlemagne, except in the cloisters.

The Normans on the West and the Hungarians in the East menaced the country, and the only important literary work of the time is a poem written by a monk at the close of the ninth century. It is called "Ludwig's Lied;" and celebrates the triumph of Louis over the Normans. Roswitha, a nun in the tenth century, wrote some Christian dramas in Latin that are remarkable as coming from the pen of a woman in the Middle Ages.

The invasions of the Hungarians and Slavs in the eleventh century effectually prevented the blossoming of any literary effort, except for some poems known as the Lombard Cycle, in which the rude pagan legends of antiquity were blended with the dawnings of Christianity. But in 1138, when Conrad III became Emperor of Germany, his accession was followed by the Crusades, which spread a flame of enthusiasm and chivalry among the Germans.

In 1149 Conrad and Louis VII of France joined forces to lead a Crusade to the Holy Land, and thus the German and French nobility became intimately acquainted, and Provencal poetry soon began to have an effect on German literature.

Emperors and nobles held court and received their foreign guests with splendid display and hospitality. Poets and singers were welcomed, and the chivalric literature was soon taken up by the Suabian minstrels who became known as the Minnesingers.

From 1150 to 1300 was the golden age of Suabian literature and German chivalry. During this period numerous romances of chivalry were translated into German.

They have been divided into different classes, or cycles.

The first, and most ancient, have to do with Arthur and the Knights of the Round Table. Their origin is Anglo-Norman, and they were probably taken from old Welsh chronicles in an early age, and were known in Britain and Brittany before the poets began to put them in rhyme.

The most popular of these romances was the San Graal, or Holy Grail, a subject that has engaged some of the best poets of all countries. In this legend the Cup, which was supposed to have been used at the Last Supper, in some way is brought to Golgotha during the Crucifixion, and is used to preserve some of the blood that flows from Christ's side, when it is opened by the soldier's spear. Joseph of Arimathea is thought to have brought this precious Cup to Europe, and to have given it into the keeping of Sir Parsifal. Knowledge of its whereabouts was then lost, so that knights and heroes make it the object of long and fruitless quests.

The second cycle of romance has to do with Charlemagne, and is mostly in the form of translations from French literature.

The third, or classic cycle, relates to the great ones of ancient times, presented in the role of chivalry. These embrace stories of Alexander the Great, the Aeneid, and the Trojan war. During this period there were two classes of songs in Germany; the minstrelsy, most in favor with the nobility; and the old ballads, which were most popular with the people. The latter were gradually collected by different poets of the time, especially by Wolfram of Eschenbach and put into epic verse, in which form they have come down to us as the Heldenbuch (or book of heroes), and the Nibelungen-lied.

The Heldenbuch relates the deeds of Theodoric and Attila and the outpouring of the Goths into the Roman Empire. In the Nibelungen-lied the hero is Siegfried, the Achilles of the North, the embodiment of beauty, courage and virtue. The same personages are met with in these German legends, as in the Scandinavian mythology, only in the latter they take on a more godlike form. The German Brunhild, in the Scandinavian story becomes a Valkyriur.

The fourteenth and fifteenth centuries witnessed the decline of the romanticists, the loss of most of the Southern culture, and all the literature of this time is at a low ebb, partly owing to the wars of the Germans against the Huns.

The fourteenth century was productive of one class of literature that was common to all Europe; namely, simple and humorous fables and satires. "Reynard the Fox" was one of the earliest of these fables, and remained a great favorite with the Germans, being finally immortalized by Goethe. The same author has made us familiar with a personage who figures in an interesting legend of the fifteenth century. Doctor Faust, or Faustus, is a magician who by unlawful arts gains a mastery over nature. This legend became the foundation of a number of stories and dramas, and was put into verse by Christopher Marlowe, the English dramatist.

The end of the sixteenth century saw a craze for Latin in Germany. The national tongue was neglected and national poetry was translated into Latin verse. German poets wrote in the same classic language, and the university lectures were all delivered in the same tongue.

The seventeenth century saw the Thirty Years' War, during which all literary activity was completely paralyzed, and in the course of these thirty years a whole generation, especially among the lower classes, had grown up unable either to read or write.

But after the Treaty of Westphalia matters began to improve, and a desire to cultivate the native language awoke. In 1688 German superseded Latin in the universities. Novels were published; and about this time appeared a German translation of Defoe's "Robinson Crusoe" that became very popular. Poets wrote plays in the style of Terence, or copied English models; and even in the present day the Germans recall with pride the fact that the Shakespearean plays were appreciated by them during and after the Elizabethan age much more than they were by the English Nation.

Science under Leibnitz also began to take shape in this century, while Opitz wrote operas in imitation of the Italian style; and translations from the Italian Marini came into vogue. In the eighteenth century arose the Saxonic and Swiss schools of literature, neither of which was devoted to national works. Gottsched, the founder and imitator of French standards in art and poetry, is known as the leader in the Saxonic school at Leipsic, and an advocate of classical poetry.

Bodmer cultivated the English style, and retired to Switzerland with his friends, where they founded the Swiss school. The English lyric and elegiac poets had a wonderful influence in Germany. The followers of this school who were, or pretended to be, poets, began to write "Seasons" in imitation of Thomson; and the novels of the time were full of shepherds and shepherdesses. The craze spread to France, where the French Court took up the fad of living in rustic lodges, and Marie Antoinette posed as a shepherdess tending sheep. Each of these poets had numerous followers, of whom Rambler is known as the German Horace.

Frederick the Great preferred French works, and no one seems to have thought of starting a German school except Klopstock, who stands almost alone in the literature of his time and country. A man of lofty ideals, he believed that Christianity on the one hand and Gothic mythology on the other, should be the chief elements in all new European poetry and inspiration. Had he been encouraged by the German Court he would have been as powerful for good in German literature during the eighteenth century, as Voltaire was powerful for evil in France. Wielland, a friend of Klopstock, and a romantic poet, might have been the German Ariosto had he not abandoned poetry for prose. He tried to copy the Greek, in which he failed to excel. During this conflict in Germany between the French and English school, German literature was much influenced by Macpherson's Ossian, and Scotch names are found in a great many German works of this period. The literature of Germany attained its highest beauty and finish in the eighteenth and nineteenth centuries; and its people may well be proud of the splendid names that adorn that period. The Gottingen School, which embraced Goethe and Schiller, includes love, philosophy and the classics for its theme, with a touch of the bucolic, modelled after Virgil, as in the "Louise" of Voss. But it remained for the Romantic School, founded by Novalis, the two Schlegels and Tieck, to oppose the study of the classic antique on the ground that it killed all native originality and power. They turned to the Middle Ages, and drew from its rich stores all that was noblest and best. The lays of the Minnesingers were revived—the true German spirit was cultivated, and the romantic German imagination responded readily, so that during the dark period of the French invasion, the national feeling was preserved pure and untouched by means of these stirring and patriotic songs of the past.

About the same time as the advent of the Romanticists in Germany appeared Walpole's "Castle of Otranto" in England, which is supposed to belong to the same school of literature and to have been influenced by the German. Scott was also numbered in this class; and it is from these old

German legends of the Minnesingers that Richard Wagner has drawn the material for Lohengrin, Parsifal, and others of his magnificent operas. In one department German scholars have attained a high standard, and that is as historians of ancient classical literature.

Their researches into the language, religion, philosophy, social economy, arts and sciences of ancient nations, has brought to light much for which the student of literature will always be their debtor.

ITALIAN

The first general language of Italy was the Latin, and so strongly was the Italian mind dominated by the influence of ancient Rome that her earliest writers sought to keep alive the Roman tradition. This spirit of freedom led to the establishment of the Italian Republics, and after the Lombard cities threw off the yoke of Frederick Barbarossa they turned their chief attention to education and literature. The spirit of chivalry and chivalric poetry never took such root in Italy as it did in other European countries. Nevertheless, Italy was not uninfluenced by the Crusades, and the Arabs, establishing a celebrated school of medicine at Salerno, gave a new impetus to the study of the classics. In Bologna was opened a school of jurisprudence, where Roman law was studied, and these schools, or universities soon appeared in other parts of Italy.

The Italians devoted more time to the study of law and history, and to making translations from the Greek philosophers, than to the cultivation of chivalric poetry, although many of the Italian poets wrote in Provencal and French; and Italian Troubadours made journeys to the European Courts.

It has been said that the only poetry that has any real power over a people is that which is written or composed in their own language. This is especially true of Italy. Following this early Latin period came Dante, the most glorious, and inventive of the Italian poets, and indeed one of the greatest masters of verse in the world. He perfected the Tuscan, or Florentine dialect, which was gradually becoming the literary language of Italy. Petrarch, who succeeded Dante, is greatest in his Italian poems, and it is by these that he is best known, while his Latin works, which he hoped would bring him fame, have been almost forgotten.

In the fifteenth century the use of the national language in literature entirely died out, through the rise of the Humanists, and the craze for Greek and Latin classics; but toward the end of the fifteenth century, under Lorenzo de'Medici and Leo X, interest in their own literature among the Italians began to revive again. Ariosto and Tasso wrote their magnificent epics; and once more Italian poetry was read and appreciated, and reached the height of its renown. Again in the seventeenth century it declined under the influence of the Marini school; whose bad taste and labored and bombastic style, was unfortunately imitated in both France and Spain. In the eighteenth century, under the patronage of Benedict XIV, the Arcadian poets of the Marini school were banished from literature, and other and more brilliant writers arose, possessed of the true national feeling. Under Pope Pius VI, by whom he was liberally patronized, Quirico Visconti undertook his "Pio Clementine Museum," and his "Greek and Roman Iconography," said to be the two greatest archaeological works of all ages.

With the rise of Napoleon, Italy was flooded with French writings, and French translations, not always of the best, and even the French language was used instead of the Italian. The Italian literature again suffered a decline, and it was not until after the treaty of Vienna in 1815 that the foreign influence was again shaken off. It will thus be seen that it was when Italian poets wrote in their own language that their greatest and most lasting success was attained. During the periods when a craze for imitating foreign works existed, the national languages deteriorated.

In Germany, under the Emperor Maximilian, a crown was publicly bestowed on any poet who achieved success in Latin verse, while no reward or emolument was given to those who wrote in German. The religion of Humanism in Italy went to such lengths that many seemed to lose not only their belief but also their good sense, as they considered it vulgar to talk of the Deity in the language of the Bible.

God was spoken of in the plural—gods. The Father was Jupiter, the Son, Apollo; and the Devil, Pluto; but these various errors had no lasting or far-reaching influence. The Divine Comedy, the most powerful and lifelike exponent of the thoughts and feelings of the age in which Dante lived—an allegory, written in the form of a vision, at a time when men believed that the things that are unseen are eternal—is the most perfect and magnificent monument of earthly love, refined and spiritualized, that has ever been written. It stands alone; for no man of any country, coming after Dante, has been able to write from the same motive, and in the same spirit, that he did. Petrarch, the next greatest after Dante, is chiefly celebrated for his lyrical poems, which were used as models by all the most celebrated poets of the South of Europe. They are written in two forms, the canzone taken from the Provencals, and the sonnet, taken from the Sicilians. Petrarch kept up a wide correspondence with the literary men of Europe; and through his influence a sort of literary republic arose which joined together the literati of many different countries. Boccaccio, next in rank to Petrarch, evolved a poetry consisting of Norman wit and Provencal love, joined to an elaborate setting of his own. He took Livy and Cicero for his models, and tried to combine ancient mythology with Christian history, the result being that his writings were not so fine as they would have been had they displayed a greater freedom a of style. His most celebrated work is the Decameron, the idea of which is taken from an old Hindu romance which was translated into Latin in the twelfth century. Most of these tales have also been found in the ancient French fabliaux, and while Boccaccio cannot be said to have really invented them, he did clothe them anew, and his tales in their turn have been translated into all the European languages.

It is due to Cosmo and Lorenzo de' Medici, and to Pope Leo X, that there was such a glorious development of the fine arts in the fifteenth century, an era whose benefits have been felt among the cultivated nations for over three hundred years.

At the same time Poliziano created the pastoral tragedy, which served to revive the study of Virgil. Other poets seizing on the old romance of the Trouveres, added to them an element of mockery, in place of the old religious belief. This new spirit was adopted by Ariosto. From the East he borrowed the magic and sorcery interwoven in the adventures of his knights and ladies, giants and magicians. It remained for Torquato Tasso to revive the heroic epic in his Jerusalem Delivered, in which he depicts the struggle between the Christians and Saracens. Neither the Siege of Trod, nor the Adventures of Aeneas could compare with the splendid dramatic element in Tasso's immortal poem, which has been said to combine the classic and the romantic style in a new and unusual degree.

In the sixteenth century Strapparola, an Italian novelist, wrote a number of fairy tales, which have been a treasure house for later writers, and to which we are indebted for Puss in Boots, Fortunio, and other stories which have now become familiar in the nursery lore of most modern nations. Bandello, in the same century, was a novelist from whom Shakespeare and other English dramatists have borrowed much material.

One thing which is peculiar to Italy, and which has found its way into nearly the whole civilized world, is Italian Opera or melodrama. It was an outcome of the Pastoral drama, and first took shape in 1594 under Rinuccini, a Florentine. But the true father of Italian opera is Metastasio, who flourished in the eighteenth century. He regarded opera as the national drama of Italy, and raised it to a plane that it has ever since retained; though of late years it has become more the fashion to cultivate German opera.

SPANISH

For six centuries before the advent of the Arabs in Spain the country was under the Roman yoke, and had adopted the language and arts of the Romans; but in the eighth century the overthrow of the Romans, the coming of the Arabs, and contact with Arabian civilization—as well as the struggle against their Moorish invaders—began to develop in the Spaniards a spirit that was the foundation of their national literature. No other people have ever possessed in so strong a degree the true national feeling—no other has produced such a uniformly pure, deeply religious, and elevated tone, in poetry and literature. Their poetry remained at all times free from any foreign influence, and is entirely romantic, while the Christian chivalric poetry of the Middle Ages remained with them longer than with any other nation, and received from their hands a more finished and elegant polish.

After the Moorish conquest the Spaniards withdrew to the mountains of Asturias; they took with them a corrupted form of the Latin language, as they had received it from the Romans; reaching these mountains, they found themselves thrown with the Iberians (the earliest of the Spanish races). These people had remained half barbaric, had resisted both Romans and Goths, and retained their original or Basque language. Coming now in contact with them, the Christian Spaniards learned their language. Later they met with another tribe of their own race who had remained with the Arabians, known as the Mocarabes, a people of superior refinement and civilization. Hence a new dialect from these contending elements was gradually formed, and became known, like the other languages of southern Europe, as the Romanic. The distinguishing feature of Spanish literature, from its birth, to the time of Ferdinand and Isabella, is religious faith and knightly loyalty. Qualities which sustained the whole nation in its struggle against the infidel Moors.

The first great Spanish work is the poem of the Cid. It is the only epic Spain has ever produced, and is the most ancient of any in the Romance language. It is also valuable as a faithful picture of the manners and characters of the eleventh century. Indeed, the chief characteristic of Spanish song and poetry is its delineation of the national life. It is said that the Cid is the foremost poem produced in Europe from the thousand years that marked the decline of Greek and Roman civilization, to the appearance of the Divine Comedy. The Count Lucanor, a work of the fourteenth century, was one of the earliest prose writings in the Spanish tongue, as the Decameron, which was written about the same time, was the first in Italian. Both are narrative tales; but their moral tone is very dissimilar—the Decameron was written to amuse, while the Count Lucanor is addressed to a grave and serious nation. These stories have frequently been dramatized, and one of them gave Shakespeare the outline of his Taming of the Shrew.

Alfonso the Wise, in the thirteenth century, was the author of a legislative code known as Las Sieta Partides, or the Seven Parts. It forms the Spanish common law, and has been the foundation of Spanish Jurisprudence ever since; and being used also in the colonies of Spain, it has, since the Louisiana Purchase, become in some cases the law in our own country. Juan Ruiz, who lived in the thirteenth and fourteenth centuries, wrote a poem, partly fiction and partly allegorical, called the Battle of Don Carnival, which strongly resembles Chaucer; both poets found their material in northern French verse.

Santob, a Jew in the fourteenth century, wrote a poem called the Dance of Death, which became a favourite subject with both painters and poets for several succeeding ages.

The literature of Spain may be divided into four classes—the old Ballads, the Chronicles, the Romances of Chivalry, and the Drama. The most interesting of the old ballads are historical; but there are also ballads that have to do with private life wherein appear the effusions of love, the shafts of satire, the descriptions of pastoral life, and the oddities of burlesque. One and all, however, faithfully represent Spanish life. No such popular poetry is found in any other language. The English and Scotch ballads belong to a more barbarous state of society, and their verse is less dignified and lofty than that of the Spaniards, who were uplifted by a deep religious sense, and an unswerving loyalty to their sovereign. A state of feeling that elevated them far above the men and events of border feuds, and the wars of rival Barons.

The great Spanish heroes, the Cid, Bernardo del Carpo, and Pelayo, are to this day a vital part of the belief and poetry of the lower classes in Spain, and are revered as they were hundreds of years ago. The wandering Mulateers still sing of Guarinos and of the defeat at Roncesvalles as they did when Don Quixote heard them on his way to Toboso; and the street showmen in Seville rehearse to this day the same wonderful adventures that the Don saw in the Inn at Montesinos. The Chronicles developed among the more refined and educated classes. The most celebrated is the Chronicle of Spain, written by Alfonso the Wise. It starts with the creation of the world, and ends with the death of Alfonso's father, St. Ferdinand. It contains all the time-honored traditions of the country, as well as exact historical truth. The story of the Cid is supposed to be taken from this work.

From the time of Alfonso the Wise to the accession of Charles V (or from the thirteenth century to the sixteenth), Spain was flooded by romantic chronicles. The most celebrated is that of Don Roderick, or an account of the reign of King Roderick in the eighth century, the conquest of the country by the Moors, and the efforts to wrest it from them. On this chronicle Robert Southey has founded most of his poem of Roderic the Last of the Goths. Whether resting on truth or fable, these old records struck their roots deep down in the hearts of the people; and their romance, their chivalry, their antique traditions, and their varied legends, form a rich deposit from which all the nations of Europe have drawn material for their own literature. It was not until the fourteenth century that the romances of chivalry—known in France two centuries earlier in the stories of Arthur and the Round Table, and the deeds of Charlemagne—found their way across the Pyrenees.

Spain, so essentially the land of knighthood, welcomed them eagerly, and speedily produced a number of like romances which were translated into French and became famous. The most celebrated is Amadis, written by de Lobeira, a Portuguese. Its sole purpose is to set forth the type of a perfect knight, sans peur et sans reproche. Amadis is an imaginative character; but he is the first of a long line of doers of knightly deeds, culminating in Don Quixote, whose adventures have charmed and delighted the Spaniards, as well as the men of other nations.

Provencal literature began to have an influence on the Spanish in 1113, after the crown of Provence had been transferred from Arles to Barcelona by the marriage of the then Provencal heiress to Beranger, Count of Barcelona. This introduction of the Provencal literature into northeastern Spain had a beneficial result on the two literatures, fusing them into a more vigorous spirit.

Spain had always maintained the closest relations with the See of Rome, and numerous Spanish students were educated at the Italian Universities, hence the Italian literature had some influence on the Spanish, more lasting as a whole than the effects of Provencal literature. From 1407 to 1454 King John II tried to form an Italian school in Spain, gathering around him a poetical court. This Italian influence extended into the sixteenth century. Diego de Mendoza, during the reign of Charles V wrote a clever satirical prose work called Lazarillo de Tormes, which became the foundation of a class of fiction of which Gil Blas, by Le Sage, is the best known and most celebrated example.

Except for the Cid, Spain had no historical narrative poems of any account, and her prose historical works, especially on the discovery and conquest of

America, are of a purely local character, and had no influence outside of Spain. The beginning of the eighteenth century saw the accession to the throne of Philip V, a grandson of Louis XIV; and this brought a strong French influence into the country, which for a time dominated the national literature.

A new poetical system founded on Boileau was introduced by Luzan in his Art of Poetry; but it did not seem to bring about any real advance in literature; and it was not until Spain threw off this foreign yoke, that any revival in her literature took place. It is due to a monk, Benito Feyjoo, in the middle of the eighteen century that a renaissance in Spanish literature took place. Feyjoo, a devout Catholic, labored to bring to light scientific truths, and to show how they harmonized with the true Catholic spirit. In the same century Isla, a Jesuit, undertook with entire success, to purify the Spanish pulpit, which had become lowered both in style and tone. His history of Friar Gerund, which slightly resembles Don Quixote, aimed a blow at bombastic oratory, causing it soon to die out. Proverbs which Cervantes had styled "short sentences drawn from long experience," have always been a distinctive Spanish product, and can be traced back to the earliest ages of the country. No fewer than 24,000 have been collected, and many more circulate among the lower classes which have not been recorded in writing.

PORTUGUESE

The earliest imitators in Europe of the bucolic poetry of Virgil, were the Portuguese; and as a people they thought that the pastoral life was the ideal model for poetry. This idea is strongly brought out by Ribeyro in the sixteenth century.

The great number of Mocarbians that settled in Portugal infused into them as a nation, a stronger Orientalism than is found elsewhere in Europe, and their poetry was of an enthusiastic order, more marked than that of the Spaniards.

Henry of Burgundy, who married a daughter of Alfonso XI of Spain, in the eleventh century, introduced Provencal poetry. The Cancioneros, or courtly ballads, in imitation of the Provencal, were sung by wandering minstrels, and Portuguese poetry retained its Provencal character until the end of the fourteenth century.

In the fifteenth century, the Portuguese invaded Africa, and Vasco de Gama pointed out to Europe the new and unknown route to India. Fifteen years later, toward the close of the century, a Portuguese kingdom was founded in Hindostan, causing a strong counter-current of Orientalism to invade

Portugal. The people awoke to a desire for greatness; and poetry and the arts flourished. This period, extending into the sixteenth century, is called the golden age of Portuguese literature.

The Os Lusiades, an epic poem, that has been called "one of the noblest monuments ever raised to the national glory of any people," was written by Luis de Camoens, a Portuguese of the sixteenth century. It is intensely patriotic, although it is touched by both Greek mythology, and the Italian style, which during this epoch had been slightly blended with the Portuguese. Portugal had little or no influence on the literature of any nation but her own, receiving her strongest impressions from outsiders. In the eighteenth century she was dominated both in taste and manners by the French, and the beginning of the nineteenth century found her a great admirer and imitator of English literature.

National songs are known to have been sung in Portugal during the earliest times; but none of them have come down to us. They were doubtless similar to the other bardic songs of Europe.

ARABIAN

The rise and development of Arabian literature occurs at an epoch when the rest of Europe was struggling through a period of transition. From the middle of the sixth to the beginning of the eleventh century, at a time when the Roman dominions were overrun by Northern hordes, and the Greek Nation was groaning under the Byzantine power, when both Greek and Latin literature was exposed to the danger of extinction, the splendor of Arabian literature reached its zenith and through the mingling of the Troubadours with the Moors of the Peninsula, and of the Crusaders with the Arabs, it began to influence the literature of Europe.

Arabia, peopled by wandering tribes, had no history other than the songs of the national bards, until after the rise of Mohammed in the sixth century. The desire of the prophet was to bring his people back from idolatry and star worship to the primitive and true worship of God. He studied the Old and New Testament, the legends of the Talmud and the traditions of Arabian and Persian mythology, then he wrote the Koran, which became the sacred book of the Arabians, and in which is traced in outline the true plan of man's salvation—Death, Resurrection, the Judgment, Paradise and the place of torment. Good and evil spirits, the four archangels, Gabriel, Michael, Azrael and Izrafeel, are all found in the Koran; but clothed with a true Oriental fancy. Besides the angels there are creatures, partly human and partly spiritual, called Genii, Peris (or fairies) and Deev (or giants). The Genii have the power of making themselves seen or invisible at pleasure. Some of them delight in mischief, and raise whirlwinds, or lead travellers astray. The Arabians used to say that shooting stars were arrows shot by the angels against the Genii when they approached too near the forbidden regions of bliss.

This fairy mythology of the Arabians was introduced into Europe by the Troubadours in the eleventh century, and became an important factor in the literature of Europe. From it, and the Scandinavian mythology spring all the fairy tales of modern nations. And these romances of the Koran form the groundwork of the fabliaux of the Trouveres, and of the romantic epics of Boccaccio, Tasso, Ariosto, Spenser and Shakespeare. Mohammed's teaching unified the different tribes of Arabia, and fostered a feeling of national pride, and a desire for learning. So rapidly did this develop that in less than a century the Arabian power and religion, as well as its language, had gained the ascendency over nearly half of Africa, a third of Asia, and a part of Spain; and from the ninth century to the sixteenth, the Arabian literature surpassed that of any nations of the same period.

This people, who, in a barbarous state had tried to abolish all cultivation in science and literature, now became the masters of learning, and they drew from the treasure houses of the countries that they had acquired by conquest, all the riches of knowledge at their command.

The learning of the Chaldeans and of the Magi, the poetry and fine arts of Asia Minor, the eloquence and intellect of Africa, all became theirs.

Greece counts nearly eight centuries from the Trojan war to the summit of her literary development. From the foundation of Rome till the age of Augustus the same number of centuries passed over the Roman world; while in French literature the age of Louis XIV was twelve centuries removed from the advent of Clovis; but in Arabian literature, from the time of the family of the Abassides, who mounted the throne in 750—and who introduced a passionate love for poetry, science and art—until the time of Al Mamoun, the Augustus of Arabia, there elapsed only one hundred and fifty years, a rate of progress in the development of literature among a nation that has no parallel in history.

Tournaments first originated among the Arabs, and thence found their way into France and Italy. Gunpowder was known to them a century before it appeared in Europe, and they were in possession of the compass in the eleventh century, and this notwithstanding the fact that a German chemist is supposed to have discovered gunpowder a century after the Arabs made use of it, while the compass is more frequently supposed to be a French or Italian invention of the thirteenth century.

Botany and chemistry were more familiar to them than they were to the Greeks or Romans. Bagdad and Cordova had famous schools of astronomy and medicine, and here in the tenth and eleventh centuries the Arabians were the teachers of the world. Students came to them from France and other parts of Europe; and their progress, especially in arithmetic, geometry and astronomy, was marvellous. The poetry of the Arabs is rhymed like ours, and is always the poetry of passion and love; but it is in their prose works, the Arabian tales of the Thousand and One Nights, that they have become most famous. Their richness of fancy in these prose tales is different from that of the other chivalric nations. The supernatural world is identical in both; but the moral world is different. The Arabian tales, like the old chivalric romances, take us to the realms of fairyland, but the human beings they introduce are very unlike. Their people are less noble and heroic, more moved by love and passion, and they depict women by turn as slaves and divinities. The original author of the Arabian Nights is unknown; but the book has become a household possession in every civilized country in the world.

THE DRAMA

The history of the drama may be divided into two classes, the Christian, which began with the Mystery and Morality plays; and the Greek, which was eminently classic. These two types were the foundation of all that came after them.

The first dawn of the drama was in Greece; for although the Hindus also had dramatic poetry, it did not arise until there had been a lengthened intercourse between Greece and India, so that the latter undoubtedly borrowed from the former. The learned writers of ancient times agree that both tragedy and comedy were originally choral song. It has been said that poetry and song are divided into three periods of a nation's history, that the Epic has to do with the first awakening of a people, telling of their legends, or of some great deeds in remote antiquity. This is followed by the second stage, which embraces elegiac and lyric poetry and arose in stirring and martial times, during the development of new forms of government, when each individual wanted to express his own thoughts and wishes; and the third is the drama, which can only be born in a period of civilization, and which, it has been said, implies a nation.

Hence Greek drama arose at the height of Grecian civilization and splendor. It originated in the natural love of imitation, of dancing and singing, especially at the Bacchic feasts. The custom at these feasts of taking the guise of nymphs and satyrs, and of wearing masks while they danced and sang in chorus, seems to have been the beginnings of the Greek drama.

Ancient tragedy was ideal, and had nothing to do with ordinary life; it arose from the winter feasts of Bacchus, while comedy was the outcome of the harvest feasts, and the accompanying Bacchanalian processions, which were more in the nature of a frolic than of real acting. The influence of the Middle and New Greek comedy, especially, that of Menander, on the Roman comedy of Terence is well defined. Under Ennius and Plautus the Roman comedy was fairly original; but Terence wrote for the fashionable set, like Caecilius and Scipio Africanus, and consequently imitated Greek models very carefully. The drama in Rome never attained any noteworthy height although the French tragic poets took Seneca for their model.

In the time of Lorenzo the Magnificent there was a great revival in Italy of the ancient classic drama, of which Poliziano was the most successful exponent. Both he and the later writers, however, made no attempt to found any National Italian drama—their works are entirely an imitation of the tragedies of Sophocles and Euripides, and the comedies of Plautus and Terence.

The Melodrama, which arose in the seventeenth century, is distinctly Italian and national, and has been extensively produced all over the civilized world. Alfieri, in the eighteenth century, is the greatest and most patriotic of the Italian tragedians, and he did as much to revive the national character in modern times as Dante did in the fourteenth century.

In France we have the dramatic representation of the Mysteries in the twelfth and thirteenth centuries, introduced by the pilgrims who had returned from the Crusades. At first these performances were given in the street, but later a company was formed, called the "Confraternity of the Passion," the suffering of Christ being its chief representation. This Mystery is the most ancient dramatic work of modern Europe, and gives the whole Gospel narrative from the birth of our Saviour until His death. Being too long for a play of one act, it was continued from day to day. What would seem irreverent on a modern stage was regarded as perfectly simple and natural in the Middle Ages, and it was a potent factor in teaching the masses the truths of their faith.

Following these Mysteries of the Passion came a host of other plays taken from the Old Testament, or from the lives of the Saints. The earliest "Miracle" on record is the Play of St. Catherine, which was represented at Dunstable about 1119, written in French; it was in all probability a rude picture of the miracles and martyrdom of the saint.

The stage was divided into three different floors, with Heaven on top, hell on the ground floor, and the earth between. Frequently the play would proceed in all three divisions at once, with angels and devils ascending and descending by means of ladders, as their help was needed in the different worlds.

The Devil generally played the part of clown or jester. The modern puppet play of Punch is a tradition handed down from these ancient miracles, in which the Evil One was alternately the conqueror or victim of the human Buffoon; who was also called by the names of Jester or Vice.

These early miracle plays were generally written in mixed prose and verse. The oldest manuscript of a miracle play in English is The Harrowing of Hell, believed to have been written in 1350.

The Morality plays were the outcome of the Mysteries; they were either allegorical or else taken from the Parables, or from the historical events in the Bible. The chief Moralities were Everyman, Lusty Juventus, Good Counsel, and Repentance.

The oldest English Morality play now extant is The Castle of Perseverance, written about 1450. It is a dramatic allegory of human life representing the many conflicting influences that surround man on his way through the world. Lusty Juventus depicts in a vivid and humorous way the extravagances and follies of a young heir surrounded by the virtues and vices, and the misery which follows a departure from the path of religion and virtue. Gradually these Moralities were corrupted and became mixed with a species of comedy called Interludes, a merry and farcical dialogue.

The Four P's, one of the best of these early Interludes, was written by John Heywood, an entertainer at the Court of Henry VIII. It turns upon a dispute between a Peddler, a Palmer, a Pardoner and a Poticary, in which each tries to tell the greatest lie; plays of this kind are seen in France at the present day. In the fifteenth century the drama in France became more secularized and included political events and satire, but the French were undoubtedly the fathers of drama in the Middle Ages. Their plays were known a whole century before Spain or Italy had any theater, while the romantic drama in other countries of Europe was founded on the early French drama. Modern drama in France during the time of Corneille, Racine and Voltaire was almost entirely classic. The French regarded the Greek standard as the highest art; and sought to imitate it faithfully, so much so that the French Academy, criticizing a tragedy of Corneille, said "that the poet, from the fear of sinning against the rules of art, had chosen rather to sin against the rules of nature."

Comic drama in France from the end of the sixteenth to the middle of the seventeenth century was borrowed from Spain, and had to do with a multiplication of trap doors, dark lanterns, intrigues, and puzzling disguises, until Moliere, in his "Precieuses Ridicules" successfully attacked these follies of his age.

The Romantic drama, which arose in the second quarter of the nineteenth century, holds at present the first place in France. Its chief exponents have been Victor Hugo, the two Dumases, Sardou and Octave Feuillet. Between them and the followers of the Classic School there was for some time a lively war. The latter wanted to exclude the Romanticists from the Theatre Francais, but without success. In spite of the beauty of its French, and the polish of its style, this latest form of the drama in France frequently offends strongly against morality. In Spain the drama was at all times thoroughly national. Even when they introduced mythological, Greek or Roman characters, it was always in a Castilian dress. In this respect Spain stands alone among the nations of Europe, as it borrowed nothing from France, Italy or England. Its earliest plays were the Mysteries, which it is supposed to have obtained from Constantinople, where the ancient theatre of Greece and Rome was kept up, in a grosser form, far into the Middle Ages. In later times this Eastern drama became so corrupt that the Christian Church tried to offset it by introducing the Mysteries, and it became a common custom every year at Christmas, for the Manger at Bethlehem, the Worship of the Shepherds, and the Adoration of the Magi, to be exhibited before the Altar, just as the Mysteries of the Passion were introduced during Lent. The Passion Play at Oberammergau and the Creche, representing the Manger at Bethlehem, as seen in Catholic Churches at Christmas, are the sole survivals of these ancient Mysteries.

The second dramatic period in Spain was pastoral and satirical. Nothing worthy of note adorns this period in the fifteenth century. In the sixteenth century de Rueda and Lope de Vega founded the true national drama of Spain. It was unlike anything of an earlier period, and yet, resting faithfully on tradition, it gave a vivid picture of the National Spanish life in all classes of society. From the gallantries of the "dramas of the Cloak and Sword," to the historical plays in which Dings and Princes figure; down to the manners and incidents of common life, all is essentially Spanish. A fourth class still represented Scriptural and sacred scenes. Calderon wrote at the height of the Spanish drama during the reign of Philip II; and after his time the drama in Spain declined until, in the eighteen century, it was at its lowest ebb. At this time plays were still held in open courtyards, and in the daytime, as in the earlier ages. Efforts were made to subject it to French and Italian rule, but this had only a limited success; stiff, cold translation from the French could not please a people who always found in the Spanish drama an essentially popular entertainment.

In Germany traces of the drama first appeared in the thirteenth century, when rude attempts to imitate the Mystery plays were conducted in churches by the priests. But when the populace tried to introduce the Burlesque, the performances were banished to the open fields. Students in the universities took part in them, and they continued until after the Reformation. Brought into Europe from Constantinople by the Crusaders and pilgrims, the Mystery plays became the chief amusement of an illiterate age. Christianity was first thoroughly impressed on the mind of Northern Europe by means of them; and the first missionaries familiarized the rude Goths and Huns with Biblical incidents at a time when reading was unknown outside of the Cloister. No change in German drama occurred until the seventeenth century, when operas after the Italian superseded the Mysteries and Moralities. The production of this age, however, were characterized by bad taste and pedantry; and it was not until Goethe brought his genius to bear on the subject, that the Germans acquired any drama worthy of the name. Whether in his national play Gotz von Berlichingen or in his classical drama of Iphigenia, this great German master stands at the summit of his art. Lessing attacked French drama as enacted in Germany prior to Goethe, and brought forward the Shakespearian plays as a model.

Schiller's Wallenstein obtained a worldwide reputation, and among the Romantic dramatists Werner's Attila and Grillparzer's Ancestress are the best examples of the extravagant and fertile mind of the German romanticist.

Modern German drama has found the highest art it has ever attained in the compositions of Richard Wagner, whose operas are entirely German and National, and mostly founded on the old German legends. Tannhauser is taken from the epic poem of "Parzifal," written by Wolfram von Eschenbach in the Middle Ages. Lohengrin, which is touched on in the "Parzifal," Wagner also found in the poem of an obscure Bavarian poet; and a more complete account of the celebrated "Swan Knight" appears in a collection of stories edited by the brothers Grimm. Lohengrin is a Knight of the Holy Grail, so part of the legend is borrowed from ancient Britain.

All dramatic effort in England before the sixteenth century was so rude as to be of little account. The Miracle and Mystery plays were introduced into England in the reign of Henry VI, and many of them had a personage called "Iniquity," a coarse buffoon, whose object was to amuse the audience. After the Reformation the Protestant Bishop Bale wrote plays on the same plan as the Mysteries, intended to instruct the people in the supposed errors of Popery. These plays, which deal largely in satire, became popular and after the era of Henry VIII were known as Interludes. In the beginning of the sixteenth century real comedy and tragedy began to exist in a rude form. The oldest known English comedy, Ralph Royster Doyster, was written by Nicholas Udall, and describes a character whose comic misadventures are somewhat akin to Don Quixote.

The earliest tragedy, Gorboduc, known also Ferrex and Porrex, was played in the Lower Temple. It is founded on the legends of fabulous British history. The tragedies of Marlowe and the legendary plays of Greene come next in order, followed by the golden age of English drama, from the dawn of the Shakespeare plays in 1585 until the closing of the theatre in 1645 on the breaking out of the Civil war in England. For a period of sixty years the splendid genius of the world's greatest dramatist gave to mankind a series of plays that have no equal in the literature of any country or age.

Contemporaneous with Shakespeare, or coming after him, were Beaumont and Fletcher, Ben Jonson, Massinger, Ford, and Shirley; these Elizabethan dramatists took their subjects from the stories and legends of all countries and ages—or else they depicted the national life. For this reason English drama has been called Irregular, in contrast to the Greek, which is called the Regular, and that of modern France, founded upon the Greek. The chief rule of the Regular is the Unity of Time, Place and Action. In the Greek, the time of action was allowed to extend to twenty-four hours, and the scene to change from place to place in the same city; but Shakespeare and his contemporaries acknowledged no fixed limit either of time, place or action. The operation of their plays covered many different countries, and the time extended over many years; but the rule that laid down in the Greek drama the principle that there should be unity of action (everything being subordinate to a series of events, which form the thread of the plot), was adopted by Shakespeare and his contemporaries. It has been called "unity of impression," as opposed to unity of time and place.

3

Romantic Poets

Coleridge, Wordsworth, Southey, and Scott had mostly ceased to produce poetry by 1815. The group of younger men, the last out-and-out Romanticists, who succeeded them, writing chiefly from about 1810 to 1825, in some respects contrast strongly with them. Byron and Shelley were far more radically revolutionary; and Keats, in his poetry, was devoted wholly to the pursuit and worship of beauty with no concern either for a moral philosophy of life or for vigorous external adventure. It is a striking fact also that these later men were all very short-lived; they died at ages ranging only from twenty-six to thirty-six.

Lord Byron, 1788-1824. Byron (George Gordon Byron) expresses mainly the spirit of individual revolt, revolt against all existing institutions and standards. This was largely a matter of his own personal temperament, but the influence of the time also had a share in it, the time when the apparent failure of the French Revolution had thrown the pronounced liberals back upon their own resources in bitter dissatisfaction with the existing state of society. Byron was born in 1788. His father, the violent and worthless descendant of a line of violent and worthless nobles, was just then using up the money which the poet's mother had brought him, and soon abandoned her.

She in turn was wildly passionate and uncontrolled, and in bringing up her son indulged alternately in fits of genuine tenderness and capricious outbursts of mad rage and unkindness. Byron suffered also from another serious handicap; he was born with deformed feet, so that throughout life he walked clumsily--a galling irritation to his sensitive pride. In childhood his poetic instincts were stimulated by summers spent among the scenery of his mother's native Scottish Highlands. At the age of ten, on the death of his great-uncle, he succeeded to the peerage as Lord Byron, but for many years he continued to be heavily in debt, partly because of lavish extravagance, which was one expression of his inherited reckless wilfulness. Throughout his life he was obliged to make the most heroic efforts to keep in check another inherited tendency, to corpulence; he generally restricted his diet almost entirely to such meager fare as potatoes and soda-water, though he often broke out also into periods of unlimited self-indulgence.

From Harrow School he passed to Trinity College, Cambridge, where Macaulay and Tennyson were to be among his successors. Aspiring to be an athlete, he made himself respected as a fighter, despite his deformity, by his strength of arm, and he was always a powerful swimmer. Deliberately aiming also at the reputation of a debauchee, he lived wildly, though now as later probably not altogether so wickedly as he represented. After three years of irregular attendance at the University his rank secured him the degree of M. A., in 1808. He had already begun to publish verse, and when 'The Edinburgh Review' ridiculed his very juvenile 'Hours of Idleness' he added an attack on Jeffrey to a slashing criticism of contemporary poets which he had already written in rimed couplets (he always professed the highest admiration for Pope's poetry), and published the piece as 'English Bards and Scotch Reviewers.'

He was now settled at his inherited estate of Newstead Abbey (one of the religious foundations given to members of the nobility by Henry VIII when he confiscated them from the Church), and had made his appearance in his hereditary place in the House of Lords; but following his instinct for excitement and for doing the expensively conspicuous thing he next spent two years on a European tour, through Spain, Greece, and Turkey. In Greece he traveled, as was necessary, with a large native guard, and he allowed reports to become current that he passed through a succession of romantic and reckless adventures. The first literary result of his journey was the publication in 1812 of the first two cantos of 'Childe Harold's Pilgrimage.'

This began as the record of the wanderings of Childe Harold, a dissipated young noble who was clearly intended to represent the author himself; but Byron soon dropped this figure as a useless impediment in the series of descriptions of Spain and Greece of which the first two cantos consist. He soon abandoned also the attempt to secure an archaic effect by the occasional use of Spenserian words, but he wrote throughout in Spenser's stanza, which he used with much power. The public received the poem with the greatest enthusiasm; Byron summed up the case in his well-known comment: 'I awoke one morning and found myself famous.' In fact, 'Childe Harold' is the best of all Byron's works, though the third and fourth cantos, published some years later, and dealing with Belgium, the battle of Waterloo, and central Europe, are superior to the first two.

Its excellence consists chiefly in the fact that while it is primarily a descriptive poem, its pictures, dramatically and finely vivid in themselves, are permeated with intense emotion and often serve only as introductions to passionate rhapsodies, so that the effect is largely lyrical.

Though Byron always remained awkward in company he now became the idol of the world of fashion. He followed up his first literary success by publishing during the next four years his brief and vigorous metrical romances, most of them Eastern in setting, 'The Giaour' (pronounced by Byron 'Jower'), 'The Bride of Abydos,' 'The Corsair,' 'Lara,' 'The Siege of Corinth,' and 'Parisina.' These were composed not only with remarkable facility but in the utmost haste, sometimes a whole poem in only a few days and sometimes in odds and ends of time snatched from social diversions. The results are only too clearly apparent; the meter is often slovenly, the narrative structure highly defective, and the characterization superficial or flatly inconsistent.

In other respects the poems are thoroughly characteristic of their author. In each of them stands out one dominating figure, the hero, a desperate and terrible adventurer, characterized by Byron himself as possessing 'one virtue and a thousand crimes,' merciless and vindictive to his enemies, tremblingly obeyed by his followers, manifesting human tenderness only toward his mistress (a delicate romantic creature to whom he is utterly devoted in the approved romantic-sentimental fashion), and above all inscrutably enveloped in a cloud of pretentious romantic melancholy and mystery. Like Childe Harold, this impossible and grandiose figure of many incarnations was well understood by every one to be meant for a picture of Byron himself, who thus posed for and received in full measure the horrified admiration of the public. But in spite of all this melodramatic clap-trap the romances, like 'Childe Harold,' are filled with the tremendous Byronic passion, which, as in 'Childe Harold,' lends great power alike to their narrative and their description.

Byron now made a strangely ill-judged marriage with a Miss Milbanke, a woman of the fashionable world but of strict and perhaps even prudish moral principles. After a year she left him, and 'society,' with characteristic inconsistency, turned on him in a frenzy of superficial indignation. He shortly (1816) fled from England, never to return, both his colossal vanity and his truer sensitive self stung by the injustice to fury against the hypocrisy and conventionalities of English life, which, in fact, he had always despised. He spent the following seven years as a wanderer over Italy and central Europe. He often lived scandalously; sometimes he was with the far more fine-spirited Shelley; and he sometimes furnished money to the Italians who were conducting the agitation against their tyrannical foreign governments.

All the while he was producing a great quantity of poetry. In his half dozen or more poetic dramas he entered a new field. In the most important of them, 'Manfred,' a treatment of the theme which Marlowe and Goethe had used in 'Faust,' his real power is largely thwarted by the customary Byronic mystery and swagger. 'Cain' and 'Heaven and Earth,' though wretchedly written, have also a vaguely vast imaginative impressiveness. Their defiant handling of Old Testament material and therefore of Christian theology was shocking to most respectable Englishmen and led Southey to characterize Byron as the founder of the 'Satanic School' of English poetry. More significant is the longest and chief of his satires, 'Don Juan,' on which he wrote intermittently for years as the mood took him. It is ostensibly the narrative of the adventures of a young Spaniard, but as a story it rambles on formlessly without approaching an end, and its real purpose is to serve as an utterly cynical indictment of mankind, the institutions of society, and accepted moral principles. Byron often points the cynicism by lapsing into brilliant doggerel, but his double nature appears in the occasional intermingling of tender and beautiful passages.

Byron's fiery spirit was rapidly burning itself out. In his uncontrolled zest for new sensations he finally tired of poetry, and in 1823 he accepted the invitation of the European committee in charge to become a leader of the Greek revolt against Turkish oppression. He sailed to the Greek camp at the malarial town of Missolonghi, where he showed qualities of leadership but died of fever after a few months, in 1824, before he had time to accomplish anything.

It is hard to form a consistent judgment of so inconsistent a being as Byron. At the core of his nature there was certainly much genuine goodness--generosity, sympathy, and true feeling. However much we may discount his sacrifice of his life in the cause of a foreign people, his love of political freedom and his hatred of tyranny were thoroughly and passionately sincere, as is repeatedly evident in such poems as the sonnet on 'Chillon,' 'The Prisoner of Chillon,' and the 'Ode on Venice.' On the other hand his violent contempt for social and religious hypocrisy had as much of personal bitterness as of disinterested principle; and his persistent quest of notoriety, the absence of moderation in his attacks on religious and moral standards, his lack of self-control, and his indulgence in all the vices of the worser part of the titled and wealthy class require no comment. Whatever allowances charity may demand on the score of tainted heredity, his character was far too violent and too shallow to approach to greatness.

As a poet he continues to occupy a conspicuous place (especially in the judgment of non-English-speaking nations) through the power of his volcanic emotion. It was this quality of emotion, perhaps the first essential in poetry, which enrolled among his admirers a clear spirit in most respects the antithesis of his own, that of Matthew Arnold. In 'Memorial Verses' Arnold says of him:

He taught us little, but our soul
Had felt him like the thunder's roll.
With shivering heart the strife we saw
Of passion with eternal law.

His poetry has also an elemental sweep and grandeur. The majesty of Nature, especially of the mountains and the ocean, stirs him to feeling which often results in superb stanzas, like the well-known ones at the end of 'Childe Harold' beginning 'Roll on, thou deep and dark blue Ocean, roll'! Too often, however, Byron's passion and facility of expression issue in bombast and crude rhetoric. Moreover, his poetry is for the most part lacking in delicacy and fine shading; scarcely a score of his lyrics are of the highest order. He gives us often the blaring music of a military band or the loud, swelling volume of an organ, but very seldom the softer tones of a violin or symphony.

To his creative genius and power the variety as well as the amount of his poetry offers forceful testimony.

In moods of moral and literary severity, to summarize, a critic can scarcely refrain from dismissing Byron with impatient contempt; nevertheless his genius and his in part splendid achievement are substantial facts. He stands as the extreme but significant exponent of violent Romantic individualism in a period when Romantic aspiration was largely disappointed and disillusioned, but was indignantly gathering its strength for new efforts.

PERCY BYSSHE SHELLEY, 1792-1832

Shelley resembles Byron in his thorough-going revolt against society, but he is totally unlike Byron in several important respects. His first impulse was an unselfish love for his fellow-men, with an aggressive eagerness for martyrdom in their behalf; his nature was unusually, even abnormally, fine and sensitive; and his poetic quality was a delicate and ethereal lyricism unsurpassed in the literature of the world. In both his life and his poetry his visionary reforming zeal and his superb lyric instinct are inextricably intertwined.

Shelley, born in 1792, belonged to a family of Sussex country gentry; a baronetcy bestowed on his grandfather during the poet's youth passed from his father after his own death to his descendants. Matthew Arnold has remarked that while most of the members of any aristocracy are naturally conservative, confirmed advocates of the system under which they enjoy great privileges, any one of them who happens to be endowed with radical ideas is likely to carry these to an extreme. In Shelley's case this general tendency was strengthened by reaction against the benighted Toryism of his father and by most of the experiences of his life from the very outset. At Eton his hatred of tyranny was fiercely aroused by the fagging system and the other brutalities of an English school; he broke into open revolt and became known as 'mad Shelley,' and his schoolfellows delighted in driving him into paroxysms of rage.

Already at Eton he read and accepted the doctrines of the French pre-Revolutionary philosophers and their English interpreter William Godwin. He came to believe not only that human nature is essentially good, but that if left to itself it can be implicitly trusted; that sin and misery are merely the results of the injustice springing from the institutions of society, chief of which are organized government, formal religion, law, and formal marriage; and that the one essential thing is to bring about a condition where these institutions can be abolished and where all men may be allowed to follow their own inclinations.

The great advance which has been made since Shelley's time in the knowledge of history and the social sciences throws a pitiless light on the absurdity of this theory, showing that social institutions, terribly imperfect as they are, are by no means chiefly bad but rather represent the slow gains of thousands of years of painful progress; none the less the theory was bound to appeal irresistibly to such an impulsive and inexperienced idealism as that of Shelley.

It was really, of course, not so much against social institutions themselves that Shelley revolted as against their abuses, which were still more flagrantly apparent in his time than in ours. When he repudiated Christianity and declared himself an atheist, what he actually had in mind was the perverted parody of religion mainly offered by the Church of his time; and, as some one has observed, when he pronounced for love without marriage it was because of the tragedies that he had seen in marriages without love. Much must be ascribed also to his sheer radicalism--the instinct to fly violently against whatever was conventionally accepted and violently to flaunt his adherence to whatever was banned.

In 1810 Shelley entered Oxford, especially exasperated by parental interference with his first boyish love, and already the author of some crude prose-romances and poetry. In the university he devoted his time chiefly to investigating subjects not included or permitted in the curriculum, especially chemistry; and after a few months, having written a pamphlet on 'The Necessity of Atheism' and sent it with conscientious zeal to the heads of the colleges, he was expelled. Still a few months later, being then nineteen years old, he allowed himself to be led, admittedly only through pity, into a marriage with a certain Harriet Westbrook, a frivolous and commonplace schoolgirl of sixteen.

For the remaining ten years of his short life he, like Byron, was a wanderer, sometimes in straits for money, though always supported, after some time generously enough, by his father. At first he tried the career of a professional agitator; going to Ireland he attempted to arouse the people against English tyranny by such devices as scattering copies of addresses from his window in Dublin or launching them in bottles in the Bristol Channel; but he was soon obliged to flee the country.

It is hard, of course, to take such conduct seriously; yet in the midst of much that was wild, his pamphlets contained also much of solid wisdom, no small part of which has since been enacted into law.

Unselfish as he was in the abstract, Shelley's enthusiast's egotism and the unrestraint of his emotions rendered him fitful, capricious, unable to appreciate any point of view but his own, and therefore when irritated or excited capable of downright cruelty in concrete cases. The most painful illustration is afforded by his treatment of his first wife. Three years after his marriage he informed her that he considered the connection at an end and abandoned her to what proved a few years of a wretched existence. Shelley himself formed a union with Mary Wollstonecraft Godwin, the daughter of his revolutionary teacher.

Her sympathetic though extravagant admiration for his genius, now beginning to express itself in really great poetry, was of the highest value to him, the more so that from this time on he was viewed by most respectable Englishman with the same abhorrence which they felt for Byron. In 1818 the Shelleys also abandoned England (permanently, as it proved) for Italy, where they moved from place to place, living sometimes, as we have said, with Byron, for whose genius, in spite of its coarseness, Shelley had a warm admiration.

Shelley's death came when he was only thirty, in 1822, by a sudden accident--he was drowned by the upsetting of his sailboat in the Gulf of Spezia, between Genoa and Pisa. His body, cast on the shore, was burned in the presence of Byron and another radical, Leigh Hunt, and the ashes were buried in the Protestant cemetery just outside the wall of Rome, where Keats had been interred only a year earlier.

Some of Shelley's shorter poems are purely poetic expressions of poetic emotion, but by far the greater part are documents (generally beautiful also as poetry) in his attack on existing customs and cruelties. Matthew Arnold, paraphrasing Joubert's description of Plato, has characterized him as 'a beautiful and ineffectual angel, beating in the void his luminous wings in vain.' This is largely true, but it overlooks the sound general basis and the definite actual results which belong to his work, as to that of every great idealist.

On the artistic side the most conspicuous thing in his poetry is the ecstatic aspiration for Beauty and the magnificent embodiment of it. Shelley is the poetic disciple, but a thoroughly original disciple, of Coleridge. His esthetic passion is partly sensuous, and he often abandons himself to it with romantic unrestraint. His 'lyrical cry,' of which Matthew Arnold has spoken, is the demand, which will not be denied, for beauty that will satisfy his whole being. Sensations, indeed, he must always have, agreeable ones if possible, or in default of them, painful ones; this explains his occasional touches of repulsive morbidness. But the repulsive strain is exceptional. No other poetry is crowded in the same way as his with pictures glorious and delicate in form, light, and color, or is more musically palpitating with the delight which they create.

To Shelley as a follower of Plato, however, the beauty of the senses is only a manifestation of ideal Beauty, the spiritual force which appears in other forms as Intellect and Love; and Intellect and Love as well are equal objects of his unbounded devotion. Hence his sensuousness is touched with a real spiritual quality. In his poetic emotion, as in his social ambitions, Shelley is constantly yearning for the unattainable. One of our best critics has observed: 'He never shows his full power in dealing separately with intellectual or moral or physical beauty. His appropriate sphere is swift sensibility, the intersecting line between the sensuous and the intellectual or moral. Mere sensation is too literal for him, mere feeling too blind and dumb, mere thought too cold.... Wordsworth is always exulting in the fulness of Nature, Shelley is always chasing its falling stars.'

The contrast, here hinted at, between Shelley's view of Nature and that of Wordsworth, is extreme and entirely characteristic; the same is true, also, when we compare Shelley and Byron. Shelley's excitable sensuousness produces in him in the presence of Nature a very different attitude from that of Wordsworth's philosophic Christian-mysticism. For the sensuousness of Shelley gets the upper hand of his somewhat shadowy Platonism, and he creates out of Nature mainly an ethereal world of delicate and rapidly shifting sights and sounds and sensations. And while he is not unresponsive to the majestic greatness of Nature in her vast forms and vistas, he is never impelled, like

Byron, to claim with them the kinship of a haughty elemental spirit.

A rather long passage of appreciative criticism is sufficiently suggestive for quotation:

"From the world of [Shelley's] imagination the shapes of the old world had disappeared, and their place was taken by a stream of radiant vapors, incessantly forming, shifting, and dissolving in the 'clear golden dawn,' and hymning with the voices of seraphs, to the music of the stars and the 'singing rain,' the sublime ridiculous theories of Godwin. In his heart were emotions that responded to the vision--an aspiration or ecstasy, a dejection or despair, like those of spirits rapt into Paradise or mourning over its ruin. And he wrote not like Shakspere or Pope, for Londoners sitting in a theatre or a coffee-house, intelligence's vivid enough but definitely embodied in a definite society, able to fly, but also able to sit; he wrote, or rather he sang, to his own soul, to other spirit-sparks of the fire of Liberty scattered over the dark earth, to spirits in the air, to the boundless spirit of Nature or Freedom or Love, his one place of rest and the one source of his vision, ecstasy, and sorrow.

He sang to this, and he sang of it, and of the emotions it inspired, and of its world-wide contest with such shapes of darkness as Faith and Custom. And he made immortal music; now in melodies as exquisite and varied as the songs of Schubert, and now in symphonies where the crudest of Philosophies of History melted into golden harmony. For although there was something always working in Shelley's mind and issuing in those radiant vapors, he was far deeper and truer than his philosophic creed; its expression and even its development were constantly checked or distorted by the hard and narrow framework of his creed. And it was one which in effect condemned nine-tenths of the human nature that has formed the material of the world's great poems."

The finest of Shelley's poems, are his lyrics. 'The Skylark' and 'The Cloud' are among the most dazzling and unique of all outbursts of poetic genius. Of the 'Ode to the West Wind,' a succession of surging emotions and visions of beauty swept, as if by the wind itself, through the vast spaces of the world, Swinburne exclaims: 'It is beyond and outside and above all criticism, all praise, and all thanksgiving.' The 'Lines Written among the Euganean Hills,' 'The Indian Serenade,' 'The Sensitive Plant' (a brief narrative), and not a few others are also of the highest quality. In 'Adonais,' an elegy on Keats and an invective against the reviewer whose brutal criticism, as Shelley wrongly supposed, had helped to kill him, splendid poetic power, at least, must be admitted. Much less satisfactory but still fascinating are the longer poems, narrative or philosophical, such as the early 'Alastor,' a vague allegory of a poet's quest for the beautiful through a gorgeous and incoherent succession of romantic wildernesses; the 'Hymn to Intellectual Beauty'; 'Julian and Maddalo,' in which Shelley and Byron (Maddalo) are portrayed; and 'Epipsychidion,' an ecstatic poem on the love which is spiritual sympathy. Shelley's satires may be disregarded.

To the dramatic form belong his two most important long poems. 'Prometheus Unbound' partly follows AEschylus in treating the torture of the Titan who is the champion or personification of Mankind, by Zeus, whom Shelley makes the incarnation of tyranny and on whose overthrow the Golden Age of Shelleyan anarchy succeeds. The poem is a lyrical drama, more on the Greek than on the English model. There is almost no action, and the significance lies first in the lyrical beauty of the profuse choruses and second in the complete embodiment of Shelley's passionate hatred of tyranny. 'The Cenci' is more dramatic in form, though the excess of speech over action makes of it also only a 'literary drama.'

The story, taken from family history of the Italian Renaissance, is one of the most horrible imaginable, but the play is one of the most powerful produced in English since the Elizabethan period. That the quality of Shelley's genius is unique is obvious on the slightest acquaintance with him, and it is equally certain that in spite of his premature death and all his limitations he occupies an assured place among the very great poets. On the other hand, the vagueness of his imagination and expression has recently provoked severe criticism. It has even been declared that the same mind cannot honestly enjoy both the carefully wrought classical beauty of Milton's 'Lycidas' and Shelley's mistily shimmering 'Adonais.' The question goes deep and should receive careful consideration.

JOHN KEATS, 1795-1821

No less individual and unique than the poetry of Byron and Shelley is that of the third member of this group, John Keats, who is, in a wholesome way, the most conspicuous great representative in English poetry since Chaucer of the spirit of 'Art for Art's sake.' Keats was born in London in 1795, the first son of a livery-stable keeper. Romantic emotion and passionateness were among his chief traits from the start; but he was equally distinguished by a generous spirit, physical vigor (though he was very short in build), and courage. His younger brothers he loved intensely and fought fiercely. At boarding-school, however, he turned from headstrong play to enthusiastic reading of Spenser and other great English and Latin poets and of dictionaries of Greek and Roman mythology and life. An orphan at fourteen, the mismanagement of his guardians kept him always in financial difficulties, and he was taken from school and apprenticed to a suburban surgeon. After five years of study and hospital practice the call of poetry proved too strong, and he abandoned his profession to revel in Spenser, Shakspere, and the Italian epic authors. He now became an enthusiastic disciple of the literary and political radical, Leigh Hunt, in whose home at Hampstead he spent much time. Hunt was a great poetic stimulus to Keats, but he is largely responsible for the flippant jauntiness and formlessness of Keats' earlier poetry, and the connection brought on Keats from the outset the relentless hostility of the literacy critics, who had dubbed Hunt and his friends 'The Cockney [i.e., Vulgar] School of Poetry.'

Keats' first little volume of verse, published in 1817, when he was twenty-one,-contained some delightful poems and clearly displayed most of his chief tendencies. It was followed the next year by his longest poem, 'Endymion,' where he uses, one of the vaguely beautiful Greek myths as the basis for the expression of his own delight in the glory of the world and of youthful sensations.

As a narrative the poem is wandering, almost chaotic; that it is immature Keats himself frankly admitted in his preface; but in luxuriant loveliness of sensuous imagination it is unsurpassed. Its theme, and indeed the theme of all Keats' poetry, may be said to be found in its famous first line--'A thing of beauty is a joy forever.' The remaining three years of Keats' life were mostly tragic. 'Endymion' and its author were brutally attacked in 'The Quarterly Review' and 'Blackwood's Magazine.' The sickness and death, from consumption, of one of Keats' dearly-loved brothers was followed by his infatuation with a certain Fanny Brawne, a commonplace girl seven years younger than himself.

This infatuation thenceforth divided his life with poetry and helped to create in him a restless impatience that led him, among other things, to an unhappy effort to force his genius, in the hope of gain, into the very unsuitable channel of play-writing. But restlessness did not weaken his genuine and maturing poetic power; his third and last volume, published in 1820, and including 'The Eve of St. Agnes,' 'Isabella,' 'Lamia,' the fragmentary 'Hyperion,' and his half dozen great odes, probably contains more poetry of the highest order than any other book of original verse, of so small a size, ever sent from the press. By this time, however, Keats himself was stricken with consumption, and in the effort to save his life a warmer climate was the last resource.

Lack of sympathy with Shelley and his poetry led him to reject Shelley's generous offer of entertainment at Pisa, and he sailed with his devoted friend the painter Joseph Severn to southern Italy. A few months later, in 1821, he died at Rome, at the age of twenty-five. His tombstone, in a neglected corner of the Protestant cemetery just outside the city wall, bears among other words those which in bitterness of spirit he himself had dictated: 'Here lies one whose name was writ in water.' But, in fact, not only had he created more great poetry than was ever achieved by any other man at so early an age, but probably no other influence was to prove so great as his on the poets of the next generation.

The most important qualities of his poetry stand out clearly:

1. He is, as we have implied, the great apostle of full though not unhealthy enjoyment of external Beauty, the beauty of the senses. He once said: 'I feel sure I should write, from the mere yearning and tenderness I have for the beautiful, even if my night's labors should be burnt every morning and no eye ever rest upon them.' His use of beauty in his poetry is marked at first by passionate Romantic abandonment and always by lavish Romantic richness. This passion was partly stimulated in him by other poets, largely by the Italians, and especially by Spenser, from one of whose minor poems Keats chose the motto for his first volume: 'What more felicity can fall to creature than to enjoy delight with liberty?' Shelley's enthusiasm for Beauty, as we have seen, is somewhat similar to that of Keats.

   But for both Spenser and Shelley, in different fashions, external Beauty is only the outer garment of the Platonic spiritual Beauty, while to Keats in his poetry it is, in appearance at least, almost everything. He once exclaimed, even, 'Oh for a life of sensations rather than of thoughts!' Notable in his poetry is the absence of any moral purpose and of any interest in present-day life and character, particularly the absence of the democratic feeling which had figured so largely in most of his Romantic predecessors. These facts must not be over-emphasized, however. His famous final phrasing of the great poetic idea--'Beauty is truth, truth beauty'--itself shows consciousness of realities below the surface, and the inference which is sometimes hastily drawn that he was personally a fiberless dreamer is as far as possible from the truth.

   In fact he was always vigorous and normal, as well as sensitive; he was always devoted to outdoor life; and his very attractive letters, from which his nature can best be judged, are not only overflowing with unpretentious and cordial human feeling but testify that he was not really unaware of specific social and moral issues. Indeed, occasional passages in his poems indicate that he intended to deal with these issues in other poems when he should feel his powers adequately matured. Whether, had he lived, he would have proved capable of handling them significantly is one of the questions which must be left to conjecture, like the other question whether his power of style would have further developed.

Almost all of Keats' poems are exquisite and luxuriant in their embodiment of sensuous beauty, but 'The Eve of St. Agnes,' in Spenser's richly lingering stanza, must be especially mentioned.

2. Keats is one of the supreme masters of poetic expression, expression the most beautiful, apt, vivid, condensed, and imaginatively suggestive. His poems are noble storehouses of such lines as these:

The music, yearning like a God in pain.

Into her dream he melted, as the rose
Blendeth its odour with the violet.

magic casements, opening on the foam
Of perilous seas, in faery lands forlorn.

It is primarily in this respect that he has been the teacher of later poets.

3. Keats never attained dramatic or narrative power or skill in the presentation of individual character. In place of these elements he has the lyric gift of rendering moods. Aside from ecstatic delight, these are mostly moods of pensiveness, languor, or romantic sadness, like the one so magically suggested in the 'Ode to a Nightingale,' of Ruth standing lonely and 'in tears amid the alien corn.'
4. Conspicuous in Keats is his spiritual kinship with the ancient Greeks. He assimilated with eager delight all the riches of the Greek imagination, even though he never learned the language and was dependent on the dull mediums of dictionaries and translations. It is not only that his recognition of the permanently significant and beautiful embodiment of the central facts of life in the Greek stories led him to select some of them as the subjects for several of his most important poems; but his whole feeling, notably his feeling for Nature, seems almost precisely that of the Greeks, especially, perhaps, of the earlier generations among whom their mythology took shape. To him also Nature appears alive with divinities. Walking through the woods he almost expects to catch glimpses of hamadryads peering from their trees, nymphs rising from the fountains, and startled fauns with shaggy skins and cloven feet scurrying away among the bushes.

In his later poetry, also, the deeper force of the Greek spirit led him from his early Romantic formlessness to the achievement of the most exquisite classical perfection of form and finish. His Romantic glow and emotion never fade or cool, but such poems as the Odes to the Nightingale and to a Grecian

Urn, and the fragment of 'Hyperion,' are absolutely flawless and satisfying in structure and expression.

SUMMARY

One of the best comments on the poets whom we have just been considering is a single sentence of Lowell: 'Three men, almost contemporaneous with each other, Wordsworth, Keats, and Byron, were the great means of bringing back English poetry from the sandy deserts of rhetoric and recovering for her her triple inheritance of simplicity, sensuousness, and passion.' But justice must be done also to the 'Renaissance of Wonder' in Coleridge, the ideal aspiration of Shelley, and the healthy stirring of the elementary instincts by Scott.

LESSER WRITERS

Throughout our discussion of the nineteenth century it will be more than ever necessary to pass by with little or no mention various authors who are almost of the first rank. To our present period belong: Thomas Campbell (1777-1844), author of 'Ye Mariners of England,' 'Hohenlinden,' and other spirited battle lyrics; Thomas Moore (1779-1852), a facile but over-sentimental Irishman, author of 'Irish Melodies,' 'Lalla Rookh,' and a famous life of Byron; Charles. Lamb (1775-1834), the delightfully whimsical essayist and lover of Shakspere; William Hazlitt (1778-1830), a romantically dogmatic but sympathetically appreciative critic; Thomas de Quincey (1785-1859), a capricious and voluminous author, master of a poetic prose style, best known for his 'Confessions of an English Opium-Eater'; Walter Savage Landor (1775-1864), the best nineteenth century English representative, both in prose and in lyric verse, of the pure classical spirit, though his own temperament was violently romantic; Thomas Love Peacock (1785-1866), author of some delightful satirical and humorous novels, of which 'Maid Marian' anticipated 'Ivanhoe'; and Miss Mary Russell Mitford (1787-1855), among whose charming prose sketches of country life 'Our Village' is best and best-known.

4

Romantic Comedies

In the second half of the 1590s, Shakespeare brought to perfection the genre of romantic comedy that he had helped to invent. *A Midsummer Night's Dream* (*c.* 1595–96), one of the most successful of all his plays, displays the kind of multiple plotting he had practiced in *The Taming of the Shrew* and other earlier comedies. The overarching plot is of Duke Theseus of Athens and his impending marriage to an Amazonian warrior, Hippolyta, whom Theseus has recently conquered and brought back to Athens to be his bride. Their marriage ends the play. They share this concluding ceremony with the four young lovers Hermia and Lysander, Helena and Demetrius, who have fled into the forest nearby to escape the Athenian law and to pursue one another, whereupon they are subjected to a complicated series of mix-ups. Eventually all is righted by fairy magic, though the fairies are no less at strife. Oberon, king of the fairies, quarrels with his Queen Titania over a changeling boy and punishes her by causing her to fall in love with an Athenian artisan who wears an ass's head. The artisans are in the forest to rehearse a play for the forthcoming marriage of Theseus and Hippolyta. Thus four separate strands or plots interact with one another. Despite the play's brevity, it is a masterpiece of artful construction.

The use of multiple plots encourages a varied treatment of the experiencing of love. For the two young human couples, falling in love is quite hazardous; the long-standing friendship between the two young women is threatened and almost destroyed by the rivalries of heterosexual encounter. The eventual transition to heterosexual marriage seems to them to have been a process of dreaming, indeed of nightmare, from which they emerge miraculously restored to their best selves. Meantime the marital strife of Oberon and Titania is, more disturbingly, one in which the female is humiliated until she submits to the will of her husband. Similarly, Hippolyta is an Amazon warrior queen who has had to submit to the authority of a husband. Fathers and daughters are no less at strife until, as in a dream, all is resolved by the magic of Puck and Oberon. Love is ambivalently both an enduring ideal relationship and a struggle for mastery in which the male has the upper hand.

The Merchant of Venice (*c.* 1596–97) uses a double plot structure to contrast a tale of romantic wooing with one that comes close to tragedy. Portia is a fine example of a romantic heroine in Shakespeare's mature comedies: she is witty, rich, exacting in what she expects of men, and adept at putting herself in a male disguise to make her presence felt. She is loyally obedient to her father's will and yet determined that she shall have Bassanio. She triumphantly resolves the murky legal affairs of Venice when the men have all failed. Shylock, the Jewish moneylender, is at the point of exacting a pound of flesh from Bassanio's friend Antonio as payment for a forfeited loan. Portia foils him in his attempt in a way that is both clever and shystering. Sympathy is uneasily balanced in Shakespeare's portrayal of Shylock, who is both persecuted by his Christian opponents and all too ready to demand an eye for an eye according to ancient law. Ultimately Portia triumphs, not only with Shylock in the court of law but in her marriage with Bassanio.

Much Ado About Nothing (*c.* 1598–99) revisits the issue of power struggles in courtship, again in a revealingly double plot. The young heroine of the more conventional story, derived from Italianate fiction, is wooed by a respectable young aristocrat named Claudio who has won his spurs and now considers it his pleasant duty to take a wife. He knows so little about Hero (as she is named) that he gullibly credits the contrived evidence of the play's villain, Don John, that she has had many lovers, including one on the evening before the intended wedding.

Other men as well, including Claudio's senior officer, Don Pedro, and Hero's father, Leonato, are all too ready to believe the slanderous accusation. Only comic circumstances rescue Hero from her accusers and reveal to the men that they have been fools. Meantime, Hero's cousin, Beatrice, finds it hard to overcome her skepticism about men, even when she is wooed by Benedick, who is also a skeptic about marriage. Here the barriers to romantic understanding are inner and psychological and must be defeated by the good-natured plotting of their friends, who see that Beatrice and Benedick are truly made for one another in their wit and candour if they can only overcome their fear of being outwitted by each other. In what could be regarded as a brilliant rewriting of *The Taming of the Shrew*, the witty battle of the sexes is no less amusing and complicated, but the eventual accommodation finds something much closer to mutual respect and equality between men and women.

Rosalind, in *As You Like It* (*c.* 1598–1600), makes use of the by-now familiar device of disguise as a young man in order to pursue the ends of promoting a rich and substantial relationship between the sexes. As in other of these plays, Rosalind is more emotionally stable and mature than her young man, Orlando. He lacks formal education and is all rough edges, though fundamentally decent and attractive. She is the daughter of the banished Duke who finds herself obliged, in turn, to go into banishment with her dear cousin Celia and the court fool, Touchstone. Although Rosalind's male disguise is at first a means of survival in a seemingly inhospitable forest, it soon serves a more interesting function. As "Ganymede," Rosalind befriends Orlando, offering him counseling in the affairs of love. Orlando, much in need of such advice, readily accepts and proceeds to woo his "Rosalind" ("Ganymede" playing her own self) as though she were indeed a woman. Her wryly amusing perspectives on the follies of young love helpfully puncture Orlando's inflated and unrealistic "Petrarchan" stance as the young lover who writes poems to his mistress and sticks them up on trees. Once he has learned that love is not a fantasy of invented attitudes, Orlando is ready to be the husband of the real young woman (actually a boy actor, of course) who is presented to him as the transformed Ganymede-Rosalind. Other figures in the play further an understanding of love's glorious foolishness by their various attitudes: Silvius, the pale-faced wooer out of pastoral romance; Phoebe, the disdainful mistress whom he worships; William, the country bumpkin, and Audrey, the country wench; and, surveying and commenting on every imaginable kind of human folly, the clown Touchstone and the malcontent traveler Jaques.

Twelfth Night (*c.* 1600–02) pursues a similar motif of female disguise. Viola, cast ashore in Illyria by a shipwreck and obliged to disguise herself as a young man in order to gain a place in the court of Duke Orsino, falls in love with the duke and uses her disguise as a cover for an educational process not unlike that given by Rosalind to Orlando. Orsino is as unrealistic a lover as one could hope to imagine; he pays fruitless court to the Countess Olivia and seems content with the unproductive love melancholy in which he wallows. Only Viola, as "Cesario," is able to awaken in him a genuine feeling for friendship and love. They become inseparable companions and then seeming rivals for the hand of Olivia until the presto change of Shakespeare's stage magic is able to restore "Cesario" to her woman's garments and thus present to Orsino the flesh-and-blood woman whom he has only distantly imagined. The transition from same-sex friendship to heterosexual union is a constant in Shakespearean comedy. The woman is the self-knowing, constant, loyal one; the man needs to learn a lot from the woman. As in the other plays as well, *Twelfth Night* neatly plays off this courtship theme with a second plot, of Malvolio's self-deception that he is desired by Olivia—an illusion that can be addressed only by the satirical devices of exposure and humiliation.

The Merry Wives of Windsor (c. 1597–1601) is an interesting deviation from the usual Shakespearean romantic comedy in that it is set not in some imagined far-off place like Illyria or Belmont or the forest of Athens but in Windsor, a solidly bourgeois village near Windsor Castle in the heart of England. Uncertain tradition has it that Queen Elizabeth wanted to see Falstaff in love. There is little, however, in the way of romantic wooing (the story of Anne Page and her suitor Fenton is rather buried in the midst of so many other goings-on), but the play's portrayal of women, and especially of the two "merry wives," Mistress Alice Ford and Mistress Margaret Page, reaffirms what is so often true of women in these early plays, that they are good-hearted, chastely loyal, and wittily self-possessed. Falstaff, a suitable butt for their cleverness, is a scapegoat figure who must be publicly humiliated as a way of transferring onto him the human frailties that Windsor society wishes to expunge.

SHAKESPEARE'S PLAY 'ROMEO AND JULIET'

Task

Look at the way conflict is investigated in *Romeo and Juliet* and in poems chosen from the selection. Throughout Shakespeare's play 'Romeo and Juliet', one of the main themes is conflict and conflict gradually escalates as the play reaches its tragic climax.

From the start of the play, in the prologue, we are told of the futility of conflict as suggested by 'ancient grudge'. The word 'ancient' suggests that the 'grudge' started long ago, meaning the real reason for it is long since forgotten, and therefore, the 'grudge' is petty though the resulting conflict is not. Additionally, the word 'grudge' suggests the consequences of the conflict are long lasting.

We are also told how contagious conflict and the 'ancient grudge' can be, 'civil blood makes civil hands unclean'. The choice of the word 'civil' shows that the 'grudge' has gone beyond private and spread into society, highlighting how infectious it can be. Moreover, the word 'blood' implies death, proving the dangerous consequences of conflict both physically and mentally. Furthermore, the word 'unclean' reminds the audience of blood stains which yet again remind us of the deadly consequences of conflict, and also the long term effects of conflict, like the scars and the lingering guilt.

The prologue inevitably ends with a Shakespearean rhyming couplet just as the tragedy will always end in the deaths of Romeo and Juliet, 'Death-marks of love'. The juxtaposition of the words 'death' and 'love', shows Shakespeare's beliefs that love isn't just a sweet thing, but also a deadly one.

At the start of Act 3 scene 1, we are informed that it's set in a public place and are immediately reminded of the Prince's warning, 'if ever you disturb our streets again, your lives shall pay the forfeit of the peace'. This immediately creates a tense atmosphere as the audience anticipate conflict. Throughout the play, the Prince is used as a voice of reason.

The first character to speak is Benvolio. His name is derived from the word 'benevolent', so it is not surprising his character acts in the role of the peacemaker. Nevertheless, this creates further tension, as when he gives a warning, it's normally because conflict is approaching: 'let's retire: The day is hot... these hot days is the mad blood stirring'. This use reflects some beliefs in Shakespeare's time, that when the days were hot, people would get hot headed, becoming animalistic and slipping down the hierarchy of being. This mirrors Shakespeare's beliefs that conflict is degrading. The use of personification creates a number of effects. Firstly, the word 'mad' further highlights the beliefs that when it was hot, you could lose your mind. Additionally, it suggests how insane conflict is and how 'mad' it is to shed blood because of a petty grudge. It also suggests loss of control, of both mind and body, showing how easy it is to get carried away by conflict.

The word 'stirring' suggests something being awoken and gradually made worse, therefore indicating that dangerous conflict is on its way.

When Tybalt arrives, the atmosphere immediately changes, becoming much tenser, because of his dangerous reputation, yet he remains polite to Mercutio as Mercutio is not his real target. Mercutio's name is derived from the word 'mercury', a fiery unpredictable element, mirroring Mercutio's fiery unpredictable personality, "by my heel I care not." The line shows how Mercutio acts with his heart, making him a loveable character but his personality is conflicting to that of Benvolio's, "by my head."

When Mercutio is stabbed, he is outraged that it's the result of such a petty 'grudge' and comments 'a plague a' both houses'. The word 'plague' links to the infectious and long lasting effects of conflict. It also shows that Mercutio wants their suffering to be long and painful, just like the 'ancient grudge' and relates to how deadly something so petty can be. The word 'both' shows that Mercutio blames the grudge for his death and wants all involved to suffer, linking to the inevitability of the tragedy and Romeo and Juliet's deaths.

We are informed once more of this inevitability, 'this day's black fate on more days doth depend; this but begins woe others must end'. The rhyming couplet inevitably suggests importance, highlighting how pivotal this scene is. Moreover, the word 'black' is pessimistic, highlighting the negative effects of conflict. It also suggests the Black Death, a deadly, fearful, and contagious plague linking to how scary and fatal conflict is, as well as how fast it spreads. Additionally, the words 'black fate' show the inevitability of death, and the pessimistic word 'black' shows what a bad thing conflict is to have to die for.

Mercutio's death makes the audience want revenge, as Mercutio was the most 'alive' character. This displays how easy it is for a conflict so petty to become so dangerous. Romeo is banished and narrowly escapes a death sentence. The conflict, based as it is on a flimsy and forgotten pretext, has ruined many lives and resulted in two deaths. Shakespeare seems to suggest that the characters' narrow-minded and childish desire for revenge leads to conflict out of all proportion to the reason for it.

Wilfred Owen in his poem 'Dulce et Decorum Est' conveys the futility of conflict on a bigger scale. He was writing during the First World War and had direct experience of the terrible suffering of the troops in the front line. He begins his poems with a comment on the soldiers returning from battle who look 'like old beggars under sacks.' The word 'old' portrays the fact that even though the people who signed up to become soldiers were young, they experienced enough to last them a life time and their youth was swiftly stolen from them unfairly. Moreover, the simile uses the word, 'beggars', showing how even though men signed up believing they would gain honour and glory, they lost their lives, in very unheroic surroundings and miserable ways, therefore making them poor like beggars. Additionally, the word also shows how desperate the men were, initially for glory, but in the end just to survive.

The word 'under' suggests being weighed down, as a result indicating, both the physical and psychological burdens conflict can bring. It also suggests how overwhelming the experience must have been, and suggests being dragged down - possibly with the guilt conflict brings.

Similarly, in Owen's poem, 'The Send Off' we are told of the negativity of conflict. The men go to battle 'Down the close darkening lanes'. The words 'down' and 'darkening' are pessimistic and create a gloomy atmosphere. Additionally, they suggest the effects of conflict worsening and becoming more and more serious. It also creates a sense of the inevitability of death as a consequence of war and conflict as the words suggest that the men are going into night, perhaps a permanent one.

Throughout 'Dulce et Decorum Est' we are also told of the serious effects of conflict: 'all went lame; all blind'. The repetition of the word 'all' shows the inevitability that everyone involved in conflict will feel its consequences. More over, the word 'all' demonstrates how throughout the traumas of conflict and war, the men were united, creating a poignant comment on their likely fate.

The iambic pentameter highlights the unity, and orderly conduct of the men as it creates a rhythm similar to that of men marching obediently. However, it also shows their lack of independence and how the soldiers rely on each other, and follow orders without question.

In the second stanza, the iambic pentameter breaks, creating a sense of disorder and chaos: 'Gas! Gas! Quick, boys!'. The use of caesura, along with varied punctuation highlights the panic and breakdown of order. Repetition of the word, 'Gas!' emphasises how serious and deadly war can be. This is a danger which must be taken seriously. Moreover, the word, 'Quick' creates an even greater sense of urgency, and the word 'boys' emphasises how tragic it is for such young people to be put in the fatal situations conflict leads to. It additionally links back to the word, 'old', showing how wasteful conflict can be. The word 'boys' also indicates the innocence of youth and the way they obey orders without question.

Similarly, we are told of the scarring effects of the conflict, 'incurable sores on innocent tongues'. Again we are informed of youth's innocence, as well as the terrible effect conflict and war can have, both psychologically and physically, indicating the tragic wastefulness of the situation.

Again, in 'The Send Off', we are told of youth's innocence, 'breasts were stuck all white'. The colour 'white' indicates purity and innocence and the soldiers' innocent acceptance of their fate, as well as their ignorance of war and conflict's consequences.

In 'Dulce et Decorum Est', we are also told of the unimaginable experience of war and conflict, 'in all my dreams... guttering, choking, drowning.' The words 'all' and 'my', link back to the fact that conflict is unforgettable and at times unavoidable. Moreover, the word 'my' shows how unimaginable the consequences of conflict are. Not only does the poor soldier suffer awfully, the writer is scarred by the experience. The wounds are not just visible; they scar the soul too.

The emotive words, 'guttering, choking, drowning', are very vivid and encourage people to imagine what the experience must have been like. Further onomatopoeia, 'gargling', helps to add emphasis on how vivid Owen's nightmares about war are. Owen uses imagery in the form of metaphors and similes in an attempt to portray how ghastly and disgusting war is: 'floundering like a man in fire or lime'. The word 'floundering' creates images of drowning, therefore demonstrating how helpless the men were and how overwhelming and powerful, as well as brutal, war can be. Additionally, the word 'lime' refers to lime gas demonstrating the deadly seriousness of conflict, as well as the inevitability that if you're unprepared you'll die. There are no second chances.

The word 'lime' could also suggest the fruit lime and the fact that lime is sour, the opposite of 'sweet' and the fact that soldiers signed up for glory but received the opposite - death. Moreover, it could also indicate the fact that the war was anything but 'sweet' and happy. Also, limes are acidic showing the fact that conflict burns and eats away at you.

Conflict's sourness is further indicated by the use of 'the old lie', 'Dulce et Decorum est pro patria mori'. Here Owen points out to those who have no experience of the realities of the war believe that it is right and proper to die for one's country but we should never pretend that it is 'sweet'. As he has described, death in wartime is likely to be ugly, cruel and painful and that those who by some miracle survive will live with the appalling images in their minds forever.

In these poems and others in the selection, the writers give a very negative impression of conflict and suggest that it rarely brings anything but misery to those involved.

Although 'Romeo and Juliet' differs in form to the poems, they all share some common ground in that they are all concerned with the unpleasant side of conflict.

In both 'Romeo and Juliet', as well as Rupert Brooke's poem 'The Soldier', the characters appear to believe that conflict is honourable. In that poem the word 'richer,' indicates the glorious rewards of conflict. Throughout 'Romeo and Juliet', characters like Tybalt and Mercutio, the main trouble makers, believe that they should fight to remain honourable and to prove their masculinity, thus they are depicted in the play as noblemen. However, Shakespeare appears to challenge this belief, as, by the end of the play, the main catalysts of conflict are dead, proving the futility and pettiness of feud.

Likewise, the use of first person narrative in 'The Soldier', engages the audience, depicting Brooke's patriotic beliefs, 'a body of England's', and as a result showing that Brooke believes that he owes his life to his country. Moreover, the fact that Brooke wrote 'The Soldier' at the beginning of the war, indicates how strongly influenced people were by propaganda at the time, 'it is sweet and right to die for your country', proving that people thought that conflict and war was going to be glorious. After reading Owen's poems, Brooke could be accused of naivety.

In contrast, Wilfred Owen's poem, 'Dulce et Decorum Est,' was written towards the end of the First world, displaying the fact that conflict is the complete opposite of 'sweet' and 'right', instead suggesting that it is bitter and acidic, eating away at you and having a scarring affect. We know this as in the poem it says, 'you would not tell with such high zest'. This displays how dangerous and unspeakable the consequences of conflict are. There is also a sense of accusation here which reinforces his bitterness. The word 'you' seems to encompass all those who have no direct experience of the fighting. We are also told of conflict's serious consequences, 'froth corrupted lungs', displaying how tainted and dark conflict is and how it plays with your mind making you think that you're being honourable when you are not. Furthermore, the pairing of 'corrupted lungs' indicates conflict's damaging affects both internally and externally, in body and mind. In addition, it also shows how conflict makes you vulnerable and less independent, as well as how deadly it is, as without our organs we could not survive.

Similarly, in 'Romeo and Juliet', we are told of how damaging and 'vile' conflict is. Using the word 'vile' displays how disgusting Shakespeare believed conflict to be and demonstrates how infectious conflict is. We are also told of this contagiousness when Mercutio realises that he is about to die, "a plague a' both your houses", therefore acting as a reminder of the black death, and Mercutio's disbelief that a conflict so petty, could swiftly become a conflict so deadly. Furthermore, 'a' both' shows that Mercutio blames the grudge itself, more than the people involved in the conflict. This is surprising as Mercutio was one of the characters that initially believed conflict noble and honourable, showing how truly deceitful conflict is.

Likewise, in Tennyson's poem, 'The Charge of the Light Brigade', at the very end we are told of his beliefs on conflict and war, "honour the Light Brigade". This suggests that Tennyson believes that the men who fight are brave and noble but that the 'blunder', which caused their horrific deaths, was the result of a misguided understanding of the word 'honour'.

In 'The Charge of the Light Brigade', Tennyson repeats the word 'hell', further highlighting conflict's deadly consequences and, therefore, its futility. It also indicates that conflict isn't rewarding to those who engage in it but instead ultimately futile, an idea Owen investigates in a poem not in the Collection called 'Futility'.

Brooke in his poem uses a different kind of imagery. Here he does not stress the awfulness of the war scene but instead writes about 'flowers', 'dreams' and a rural dream world of 'ways to roam'. He also tells us how patriotic he believes conflict to be, indicating his beliefs that sometimes conflict is the key to peace, and that you have to make sacrifices for the 'greater good', and in order to achieve your 'dreams'. This would be unlikely to impress Owen with his more realistic picture of death on the battlefield.

In 'The Charge of the Light Brigade', the inevitability of conflict is hinted at from the very start of the poem, 'all in the valley of death'. The fact this line is situated towards the beginning of the poem, illustrates the fact that the men are already destined to die. Moreover, the word 'all' shows how no one can escape the death that conflict brings, and the word 'in' demonstrates how in a way the men are already dead, yet they're noble as they continue fighting despite their helplessness.

Similarly, in the Prologue of 'Romeo and Juliet', we are told that Romeo and Juliet are destined to die, 'star-cross'd.' The phrase indicates that Romeo and Juliet's destinies are mapped out in the stars and are unavoidable. This links clearly with most of the poetry mentioned where inevitability and fate lead the soldiers to a similar terrible conclusion.

Moreover, the word 'cross'd' could also have a reference to biblical teaching, as in Christianity, it is believed that Jesus was crucified as a sacrifice for the 'greater good'. Correspondingly, at the end of 'Romeo and Juliet', Capulet uses the word 'sacrifices', which further demonstrates the fact that Romeo and Juliet's deaths were a sad necessity in order to end the conflict.

In 'Romeo and Juliet', we are also informed that conflict is animalistic and degrading, as Mercutio says, 'a cat, to scratch a man to death'. The word 'cat' demonstrates how those involved in conflict slip down the hierarchy of being, which is shocking for the audience as Mercutio was one of the initiators of conflict, demonstrating how truly dishonourable conflict can be. Moreover, the ironic word Mercutio uses about his injury, 'scratch', stresses the fact that such petty conflict can have such serious consequences.

In contrast, throughout 'The Soldier', Brooke reveals his beliefs that conflict is glorious and rewarding, 'hearts at peace under an English heaven'. These words demonstrate Brooke's belief that in order to get to heaven you must first prove your bravery and masculinity, through conflict and appropriate conduct within it.

In Shakespeare's play, 'Romeo and Juliet', throughout the orderly iambic pentameter, there are numerous scenes of conflict, demonstrating how conflict may seem ordered and noble at times but really it's manic and dishonourable. Most of the pieces of literature that I have studied are similar in that they depict conflict as futile and dishonourable. Even 'The Soldier' has a melancholy tone despite Brooke's claims that conflict is glorious, indicating that deep down, at some level, we are all aware of conflict's inevitable, deadly consequences.

Commentary

This student gets straight to the language making sensible comments about the implications of the Prologue. She then moves to Act 3 scene 1 making some good analysis of the language at the opening of the scene. The Shakespeare section is strong with its consistent stress on the way Shakespeare has used language to shape our responses about the idea of conflict. However, it ends rather abruptly. In the poetry section she easily moves between the texts and makes clear and interesting points. Although the reference to the significance of 'lime' as a fruit is questionable, it is pleasing that she is trying to probe the text. The final section of the essay is very good. The student moves between the poems she has studied and the Shakespeare text with ease drawing on her extensive knowledge of the verse and the play to weave a convincing linking section.

This student easily fulfils the Band 5 assessment criteria. Her work demonstrates good selection, detailed reference to the texts, character evaluation and assured exploration and evaluation of the ways in which the language of the works is shaped for effect. The work is well organised and the final section is detailed and developed. Able candidates will have little difficulty in writing more than the 1500 word guide within the 4 hours allowed – in this case nearly double. This itself is not an issue: the only consideration is the quality of the response as judged by the criteria, and it would be quite possible for work much nearer the word guide to reach the top end of Band 5. In this case there is no sense of over-writing in what is a cogent, critical response which demonstrates flair and originality of interpretation. Subtle links are established between texts supported by apt textual references. It deserves the highest mark.

Task

Look at the way conflict is investigated in *Romeo and Juliet* and in poems chosen from the selection.

Conflict is a recurring theme throughout 'Romeo and Juliet'. It is a vital component in the plot and determines the fare of many characters including both Romeo and Juliet. Conflict escalates rapidly from verbal conflict to physical conflict throughout 'Romeo and Juliet'. For example in Act 3, Scene 1, verbal sparring between Mercutio and Tybalt escalates and intensifies, ultimately resulting in Mercutio's death. The rate at which the conflict speeds up portrays the impulsive nature of the characters. It also suggests that the young men feel sensitive to any insults to their family honour and pride, and they are quick to defend their houses; they are loyal to their houses and pride is their main priority. Mercutio refuses to avoid conflict, and therefore seems excited about the prospect of potential conflict. When Benvolio tells Mercutio that the Capulets are coming his response is 'By my heel I care not'. His stubborn attitude and excitement creates an aura of anticipation and also suggests that Mercutio is hungry for conflict, like an animal. Their quick reaction when defending their honour is like that of animal instinct, which is reinforced in the Prince's speech, 'You men, you beasts!' The rapid rate of escalation also suggests a lack of thought process. The way in which Shakespeare refers to the young men as 'beasts' indicates that they don't take conflict very seriously and treat it is a competition, and that the young men are wild, uncontrollable and vicious. Additionally, Mercutio uses the repetition of 'quarrel' during Act 3, Scene 1, which creates a 'domino effect.' The repetition suggests the alarming rate at which the conflict spreads and escalates, and also that conflict only leads to more conflict.

In addition, conflict is not only between the two houses and between members of houses, but conflict also occurs within characters. Romeo experiences severe conflict of his emotions in Act 3, Scene 1, 'My reputation stained With Tybalt's slander - Tybalt, that an hour hath been my cousin. O sweet Juliet,' after the murder of Mercutio. Shakespeare uses caesuras to portray the battling of different emotions and opinions within Romeo. Both the dash and full stop break his speech, making him appear confused and unsure. The caesuras make Romeo's speech unpredictable and spontaneous, which conveys the unpredictability of conflict. However, the caesuras could also give the effect of Romeo sobbing, because of the breaks in between his speech and the lack of pattern with the use of the caesuras. Also, the fact that there is conflict both surrounding Romeo and within Romeo shows that conflict invades personal life, like a poison, and you cannot escape from it. He feels he has to revenge Mercutio's death even though this means killing the cousin of the woman he has just married. Additionally, Romeo's decision to avenge Mercutio's death implies that conflict and hatred always prevails.

For the duration of 'Romeo and Juliet' conflict is foreshadowed and there are repeatedly references to fate. Benvolio has a premonition at the beginning of Act 3, Scene 1, which does - later on in the scene - come true, 'We shall not 'scape a brawl' and he refers to the 'mad blood stirring'. Here Benvolio is stating that hot days cause madness, which implies that a character will do something crazy or reckless that they'll later regret. The personification of 'blood' indicates that there will be blood spilled and foreshadows violence and physical conflict. Also, the personification used could suggest excitement, as scientifically when a liquid (like blood) gets excited it vibrates and moves; this suggests that the young men are excited for conflict and enjoy it, and also that they are bloodthirsty. 'Stirring' could imply that the characters are hungry for violence and conflict (like animals). This indicates that the characters get a sense of satisfaction from conflict and bloodshed - this shows their twisted ideas and maliciousness. Later in Act 3, Scene 1 (once Romeo has killed Tybalt) Romeo professes, 'O, I am fortune's fool.' He has realised the outcome of the conflict is anything but good and he is claiming that he has been cheated by fortune and that he has no control over his actions. This is not really true and he should blame his own impetuosity rather than fortune for what he has done. Romeo's reluctance to blame the houses and the feud portrays how he is blinded by conflict and misguided honour, for he believes that his house and its doings are righteous. The alliteration, 'fortune's fool' sounds as if Romeo is spitting out the words to convey his bitterness towards the conflict. The personification of fortune suggests that Romeo is like a puppet and that fortune is powerful and malicious. In this case, fortune and conflict are very closely linked. Additionally, in the Prologue the fate of both Romeo and Juliet is foreshadowed, 'Star-cross'd lovers.' This shows the inevitability of the fate of the characters and also the futility of conflict. Also, in Elizabethan times astrology was an integral part of Italian society, so the audience would have believed fate and be shocked about the foreshadowing.

Logic is ignored in the face of conflict, which is seen in Act 3, Scene 1, when Benvolio's reasonable and logical suggestions are ignored. Benvolio personifies reason, and he frequently has sensible ideas, 'Withdraw into some private place,' which however no other characters appear to take note of. Also, the fact that Benvolio survives the duration of the play supports this statement, whereas other reckless characters - such as Tybalt and Mercutio - die as a result of their foolish actions. Benvolio speaks in structured verse, 'I pray thee... blood stirring', which provides a sense of order and organization. This is much in contrast to Mercutio's prose, 'Come, come thou art as hot a jack in thy mood as any in Italy.' Mercutio's words seem designed to raise the temperature and create conflict. In addition, when there is a scene of conflict, Benvolio is not present or doesn't predominantly feature; this symbolises the absence of logic amidst conflict.

Conflict in the play is powerful and dictating; however, whether conflict can defeat love is still questionable. At the end Romeo and Juliet are dead but they are still celebrated for their love.

Conflict is a predominant theme in many of the poem; however, conflict is portrayed differently in each poem, depending on the poet and the purpose of the poem.

Firstly, conflict is presented as horrific. In 'Dulce et Decorum est' the first stanza has a slow and peaceful rhythm, like that of a lullaby. 'Distant rest... asleep... drunk with fatigue... gas shells dropping softly...' Owen uses a number of references to sleep in the first stanza to show how brutal and hard war is, and the tiring effect it has on the soldiers. In addition, in Stanza 4 Owen states, 'If in some smothering dreams...' which – as well as the references to and words about sleep - suggests that war is like a nightmare. This indicates that war is dominating and that there is no escape from conflict, even in unconsciousness. Also, likening conflict to a nightmare implies that conflict is extremely horrific and recurring - it doesn't go away. Additionally, the first stanza is written in past tense, which gives the effect of a story being told. This could suggest that the reality of conflict is so terrible and horrific that is has to be told in a story format.

Also, conflict is unpredictable and chaotic, particularly in 'Dulce et Decorum est'.' 'Gas! Gas! Quick, boys!' The use of caesuras adds spontaneity and irregularity, which reflects on the nature of war. Also the caesuras portray the conflicting emotions of the soldiers amidst the chaos - they are panicking, which is evident in the use of exclamation marks to show desperation. In addition, the structure of the poem is irregular, suggesting the unpredictability of conflict and also the fast pace at which conflict can change.

Conflict is fatal and leaves a lasting impact on all involved. For instance, in 'Dulce et Decorum est' powerful verbs are used to convey the brutality and emphasise the fatality of conflict, 'Guttering, choking, drowning.' Powerful verbs relating to death emphasize how destructive and impacting conflict is. Also, the repetition of three powerful verbs suggest the horror of the death and that conflict only leads to more conflict, that it is infectious and spreads. The decline of the man's life is strongly suggested by the gradation of the verbs. The horror is made more real by the focus on a single death amid many others.

In 'The Charge of the Light Brigade,' the short final stanza capitalizes that futility of conflict, 'Honour the... Six hundred!' The short final stanza both emphasizes the fatality and the lasting impact of conflict. Tennyson is suggesting that we should 'honour' the six hundred but he is not suggesting that the order for them to go into the 'valley of death' was a wise or good one. On the contrary, he seems to suggest that their lives were wasted by a 'blunder' that should not have happened. The conflict and death here are partly the result of arrogance and stupidity. Owen supports this idea in his poem where it is clear that he does not think it is particularly 'sweet and right' to die in a hideous way for one's country. He seems to be suggesting that nothing has been learned.

Conflict is portrayed as inevitable and brave, yet malicious. This is seen in 'The Charge of the Light Brigade.' The men ride 'Into the jaws of Death'. The personification of death suggests that death is more powerful than the soldiers, and that death is like a beast. As death is referred to like an animal, it implies that 'death' is hungry, and so the soldiers can't escape their fate. It also suggests that conflict is reckless and instinctive, because animals act rashly owing to animal instinct. The fact that the soldiers are riding 'into' the jaws of death suggests that the soldiers are brave and accepting of their fate. It also implies that conflict is inevitable and that the fate of the soldiers has already been decided.

Conflict is devastating and leaves those involved feeling bitter. In 'Dulce et Decorum est' - it seems even the devil is sickened by conflict, 'Devil's sick of sin.' Here Owen is suggesting that there is so much conflict that even the devil is fed up, which implies that the conflict is extremely devastating and malicious. The use of sibilance makes it sound as if the words are spat out in spite, which suggests that Owen is bitter about war. However, it could also be interpreted as hissing, which suggests evil and could sound like gas, which was one of the most devastating components of the war and central to the poem's effect. Another reason to believe that conflict is malicious would be in 'The Send-Off', 'a lamp winked to the guard.' This implies that the lamp and driver share a secret that the soldiers are unaware of. This creates an air of conspiracy and shows how the fate of those involved was already planned and therefore inevitable.

Finally, conflict involves numerous sacrifices. In 'The Send-Off,' the soldiers are described as animals and are dehumanized with the reference to the 'siding-shed.' Similarly, 'The Conscript' implies a sense of sacrifice with an allusion to the crucifixion, 'Arms outstretched and drooping thorn-crowned head.' Here Gibson could be suggesting that the men were sacrificing their lives for others. But he is also perhaps suggesting that the sacrifice is without point, unlike Christ's. However, it could also be implying that the men of higher authority (like God) were sacrificing the men for the good of the remainder of the population. Additionally, mentioning Christ could be to suggest that war and conflict are good, justified and righteous or that sacrifice needs to be made before the world can become good.

In conclusion, Owen presents conflict negatively, whereas Tennyson suggests the nobility of those who die. Despite this, both poems share numerous qualities and are both effective in conveying their message.

There are many similarities between the poems and the play 'Romeo and Juliet' concerning the theme of conflict. However, there are numerous differences too, which are portrayed through various poetic techniques and use of language.

First of all, conflict is fatal. The fatality of conflict is conveyed in Romeo and Juliet, with the death of Mercutio. As he is dying, he curses the houses, 'A plague a' both your houses!' The reference to a disease indicates that conflict is both futile and horrific. Also, in 'Dulce et Decorum Est', there is reference to disease, 'obscene as cancer.' Diseases such as the plague and cancer are gruesome and fatal, and so this provides graphic imagery, especially with the use of the simile, 'Obscene as cancer.' In my opinion, I think that Shakespeare's reference to a contagious disease (as opposed to Owen's simile involving cancer) has a greater effect, as it shows how conflict can spread and the rate at which conflict escalates.

On the other hand, conflict is honourable. Honour appears repeatedly throughout 'Romeo and Juliet', and is a vital component. Again, at the scene of Mercutio's death, Benvolio describes Mercutio as, 'Brave Mercutio.' Additionally, the six hundred who die in 'The Charge of the Light Brigade' are named the 'Noble six hundred!' By describing both Mercutio and the soldiers (who all died as a result of conflict) as 'noble' and 'brave', this is indicating that they are heroes, which suggests that war is honourable and glorifies. The use of an exclamation mark '...hundred!' implies that the death of the soldiers is not shameful, rather something to be proud of. Despite the fact that it was Mercutio's fault that he died, Benvolio seems to forget his taunting and proclaims that he is 'brave', which suggests that conflict glorifies those in death. I can relate to the glorifying of soldiers in conflict, as presently there are rewards for soldiers for their bravery. However, I believe that conflict should be something to be ashamed of, as in 'Dulce et Decorum Est', 'Like old beggars under sacks.' Likening young men to 'old beggars' suggests that war makes one weak, and is not glorifying at all. Similarly, in the 'The Send Off', the soldiers 'creep back' from conflict. This implies that they are ashamed of what they have done and wish to return to normality unnoticed. 'Creep' could imply a cowardly attitude, as opposed to honourable bells and parades for bravery upon return. Also, it suggests that the soldiers are not proud of what they have done. It also suggests that they return to a nation ungrateful for their sacrifice.

In addition, the fate of those involved in conflict is not due to their actions, but to another force or power. For instance, the doctors in 'The Conscript', 'Pronounce each doom with easy indifferent breath'.

The men are vulnerable, and their fate is decided by the doctors. In 'Romeo and Juliet', Romeo blames fortune for his tragic fate, 'Fortune's fool.' Romeo believes that he has no control over his actions, and therefore does not claim responsibility for them. Shakespeare uses alliteration to convey Romeo's bitterness towards the power which he believes is controlling and deciding the outcome of his life. The metaphor suggests that 'Fortune' is messing with Romeo for entertainment. Correspondingly, in 'The Send-Off', the fate of the soldiers is unknown by the soldiers, however it is seemingly known by all other objects and the guard, 'Unmoved signals nodded and a lamp winked to the guard.' The personification of the signals and lamp could imply that there is some sinister magic or other-wordly force involved. This creates a malicious atmosphere, and suggests a conspiracy between the guard, signals and lamp know of an evil secret involving the fate of the soldiers.

Finally, conflict is portrayed as a duty. For example, in 'Romeo and Juliet', Romeo does not want to kill Tybalt, yet he does so as he feels compelled to avenge Mercutio's death. This shows the power of conflict and how conflict is more important than Romeo's personal feelings. Also, in 'Charge of the Light Brigade', the soldiers know a mistake has been made, yet continue with their advance, 'Theirs not to reason why, Theirs but to do and die'. The repetition of the negative 'theirs not' suggests that the result of the conflict is futile, but also that they have no control over what they are to do and have, like puppets, no rights. In addition, the duty of conflict is enforced by the fact that Wilfred Owen despised conflict, yet returned to war out of duty. His death reinforces the fatality of conflict too.

In conclusion, conflict is both fatal and horrific, and after reading the poems and the play, conflict is definitely mostly portrayed in a negative light. The negatives outweigh the positives, and conflict is only conveyed positively by a poet who did not experience conflict himself, so both the poems and the play are more successful in portraying conflict negatively.

Commentary

This student chooses to centre her work on Act 3 scene 1 of *Romeo and Juliet*. She begins by noting the nature of the conflict and the various ways it is revealed through both the actions and thoughts of the characters. A number of good points are made about the conflict in the play though the range of reference is not wide. When she deals with the poetry, she refers to a number of poems, showing wide reading and the ability to select the aspects that fit her argument. The final section is the strength of the piece. Here she makes intelligent and cogent comments about the relationships between the poetry and Shakespeare's play, though again her work is stronger on the poetry than the drama.

This is sound work and suggests an active and mature mind at work. The Shakespeare section could be more wide ranging in reference and detail and perhaps she spends rather too long in her discussion of caesuras and rather too little time, relatively, on the words and how they shape our responses. The work is of a similar length to the first example, and the same comments on length and quality apply, though in this case the work is not quite of such consistently high quality. Nevertheless, this deserves a good mark towards the top of Band 5 (18 in a GCSE English folder and 36 in a GCSE English Literature folder). It represents a considerable achievement.

Task

Examine the way Shakespeare presents conflict in Act 3 Scene 1 in *Romeo and Juliet*. In your response make reference to other parts of the play.

Then look at the way conflict is presented in the selection of verse you have studied.

Finally, make links between the ways the writers present the theme of conflict.

In 'Romeo and Juliet' William Shakespeare writes about different types of conflict, and how the conflict affects those around it.

Conflict is one of the main themes, throughout the play, and its presence is certainly felt in Act 3 Scene 1. This scene is a prime example of how playful banter, can turn to verbal warfare, which can turn to physical conflict, all in a matter of seconds. It is a mere twelve lines after Tybalt returns furiously, that he falls, after fighting with Romeo, to his death. What Shakespeare is trying to show is how easy it is to manipulate someone. All you have to do is use the right words. It is Mercutio's use of insults like 'rat-catcher' that really annoy Tybalt, and make him want to get out his sword.

In this play Shakespeare shows how easily conflict can occur. He shows us this by creating conflict between family members from the same house. At the very start of Act 3 Scene 1 Benvolio and Mercutio are having a difference of opinion. These two are very good friends, but it shows how the slightest thing playing on someone's mind can make them act differently to those around them. 'I pray thee, good Mercutio' says Benvolio at the very start of the scene. They are best friends but Benvolio has to beg of Mercutio to calm down, and this is before the Capulets even arrive.

Conflict is seen throughout this work as a noble thing. All of the characters, some more than others, are led to believe the any type of conflict is the way to go. Verbal or physical, the characters all push forward, disagreeing with each other and thinking that the mentally and physically stronger will come out on top. This is even true of the lesser characters as we see at the beginning of the play when the servants of both houses insult each other. They are more interested in defending their honour than keeping the peace. Because of the pride these characters hold in their houses, they are willing to die. I think this is most clearly shown in Mercutio's famous line 'a plague a' both your houses'. This is possibly the biggest insult that he could have said to either of them, but he takes no caution in saying it, as he is on his deathbed. Raw passion for their house is seen virtually in every scene, such as what we see in Act 1 scene 5, when Tybalt is furious with the Romeo's presence at the party at the Capulet house, and is positive he must leave. It is only when he is forced by Capulet to ignore his presence that he does so. Even then he is determined to get revenge. He says: 'but this intrusion shall, Now seeming sweet, convert to bitterest gall.' This seems to put a black feeling on to the meeting of Romeo and Juliet which happens as soon as he has spoken.

It is shown that characters feel so strongly about conflict and protecting their family honour because they believe it is their destiny. We see throughout the play that astrology and fate means a lot to the characters, as it did to most people at the time. Romeo and Juliet are described in the prologue as 'Star-crossed lovers', something that turned out to certainly have elements of truth in it. These were two people who paid the ultimate price of death, just because it wasn't their destiny to be together.

Throughout the entire play we see what conflict is and how it can occur, but in the end, at least some of the characters realize that all of their loyalty was worth nothing. After Romeo and Juliet's deaths, their fathers agree to drop the feud. But conflict has resulted in a number of avoidable deaths and Shakespeare seems to be saying that it is in the end wasteful and tragic that mindless conflict can do such damage.

In the historical poems, 'Dulce et Decorum Est' and 'The Charge of the Light Brigade' we are given a good idea of how two writers can have different opinions about war and conflict. In 'Dulce et Decorum est' the first line is 'Bent double, like old beggars under sacks' suggesting war ages men before their time. Wilfred Owen is trying to get across the fact that these soldiers and being treated disgracefully by the army. It is one of the many points made to show how unfair and brutal this conflict was to the men fighting in it. In 'The Conscript' Wilfrid Gibson writes of a man 'Standing before them wearily'. This shows that before the men even went to war many of them weren't in the best mental or physical state, and that doctors were willing to ship almost anyone off to war. Here conflict seems to be without honour or glory.

But, war is spoken of in a very different light in Alfred Lord Tennyson's 'The Charge of the Light Brigade'. He is trying to tell us how noble it is for these six hundred men to go into battle, almost certain to not return, just for the pure love and passion they have for their country. The final line 'Noble six hundred!' tells us all we need to know about what Tennyson is trying to say. Even though these soldiers have died for an extremely questionable cause, it is being exclaimed that they are noble. It is almost as if Tennyson is saying that these soldiers reward for dying in battle is that they are being recognised by the people as 'heroes'.

Despite the vast differences between the two poems, there is one strong common theme that is ever present throughout; and that is the fact that war is simply horrific. We are told, quite graphically at some points, of the sheer violence of the conflict that these soldiers are partaking in. As a man is choking to death in 'Dulce et Decorum est', Owen describes the scene as him 'gargling from the froth-corrupted lungs'. This line is enough to make some people's stomachs churn, but we can only imagine the feelings of the man himself, and what is going through Wilfred Owen's mind as he watches someone who could so easily have been him, come to a sorry end. In 'The

Charge of the Light Brigade' it is written of more than once that they are about to enter the 'Jaws of death'. This lets our imaginations run wild as to what terrible fate these soldiers were about to come to.

Another theme which is constant throughout is one of futility. Wherever in Literature we find conflict, we will almost definitely find futility. In 'The Charge of the Light Brigade' the six hundred know they if they go into battle they will probably not return, so it seems an absurd idea that they would go anyway. Whether it is their patriotism or they think it's their 'destiny' it still seems almost pathetic that these men would fight. The horrible death described in 'Dulce et Decorum est' makes us wonder what could he or his country have possibly done to make him deserve a death this brutal. At the end of the day, the war can't possibly mean that much to anyone.

These four wartime poets may differ in their beliefs about war, but the lesson learnt could not be more similar. Whether you think conflict is noble or childish, it is agreeable that it is horrific, futile, and to sum up, pointless.

We can interpret conflict in many ways from these pieces of literature. We can see the different viewpoints and this teaches us a lot.

Despite the vast differences between these works, there is one definite common theme and that is the idea of conflict as a thing of futility. Not one of these pieces of literature ends up with conflict that was actually worthwhile. We see this type of futility in Act 3 Scene 1 of 'Romeo and Juliet'. Tybalt is out to confront Romeo, after the previous nights events, but because of his fury and stupidity, two men, including himself, end up dead within hours. Wilfred Owen, the poet who wrote 'Dulce et Decorum est' and 'The Send off' was a soldier in World War one and he died as a result of the conflict and warfare. Surely no type of conflict is necessary if the ultimate price to pay is the lives of people. This lesson is one not learnt even by some who have seen it happen themselves.

We can see in these pieces of literature conflict as being a very controlling thing. Men are forced to go to war in poems like 'The Conscript' even though they are not fit to do so and even if they do not desire to. Similarly in 'Romeo and Juliet' all of the characters are bound by the love of their house, and would do anything to protect its pride and would never dare to dishonour them.

It is the case that these people must have unquestionable loyalty for their house or country. I think what this shows us about conflict in these pieces of literature is that it is very predictable. 'Romeo and Juliet', is possibly one of the most predictable pieces of work of all time. We are told in the prologue that 'a pair star-crossed lovers take their life' so we know from here on what is going to happen and why. There is also a huge sense of inevitability throughout Alfred Lord Tennyson's 'The Charge of the Light Brigade'. We are told in the first stanza that they are charging into 'The Valley of Death'. This makes us question why they would do this, with the probable answer again of patriotism. This shows once again that patriotism or in the case of 'Romeo and Juliet' family honour, which is only patriotism in miniature, rules in a game of conflict.

This is also linked to the fact that in conflict, your life is often not in your own hands. In Wilfred Gibson's 'The Conscript' we can see that these men really have no choice but to enter into the war. It seems extremely unfair that these men have been robbed of their free will and for some of them, their lives. Also, in 'Romeo and Juliet' some of the characters like Benvolio express their desire to not engage in conflict, but it is almost as if they are peer pressured into it or almost accidently involved despite their innocence.

All of these pieces of literature are not too dissimilar in the lessons we learn about conflict. Despite the differences in how they try to get it across they are all crying out with the fact that conflict is horrific, futile, and has no place in today's society.

The work on Shakespeare is well-focused on the theme but a little vague in detail and the student misses some opportunities to examine the language of the play. Nevertheless, what he writes is sensible and on task. It could be a little more wide ranging. In the poetry section, he moves between the poems with ease and makes reference to key aspects within his chosen verse. He perhaps could have looked at one poem in a little more detail and the fact that he has not done this makes his work a little generalised. In the linking section, he makes clear, thoughtful and well supported points which sum up his views throughout the piece.

There is much to commend in this essay. The strength lies in the final section and the Shakespeare section is the weakest part. What is admirable is the way the student can move around, between and within texts thus displaying a mature grasp of the works and their various significances. This essay deserves a mark at the top end of Band 4 (in a GCSE English folder 15 and in a GCSE English Literature folder 30). More detail in the Shakespeare section and a closer examination of one of the chosen poems would push it easily into Band 5.

Task

Examine the ways Shakespeare presents the relationship between men and women in *Romeo and Juliet* and any two poems of your own choice. Try to make links between the ways the writers display the relationship between men and women.

Romeo and Juliet is one of the most romantic love stories ever written. Shakespeare uses different types of love to show the relationships between characters in the play. The language used helps make the play more dramatic and interesting. He also uses many mythological and Biblical allusions which help elevate the love between two people, and show the nature of love.

At the beginning of the play, we see Romeo is in a "relationship" with Rosaline, and we can tell that it is an infatuated love and that Romeo is in love with the idea of being in love. We can tell by the number of negative oxymorons used that he is actually very depressed and miserable. "O heavy lightness, Serious vanity"- these suggest that Romeo is also very confused about his own feelings. "Misshapen chaos of well seeming forms" also suggests that life is actually quite chaotic and that their love seems to be full of beautiful things but it is all muddled together in an ugly mess. He uses other words like "grief", "lovers' tears" and "madness" which all suggest the love problems Romeo has.

Biblical allusions are also used in the play, for example when Romeo and Juliet first meet. Romeo woos her by calling her a "holy shrine" and refers to himself as a "pilgrim" as if they are visiting a holy place. This makes Juliet feel beautiful and valued. There are other religious phrases such as "holy Shrine" "Pilgrims" "Sin" and "Saints" which all suggest the honesty and sanctity of their love.

These religious images continue into the Balcony Scene where Romeo calls Juliet a "bright angel" and a "winged messenger of heaven". These all make Juliet feel valued and beautiful. There is also a link to Juliet's birth because she is born "on Lammas Eve". This links to Christ's suffering, and how Juliet will also have to suffer in the future.

There are not only biblical allusions but also mythological allusions to gods such as "Phaeton" suggesting recklessness, "Cupid" suggesting love that it is blind, "Aurora" Goddess of Dawn meaning the light and dark motif. Shakespeare also refers to the goddess of the moon Diana. She is also known for her chastity and staying pure. Romeo accuses Rosaline of having "Diana's wit"- the main focus of this allusion being chastity. At the famous balcony scene Romeo says to Juliet "arise fair sun and kill the envious moon". This shows that Juliet is brighter and better than the Goddess of the moon. This elevates their love. Shakespeare describes their love that it is "too like the lightning" and how it is "too rash, too sudden". This shows that their love may be beautiful but it can end quickly and be very destructive. Again there is a warning about the future.

We all know that Juliet is the daughter of Lady Capulet, and in Shakespeare's time, arranged marriages were very common. It is suggested that Juliet should marry Paris. The Nurse once said that "he that shall lay hold on her shall have the chinks". This links to money and could be the reason Paris is marrying her, though later in the final scenes of the play we do get the feeling that he loved her. We also learn that in the Capulet family the parents have a very distanced, formal relationship with their daughter.

To conclude we can learn a lot about Romeo and Juliet as a couple from the language Shakespeare uses. We can also tell a great deal about their relationship by the number of Biblical and mythological allusions used. These images make the relationship more important and give it status. We also learn from the Prologue that they are "star cross'd lovers" linking them to fate and that they "take their lives" and they do "bury their parents' strife". This suggests that the male female relationships between the lovers in the play, Rosaline, Romeo and Juliet, are set for tragedy. The language Shakespeare uses leads us to think that they are utterly fated to die.

Male and female relationships are portrayed very differently in the two poems I have chosen: "A Passionate Shepherd to his love" by Christopher Marlowe and "A Married State" by Katherine Phillips. There are some similarities and some differences between the way relationships are investigated in the two poems, I have chosen. For instance "A passionate Shepherd to his love" is a pastoral poem whilst "A Married State" is not. The poems display different attitudes and viewpoints towards love.

"A Passionate Shepherd to His Love" was written by one of Shakespeare's contemporaries, Christopher Marlowe. He was a very talented male poet and playwright but unfortunately his talent was wasted when he was killed in a tavern brawl in London. The theme of the poem is love and courtship and it is linked to a Shepherd who is trying to persuade his "love" to come and live with him in the countryside- "Come live with me and be my love". The common topics in a pastoral poem are Shepherds and rustic life. In the poem, Marlowe suggests that their life together will be without any kind of unhappiness. They will "sit upon rocks" and watch others work. "Melodious birds" will sing them love songs and their clothes will be made of the "finest wool". They will have "buckles of the purest gold" and the poem is set in the springtime when people feel most hopeful and positive as it suggests the beginning of new growth. Marlowe really paints an unrealistic picture of married love since the idealism is unlikely to be matched by the reality.

My other chosen poem is "A Married State" by Katherine Phillips. She has a completely different perspective towards love and marriage. Her poem suggests that a "married state affords but little ease" which is a direct contradiction of what Marlowe says and she is very pessimistic about her prospects for happiness in marriage. She focuses on the bad points rather than the good unlike Christopher Marlowe. She shows the harsh realities rather than the idealised fantasies in Christopher Marlowe's pastoral poem. For instance she writes about "the best husbands are so hard to please" and she also writes about childbirth and uses words like "pangs" and "extort your tears" to describe it. These are all very critical comments. She seems to have a low opinion of men and has quite feminist views. She uses words like "blustering" suggesting that they are always complaining and that they "create your fears". She concludes by writing "there's no such thing as leading apes in hell". This links to religion but it is a bad link because it links to "hell" rather than Heaven.

It is based on a saying that an unmarried woman will not go to heaven. She rejects this. Katherine Phillips uses different language to Christopher Marlowe e.g. "apostate" and "blustering" instead of "pleasures" and "delights". Her language is negative while Marlowe's gives an idealised and positive view of love. This poem was written by a woman in the 18 Century so this may be one of the reasons why she is so negative since in those days women were forced into marriages even when they did not want to become under the direct control of men.

"Romeo and Juliet" is a tragic tale of love and treachery. Two lovers "both alike in dignity" must be prepared to risk their own lives to be together because their families are arch enemies, So they have to disobey their parents to allow their relationship to bloom. A young man Romeo strives to fulfil his fate and tries to control his destiny but he soon realises that fate conquers all. Shakespeare's classic drama also links to both modern and classical poetry where the poets have looked at the way men and women relate to each other and the problems relationships can bring.

William Shakespeare was not the first man to write 'Romeo and Juliet'. Arthur Brooke's wrote a similar storyline but it was in the form of a long poem where the story runs over many months. A young man and woman deceive their parents and marry in secret without their parents' consent. They are then punished for their defiance of the proper authority. Shakespeare took some of Arthur Brooke's ideas such as the first meeting, the secret marriage and Tybalt's death. He condensed all the main details down so the play had a shorter timescale. This then crushed all the lovers' emotions so they seemed more passionate and reckless owing to him shortening the play.

"A married State" has a different social circumstance. In Philips' poem, she does not want to marry and her situation is a bit like Juliet's when her father wants her to marry Paris. Katherine Philips also uses religious terms like "prayers" and "crosses" and "Matrimony", a joining by God in her poem and this is similar to the way Shakespeare uses religious imagery when the lovers meet. She concludes by writing "There's no such thing as leading apes in hell" and this links again to religion. In "Sonnet 18" William Shakespeare writes about a "Summer's day". It is a courtship poem. He is trying to flatter his love by comparing her to the seasons "thou art more temperate". This is like Marlowe's Shepherd's invitation to his lover where he uses compliments to gain love. This elevates the love just like the way love is elevated in "Romeo and Juliet".

The play is very passionate and irrational. Their relationship goes from a chaste love to a passionate love. An affect of this is that Romeo becomes very reckless and acts before he thinks for example when he proposed and gets married. There are lots of foreshadowing comments but the couple ignore the warning signs- "those stumble who run fast". Friar Lawrence warns them not to act too quickly. This also links to Phaeton because if Romeo acts too impulsively he will stumble at the final hurdle. This links to Duffy's "Valentine" because the poem is trying to warn people about the future. She uses words like "lethal" which links to death and Romeo and Juliet dying and "Possessive" and "faithful". She also says it "will blind you with tears" which shows the side effects of an onion and that there are consequences in a relationship.

Arthur Brookes believes that Romeo and Juliet are wicked and deserve to die, due to their "unhonest lyfe" and "unhonest desire" because they betray lots of people during their lifetime, mainly their parents, by getting married in secret. Arthur Brooke's thinks they abused "the honourable name of lawful marriage".

Shakespeare has a different view of Romeo and Juliet. He believed they were a heroic couple who by their deaths stopped their families' everlasting feud. This shows how differently two people can portray characters for instance. In Sonnet 18 Shakespeare tries to compare his lover to the seasons- this contrasts to "Romeo and Juliet" because Shakespeare believes their love is long lasting and it will not end like a season and in "Romeo and Juliet" their love does end like a season. I think that Christopher Marlowe's pastoral poem "A Passionate Shepherd to His Love" was the best out of the selection of poems I studied mainly because of the interesting form of the poem and the idealised views in Pastoral poetry. I also like the way the Shepherd is trying to persuade his love and is using amazingly rich language e.g. "Amber studs" and "coral clasps".

Commentary

The first paragraph introduces the essay with a number of assertions which are unsupported. The student then looks at Romeo's relationship with Rosaline commenting upon and illustrating the 'negative oxymorons'. Perhaps more could be done here to examine exactly how Shakespeare is using language. However, later in the essay, she does look more closely at phrases and words. She then goes on to make some simple observations about Juliet's relationship with her parents before concluding this section with a generalised statement.

The Shakespeare part of the essay never seems to settle. Instead it is made up of bits and pieces of information which have little cohesion. However, the student makes reference to many areas of text thus displaying her knowledge of the play as a whole as opposed to a single scene.

In the second section on the chosen verse, the student focuses on two contrasting poems. She includes some rather unnecessary biographical work on Marlowe but her early work on the poem is reasonably detailed. She then writes about Katherine Philips' poem occasionally looking back at Marlowe's. Her comments are sensible and she has a reasonable grasp of the themes and the ways they are presented in both poems. In the final section, she gets a little sidetracked into thinking about Brooke's original poem losing focus on the task. After this she begins to draw in other poems, making sensible comments upon them. She then moves to the play again and links it quite successfully to Duffy's 'Valentine'.

The section on Shakespeare seems to be unfocused and a little directionless but the work on the poetry is reasonably detailed. The final section seems a bit disorganised with references being made, in a rather rushed way, to other poems. This is an interesting piece, nevertheless, and deserves a mid range Band 4 mark (in a GCSE English folder 14 and in a GCSE English Literature folder 28). The lack of organisation and direction plus the rather intermittent attention to language are the main weaknesses. The lengthy section on Brooke does not help a great deal and this time may have been better spent on looking at more of the writers' language.

Task

Many plays and poems are concerned with the experience of fighting or Warfare. Chose a situation where conflict and death occurs in a Shakespeare play and link it with poetry where there is a similar situation.

Examine the way Shakespeare presents conflict in a section of 'Macbeth'

Examine the way Thomas Hardy presents conflict in 'Drummer Hodge.' Refer to other poems about conflict in your answer.

Make links between the two pieces of literature.

Macbeth was confronted by three witches on his journey back from his victorious win in the war between Scotland and Norway. After Macbeth won the war, the Scottish king Duncan decided that he would hand over Cawdor's land and his title over to Macbeth because Cawdor had been a traitor. When Macbeth is greeted by the three witches, coincidentally they predict that he will become King someday.

Lady Macbeth sends Macbeth a letter telling him to not trust the King and saying that they should kill him for his title. The Witches' predictions and Lady Macbeth's persuasion encourage Macbeth to kill Duncan. The King's death is then blamed on the guards.

I have been looking at Act one, scenes one two from 'Macbeth' by William Shakespeare. In this section we have been analysing the text and looking how conflict is brought up in the Warfare situation.

In the first act scene one we are confronted with what the atmosphere is like 'Thunder and lightening'. This is showing us that the weather reflects what the witches are like when they enter setting a dark and gloomy mood. The weather is again repeated by the witches. We can now see that they control the weather as they ask 'In thunder, lightening, or in rain?' so the witches are magical and mysterious. As the witches reply to each other their answers are in riddles. The second witch replies in a strange riddle 'When the battle's lost and won' which makes you realise that obviously there are two sides of the battle, one will win and the other will lose. They may be referring to the battle for Macbeth's mind. The witches are mysterious characters who know a lot about the battle, maybe they can see into the future. We get this particular information from the text - First witch: 'Where the place?' and the second Witch replies: 'Upon the heath'. From this they know where Macbeth is going to appear where they greet him later on in the play. The witches have a cat 'Graymalkin'. People believed that witches could take over animals and possess them. All of the witches then say a riddle. 'Fair is foul, and foul is fair.' This could refer to Macbeth who starts off good by mysteriously changes to bad. Could the witches be powerful enough to curse him and make him do wrong?

In scene two, the scene is set in a camp near Forres. Duncan the King of Scotland and his two sons Malcolm and Donalbain enter with the Scottish Lord Lennox. They enter to meet a 'bleeding Sergeant'. This Sergeant had been fighting in the war so has been injured during his experience. The King Duncan questions the man. 'What bloody man is that? He can report - as seemeth by his plight of the revolt, The newest state'. When the King mentions 'Bloody man' he is talking about the Sergeant physically covered in blood. Duncan thinks that the Soldier would have good knowledge and information about the war, so Duncan approaches him, as this Sergeant would have much first hand experience.

Malcolm has a positive image of the soldiers who fought in the war as it states in the quote: 'Who like a good hardy soldier fought' 'Hail brave friend!' This is showing he felt being a soldier is a brave thing to be. He also refers to the Sergeant as his friend being kind to him and showing he is proud to call him his friend.

The Sergeant replies to the King: 'Doubtful it stood' which means that he couldn't tell who would win. The Sergeant then explains why he couldn't tell who'd win, 'As two swimmers, that do cling together, And choke their Art,' which is making us build an image of the battle in our heads and how tired people were getting near the end. Men were clinging on to each other, in a desperate attempt to gain the upper hand.

King Duncan wants to know more information and the Sergeant explains how they won thanks to Macbeth 'for brave Macbeth - well he deserves that name' so the Sergeant is suggesting that Macbeth was a great and brilliantly brave soldier who deserved that title. 'Disdaining fortune, with his brandished steel which smoked with bloody execution'. This explains how Macbeth was so strong and how he killed many men easily, ignoring luck. Macbeth is also described as a servant to fighting as he is so determined and gets stuck right in. I get this information from 'Like valour's minion'. 'Minion' means servant.

We also know that in war, Macbeth is seen as a brave hero and he is respected, giving soldiers in a war battle a good image. 'Till he unseam'd him from the nave to the Chaps, And fixed his head upon our battlements'. The Sergeant is giving Macbeth his respect and credit for killing so many warriors in such a ferocious way. Then King Duncan interrupts the Sergeant with these words: 'O valiant cousin! Worthy gentleman!' meaning good soldiers are valiant. Duncan shows his admiration for Macbeth, making Macbeth seem unique, and something special about the way he killed many opponents. As Duncan uses words such as 'cousin' and 'gentleman' this makes his and Macbeth's relationship seem close, or that Duncan wants to seem close to this noble man Macbeth.

The next speech is back to the Sergeant. Imagery is used in this particular line: 'As sparrows eagles, or the hare the lion' using imagery to create a fighting effect of Macbeth- Macbeth being a vicious eagle, killing and hunting, praying on victims, killing then triumphantly.

Death occurred a lot as Macbeth and Banquo killed so many people. I get this information from 'They meant to bathe in reeking wounds'. This suggests bathing in all the pools of blood from the dead bodies. There must have been a lot of blood to be able to bathe in it, meaning there must have been strong conflict between rivals. Another quote supporting the fact death occurred a lot is 'Memorise another Golgotha' which tells me that Macbeth and Banquo killed so many men it was like a massacre, 'Golgotha' being a deathly word meaning the horrific place where Jesus was crucified. 'Golgotha' brings a gothic image of death into mind. Shakespeare used good words such as Golgotha to build a picture in our head of something we can relate to, and also used as comparisons to glorify Macbeth.

King Duncan then shows his appreciation and admiration: 'So well thy words become thee as thy wounds; They smack of honour both' Duncan mentions that he is proud of Macbeth and Banquo and these both men are honoured. They are honoured for being such brave men. The Sergeant's words push images into our mind of Macbeth winning the king a glorious victory.

To sum up, in 'Macbeth' the battle is seen as a glorious conflict where valiant men do outstanding deeds of bravery proving themselves to be heroic. Later in the play Macbeth is less heroic when he kills Duncan to get the throne.

The poem that I am comparing with the extract from 'Macbeth' is 'Drummer Hodge' by Thomas Hardy. The Drummer boy was a young soldier who had to fight in a war. 'Drummer' is a nickname given to young boys who lead at the front of a marching order beating a drum.

The poem is about a West Country boy who fights during the Boer war. Hodges' grave is brought up constantly describing the soil and strangeness of the terrain. In this poem we feel sorry for Drummer Hodge. Hardy uses African words to make the story more real.

In the first sentence of the first verse I can see that this drummer boy is dead 'to rest uncoffined - just as found' so the boy was obviously buried but with no respect. 'Uncoffined' means without a coffin- just thrown into a pit. This is also building a picture of such grim surroundings that there must have been so many dead bodies that they were not able to coffin them. This shows a lack of respect for the brave men who had died.

We then find out whereabouts this is taking place as 'Kopje-crest' is a hill in South Africa, but despite the lack of respect the young boy can be remembered for evermore like a hero. This relates back to 'Macbeth' and the way in which Shakespeare emphasises how brave and great Macbeth was in the early part of the play. Drummer Hodge has also been brave but nobody recognises that fact as e is thrown into a grave without any care. Hardy makes us realise that Hodge is buried far from home under different stars- 'And foreign constellations West'.

We can also get a sense of Hodge's age from the poem- 'Young Hodge' is emphasised so we know how young this boy is and dying so far from home must have been dreadful. This is commented upon by Hardy to create more of an atmosphere and us feel sympathetic to this young boy brought into a war where he did not belong. The young drummer wasn't very well educated as 'the drummer never knew' so he might have been unaware of what he was going into unlike Macbeth who was an older, stronger and experienced soldier. In this same verse I can also get where the boy is from and how sad that he was buried far from his homeland, 'Wessex home' meaning he is from England but buried in Africa with no respect.

The fact that the 'Drummer Hodge' is a teenager makes my views more strongly sympathetic as a young boy isn't strong enough to cope unlike Macbeth and this creates a negative attitude and gives a bad impression of the unfairness of war.

The young Drummer boy must feel confused as to why he was there in a war so far from home. We can also get this from the strange scenery: 'strange stars' meaning he hasn't seen them before. Macbeth has an understanding unlike 'Drummer Hodge' as Macbeth knows his purpose and fights strongly to prove he can't be defeated.

'Yet portion of that unknown plain. Will Hodge forever be,' is telling me even though Hodge is buried far from home he will still be forever there and remembered as all wartime soldiers should be. 'And strange-eyed constellation reign, His stars eternally'.

Drummer Hodge is like the soldiers who are sent to war in Wilfred Owen's poem 'The Send Off'. In both poems, the writers say that once they are dead the soldiers will be forgotten. We could see Hodge as one of the men referred to at the end of Owen's poem:

'Shall they return to beatings of great bells

In wild train loads?

A few, a few, too few for drums and yells...'

In my opinion conflict and death occurs in both pieces of literature but 'Macbeth' understands why whereas the 'Drummer' doesn't. This shows the difference between the roles they play in war. Also the young boy dies making him seem innocent with his life wasted for something he didn't even understand whereas Macbeth knew and survived.

Hardy and Shakespeare both create a good wartime image. Both men are respected for being in the war but in different ways. Macbeth gets all the praise from Duncan but the Drummer Boy's heroism is only noticed by Hardy, the writer of the poem, not the other soldiers in the battle. The Drummer Boy is not important enough for that.

Hodge's burial seems to be rushed. Maybe as there were so many deaths there was not enough time. Hardy has brought this up to emphasise the lack of respect given and how much death occurs for there not to be enough time for each soldier to be respected and honoured.

'Drummer Hodge' is an interesting poem to be compared with 'Macbeth' as Hodge has a different role and being from England, yet dying in a foreign country makes it more interesting especially when Afrikan terms are used.

The war circumstances in 'Drummer Hodge' weren't described in much detail but Hodge's confusion and age gives us that along with the burial where we can guess from Macbeth what's happening.

Commentary

This piece is of a good length and the student tries hard to investigate detail. Some of what he writes is concerned with the superficial aspects of the chosen texts and the consideration of the theme is not fully developed. There is some repetition in the poetry section and there is little reference to the rest of 'Macbeth' but the student does mention briefly another poem from the selection. In the linking section, he makes some sensible if basic points about the way the two men are treated. The student does pick up and consider some language aspects in the works but again this skill is not consistently displayed. This essay just gets into Band 4 with a mark of 12 in a GCSE English folder and 24 in a GCSE English Literature folder. There is some detailed reference to the texts and evaluation of the subject and theme. The student begins to explore links between the texts. The expression is reasonably clear.

Task

In the first Act of 'Macbeth' Shakespeare presents us with a picture of a battle as told by the captain. Consider the way Shakespeare describes the battle with Owen's thoughts on the same subject in 'Dulce et Decorum Est'.

Wilfred Owen's poem title 'Dulce et Decorum Est.' is a misleading title because 'Dulce Et Decorum Est' means 'it is sweet and right' when Owen's poem is about the horrors of the war. Jessie Pope, who wrote a recruitment poem for the war making it out it as a 'game' and a wonderful experience, is wrong. Jessie Pope's poem was named 'Who's for the Game?' which is a rhetorical question but Wilfred Owen's poem was like a reply to Jessie Pope's poem and Wilfred Owen wrote his poem on the realistic side of the war saying it is not a game it is a traumatic experience.

'Dulce et Decorum Est' is a Latin saying meaning it is sweet and right but at the end of the poem it says 'Dulce et Decorum Est Pro patria mori' meaning it is sweet and right to die for your country which is ironic because Owen's poem is about how horrific war is.

Owen starts his poem with a picture of the soldiers returning from battle. 'Bent double, like old beggars under sacks': Wilfred Owen is trying to say that the soldiers are sick in health and are utterly exhausted. They don't look very proud of themselves. 'Coughing like hags' is another simile. Owen is describing the sickness of the soldiers. 'Distant rest'- The soldiers have hardly any rest and it will be sometime before they get any. 'Men marched asleep' suggest that the men were so tired they were basically marching asleep and again this suggests their exhaustion. 'Many had lost their boots but limped on, blood shod'- This means that they are not even properly equipped because their feet are covered in blood. 'Drunk with fatigue' means they had no focus and they can hardly stand. 'Gas! Gas! Quick boys!' The word 'boy' suggests that the soldiers are young. Owen makes the poem suddenly liven up at this point because the soldiers know that a gas attack could easily kill them. 'But someone was yelling out and stumbling' shows Owen's fear. He knows that the man will die quickly and he cannot do much about it. 'Under a green sea, I saw him drowning': green represents the gas covering the field and the effect of the gas is their lungs filling with blood as if they are drowning. 'Before my helpless sight'- Owen could only watch him dying. He could not help him.

'Behind the wagon we flung him': He's not being treated like a hero. 'Watch the white eyes writhing' is a horrible picture of how he surrendered his life. 'His hanging face'- this is a sick face. He has no control over his body because he is dying. 'Like a devil's sick of sin' means that the soldiers have had enough of the war and just wanted it to end. 'Obscene as cancer' the condition the soldiers are in is just like having cancer. At then end of the poem Owen tells us that it isn't 'sweet and right' die in these terrible conditions.

I have also looked at 'The Charge of the Light Brigade,' written by Alfred, Lord Tennyson and his poem was also about the horrors of war but Tennyson's poem is not as horrific as Wilfred Owen's poem. Alfred, Lord Tennyson was describing a specific moment of the war that was reported in a local newspaper but Tennyson's poem is in between the middle of Jessie Pope's poem and Wilfred Owen's poem because Tennyson's poem talks about both sides of the war where it is like a game but you only get one life.

In 'Macbeth' the King of Scotland has seen one of his soldiers return to him covered in blood from a massacre of a war. 'What bloody man is that?' The quotations 'Like a good and hardy soldier fought' and 'Hail brave friend!' both say that Malcolm the Prince of Scotland thinks that fighters are heroes.

'For brave Macbeth - well he deserves that name ... Disdaining fortune,' this quotation is trying to say that Macbeth doesn't need luck to win as he is an outstanding soldier. He deserves to be called brave and everyone thinks he's special.

The quotation 'Like valour's minion' is trying to say that Macbeth is a servant to bravery. 'Till he unseam'd him from the nave to the chops, And fix'd his head upon our battlements'. Duncan thinks Macbeth is untouchable because he is slaying the opposition and doing it a particularly brutal way. When Duncan says, 'O valiant cousin! worthy gentleman!' he is pleased with Macbeth and admires Macbeth's bravery. When the Captain says, 'As sparrows eagles, or the hare the lion' he is comparing Macbeth to an eagle or a lion and all others are compared as sparrows and hares. 'Doubly redoubled strokes upon the foe': The Captain is trying to say that Macbeth is trying four times harder than anyone else. All the way through the description of the battle Shakespeare is writing about how brave Macbeth is and he does not want us to be sympathetic to the people he has killed.

In these two pieces of literature, there are similarities such as the use of similes and metaphors and they are both on war but there is a big difference on the views of the war. Wilfred Owen's view of the war was from his own experience mentioning the horrors of charging the enemy and sleeping in poor conditions but William Shakespeare thinks that being in the war is a wonderful experience and if you come back from the war you will be treated like a hero.

My favourite piece out of the two was Wilfred Owen's poem 'Dulce Et Decorum Est' because Wilfred Owen was writing whilst he was in the war and it is a more descriptive poem.

Commentary

This student looks at lines in Owen's poem and makes brief comments upon them either paraphrasing or explaining meaning. His work is mostly accurate in terms of content but there is more to be written about the way Owen structures and uses language to shape our response. He sums up his view of the poem and its effect but again this aspect is short of development. He makes reference to another poem in the Collection with a brief commentary and he links both poems with Jessie Pope's 'Who's for the Game?' Although this poem is not in the Collection, it is a useful reference.

At the beginning of the Shakespeare section, he assumes the approach of making notes on some lines and, while this keeps his work closely linked to text and prevents him from straying into generalisation, it does have the negative effect of making the work very fragmented. Even though the title of the task focuses on one scene from 'Macbeth', the student could have made reference to other occasions when battles feature in the play. The linking section is brief and undeveloped and he misses the chance to draw the threads together and look at the ways the writers think about the horror of war in more general terms. However, there is close if not detailed, reference to texts and the work is worthy of a mid Band 3 mark (10 in a GCSE English folder and 20 in a GCSE English Literature folder). The student has shown that he can begin to select relevant detail and show a basic awareness of how the texts achieve their effect through the writer's use of language.

Task

Discuss the treatment of women in 'Much Ado about Nothing' (Shakespeare) and 'Cousin Kate' (Rossetti) with reference to text and context. (NB Since 'Much Ado About Nothing' is a set text for GCSE English Literature, it would not be permissible for this essay to be entered for GCSE English Literature Controlled Assessment.)

Elizabethan society was patriarchal, which means men were considered to be the leaders and the women were regarded as 'weaker sex', not just in terms of physical strength, but emotionally too. The roles of women in patriarchal society were very limited. Women were supposed to marry well, be loyal to their husbands and give birth to children.

Many rich women in that period were highly educated, like the Queen herself and Mildred Cecil - wife of William Cecil, and Mary Herbert - Countess of Pembroke. Women were not allowed to go to school or to university, but they could be educated at home by private tutors. Elizabeth was tutored by the famous Elizabeth scholar Roger Ascham.

Women were not allowed to take any professional occupation, such a law, but they could work in domestic services as cooks, maids etc, and a female painter. Levina Teerline, the artist, was employed by Henry VIII and later by Mary and Elizabeth respectively. Women were not allowed to act on the public stage or write for the public stage. Women did not appear on the stage in England until the eighteenth century. In Shakespeare's play, the roles of women were played by young boys.

Women in that time didn't have any social position. They were not allowed to vote, only men of a certain social position were allowed to vote. Women could not acquire their father's titles. All titles would pass from father to son or brother to brother, depending on the circumstances.

William Shakespeare's play 'Much Ado About Nothing' reflects the society at that era. During that time, a woman's honour was based upon her virginal chastity. They would lose all their social standing if the honour were to be destroyed. The climax of this play is the aborted wedding ceremony where Hero's honour was questioned in public. Claudio rejected Hero openly, accusing her of infidelity and blatantly shaming her in front of her family. Unlike men, women couldn't defend themselves.

The treatment of women didn't change much. In Victorian era, a woman's place was in the home, to have children and tend the house. The legal rights of married women were similar to those children. They could not vote, sue or own property. They could not hold a job unless it was that of a teacher, nor were they allowed to have their own checking accounts or saving accounts. In the end, they were to be treated as saints, but saints that had no legal rights.

The poem 'Cousin Kate' is told from the viewpoint of a first-person narrative. The poem is about the pretty blonde narrator, who is from a humble working family and is seduced by a 'great lord.' When he 'changed me like a glove,' it is partly because he had found another attractive girl of poor estate - the narrator's cousin, Kate.

Because Kate was 'so good and pure' and won't allow herself to be seduced, the lord marries her. The bitter narrator, 'an outcast thing' in her community, believes that she has the greater happiness because she has the lord's child whereas Kate is childless.

In this poem, Rossetti gives the narrator several oxymorons, such as 'shame-less shameful' and 'my shame, my pride'. Rossetti used strong verbs in 'Cousin Kate.' Most single-syllable words derived from Old English rather than from Latin or French, such as 'lured', 'chose', 'cast' and 'howled'.

The narrator was happy about herself. From 'Contented with my cottage mates, Not mindful I was fair' it shows she was not vain. Her willingness to have a relationship with the 'Great Lord' was because she loved him. However the 'Lord' didn't really love her.

The lord dehumanised her as his 'plaything' and his 'silken knot', then he changed her 'like a glove'. Now, the narrator became 'an outcast thing' in the society. The lord then found another girl - the narrator's cousin Kate, and because she was 'so good and pure' the lord wanted Kate to marry him.

I have studied both texts 'Much Ado About Nothing' and 'Cousin Kate', I am aware of similarities and differences between them in the way that they reflect the treatment of women in patriarchal society. The women were most unfairly treated in 'Cousin Kate', because the narrator had been seduced by a man, she becomes an 'outcast thing' and nobody cares about her. In 'Much Ado About Nothing', Hero also appeared to have been 'seduced' by a man but people were trying to find out the truth. Female victim is 'outcast' by society because of the seduction, but the man is unpunished.

I have studied these texts, I understand how are women treated in patriarchal society now.

Commentary

The student, in his concentration on the position of women, goes down the wrong route. There is a great deal of background material which, while being interesting and informative, will not gain the student many marks since the focus of the task should be on the study of the way the chosen theme is considered by the writer through close textual analysis. Much of this essay therefore is irrelevant since the student has not investigated the language in the Shakespeare text but instead written in general terms about the position of women in Elizabethan society. When the student reaches the poem, he writes intelligently but without a great deal of detail. The linking section is brief and undeveloped. It relies on a single point of similarity. The original marker of this piece correctly made the comment: 'All context; little content.' This accurately reflects the student's achievement. This essay deserves a low Band 3 mark (8 in a GCSE English folder). If he had considered the way that Hero is treated in the Shakespeare play with close textual reference, he could have pushed his mark up considerably. In the essay, he has made straightforward links between texts, commented upon particular features of the poetry text, and has shown some understanding of the main features of the play.

Task

Many plays and poems are concerned with the experience of fighting or warfare. Choose a situation where conflict and death occurs in 'Macbeth' and link it with poetry where there is a similar situation.

- Examine the way Shakespeare presents conflict in a section of 'Macbeth'
- Examine the way Thomas Hardy presents conflict in 'Drummer Hodge'. Refer to other poems about conflict in your answer.
- Make links between the texts

William Shakespeare was born on the 26th of April 1564. He was an English poet. He was also a play writer. Shakespeare was said to be the greatest writer in the English language. He was also known as the 'Bard of Avon'. Shakespeare wrote 38 plays, 154 sonnets, two long narrative poems and several other poems. At the age of 18 he married Anne Hathaway who had three children. Between 1585 and 1592, he had began a successful career in London as an actor. He retired in 1613, and died three years later.

I will start by summarising the plot. Macbeth and Banquo came across three witches. The witches tell Macbeth that he will be the next King of Scotland, while Banquo's heirs will be kings. The generals want to hear more, but the weird witches vanish in to thin air.

Lady Macbeth receives the news and makes a plan. They plan to kill the King. His wife assists him in the murder and spreads the King's blood in the guards' daggers and bodies to frame them. Lady Macbeth starts to imagine her hands covered in blood. She starts feeling guilt.

Later on in the story Macduff plans and kills Macbeth with a small army. Now everyone knows exactly what Macbeth has done. He is now a villain. If he hadn't had the pressure of Lady Macbeth none of this probably would have happened.

The poem that I am comparing with the extract from Macbeth is "Drummer Hodge", by Thomas Hardy.

Thomas Hardy was born on the 2nd June 1840. He was born at Higher Bockhampton, Dorset, where his father worked as a master mason.

Thomas Hardy gained an appreciation of music from is father and from his mother an appetite for learning and the delight of the countryside, where he lived in his rural home. He started school at the age of eight and then at the age of sixteen he worked with his father. In 1870 Hardy was sent to plan a Church restoration at St. Juliot in Cornwall. He met Emma Gilford who encouraged him in his writing, and they were married in 1874.

The poem is about a West Country boy, who has gone to battle in South Africa during the Boer War. The terrain was terrible which covered Drummer Hodges grave. Thomas Hardy uses African words to emphasize this strangeness. This poem shows great sympathy towards Drummer Hodge. Thomas Hardy is skilful in what he writes because we can gather a great amount of information about what's happened.

Thomas Hardy's poem "Drummer Hodge" starts off with the phrase "They throw Drummer Hodge to rest". This gives me a clear idea that Drummer Hodge has been put in his grave. The word "throw" shows that they had no respect for Drummer Hodge. "Uncoffined" is been mentioned in the second line and this shows he's just been thrown in a hole.

This makes me feel angry because a young boy, who isn't meant to be in the army has been killed and no respect has been shown. At the end of the first verse it quotes "foreign constellations". This shows he's in a foreign country, the stars are in a different arrangement. This shows that Drummer Hodge is far, far away from home.

In verse two it says where he is from because it quotes "fresh from his Wessex home". It then quotes "The meaning of the broad karoo". This mean's that Drummer Hodge is not educated. I know from the text that he hasn't had the chance to live his life because it says "And why uprose to nightly view".

In the last line of the second verse it quotes "Strange stars amid the gloam". This shows that it is turning to night. This creates an eerie atmosphere.

"Will Hodge forever be". This is a reply to Rupert Brooke. The last line of the third verse says "His stars eternally". This explains that his star will always be there.

The similarities between "Drummer Hodge" by Thomas Hardy and "Macbeth" by Shakespeare are that they are both about war. On the other hand, "Macbeth" talks about how glorious war is and how much respect soldiers have for each other. In "Drummer Hodge" there is no respect for soldiers. Overall my favourite story is "Macbeth". This is my favourite because I like the way that he is a hero at the start of the story and a villain at the end. I like the way that the Macbeth and Lady Macbeth go mental in the head. This makes the scene more effective.

Commentary

The student begins with some totally unnecessary biographical work. This gains him no marks and only delays his study of the texts. When he reaches the play, he spends time telling the story before making some useful if very simple comments. The words of the text are not considered and the student confines himself to surface content. There is more biographical work on Hardy which again does not benefit the student in any way. However, his work on the Hardy poem is a little more detailed and here he does refer to text and occasionally shows how the effects are achieved but there are also occasions when he misreads. The essay ends with a personal preference and some very simple links are made. It seems a pity that he did not do much more work on the play where he hardly moves beyond plot summary. The essay is out of balance. This piece deserves a high Band 2 mark (7 in a GCSE English folder and 14 in a GCSE English Literature folder).

5

Victorian Literature

It was in the Victorian era (1837-1901) that the novel became the leading form of literature in English. Most writers were now more concerned to meet the tastes of a large middle class reading public than to please aristocratic patrons. The best known works of the era include the emotionally powerful works of the Brontë sisters; the satire Vanity Fair by William Makepeace Thackeray; the realist novels of George Eliot; and Anthony Trollope's insightful portrayals of the lives of the landowning and professional classes.

Charles Dickens emerged on the literary scene in the 1830s, confirming the trend for serial publication. Dickens wrote vividly about London life and the struggles of the poor, but in a good-humoured fashion which was acceptable to readers of all classes. His early works such as the Pickwick Papers are masterpieces of comedy. Later his works became darker, without losing his genius for caricature.

An interest in rural matters and the changing social and economic situation of the countryside may be seen in the novels of Thomas Hardy, Elizabeth Cleghorn Gaskell, and others.

Leading poetic figures of the Victorian era included Alfred Tennyson, Robert Browning and his wife, Elizabeth Barrett Browning, Matthew Arnold and Dante Gabriel Rossetti and his sister, Christina Rossetti.

Literature for children was published during the Victorian period, some of which has become globally well-known, such as the work of Lewis Carroll who was a proponent of nonsense verse, as was Edward Lear.

MODERNISM

First edition of Ulysses, James Joyce's masterpiece, and landmark of high modernism (1922).

The movement known as English literary modernism grew out of a general sense of disillusionment with Victorian era attitudes of certainty, conservatism, and objective truth. The movement was greatly influenced by the ideas of Romanticism, Karl Marx's political writings, and the psychoanalytic theories of Sigmund Freud. The continental art movements of Impressionism, and later Cubism, were also important inspirations for modernist writers.

Although literary modernism reached its peak between the First and Second World Wars, the earliest examples of the movement's attitudes appeared in the mid to late nineteenth century. Gerard Manley Hopkins, A. E. Housman, and the poet and novelist Thomas Hardy represented a few of the major early modernists writing in England during the Victorian period.

The first decades of the twentieth century saw several major works of modernism published, including the seminal short story collection Dubliners by James Joyce, Joseph Conrad's Heart of Darkness, and the poetry and drama of William Butler Yeats.

Important novelists between the World Wars included Virginia Woolf, E. M. Forster, Evelyn Waugh, P.G. Wodehouse, D. H. Lawrence and T. S. Eliot, the preeminent English poet of the period. Across the Atlantic writers like William Faulkner, Ernest Hemingway, and the poets Wallace Stevens and Robert Frost developed a more American take on the modernist aesthetic in their work.

Perhaps the most contentiously important figure in the development of the modernist movement was the American poet Ezra Pound. Credited with "discovering" both T. S. Eliot and James Joyce, whose stream of consciousness novel Ulysses is considered to be one of the century's greatest literary achievements, Pound also advanced the cause of imagism and free verse, forms which would dominate English poetry into the twenty-first century.

Other notable writers of the period included W. H. Auden, Vladimir Nabokov, William Carlos Williams, Ralph Ellison, Dylan Thomas, R.S. Thomas and Graham Greene. However, some of these writers are more closely associated with what has become known as post-modernism, a term often used to encompass the diverse range of writers who succeeded the modernists.

BRITISH LITERATURE

British literature is literature from the United Kingdom, the Isle of Man and the Channel Islands. By far the largest part of this literature is written in the English language, but there are also separate literatures in Welsh, Scottish Gaelic, Scots, Cornish, Manx, Jèrriais, Dgèrnésiais and other languages.

Northern Ireland is the only part of Ireland still part of the United Kingdom and it possesses literature in English, Ulster Scots and Irish. Irish writers have also played an important part in the development of English-language literature.

Old Celtic Literature

Literature in the Celtic languages of the islands is the oldest surviving vernacular literature in Europe. The Welsh literary tradition stretches from the 6th century to the 21st century. The oldest Welsh literature does not belong to the territory we know as Wales today, but rather to northern England and southern Scotland. But though it is dated to be from the 6th, 7th, and 8th centuries, it has survived only in 13th and 14th century manuscript copies. Irish poetry represents a more or less unbroken tradition from the 6th century to the present day.

Old English Literature

The earliest form of English literature developed after the settlement of the Saxons and other Germanic tribes in England after the withdrawal of the Romans and is known as Old English or Anglo-Saxon. The most famous work in Old English is the epic poem Beowulf. (The oldest surviving text in English is Caedmon's hymn of creation.) The precise date of the manuscript is debated, but most estimates place it close to AD 1000.

Chronicles contained a range of historical and literary accounts, for example: Historia ecclesiastica gentis Anglorum by Bede and the Anglo-Saxon Chronicle.

Late Medieval Literature in England

Latin literature circulated among the educated classes. Following the Norman conquest, the development of Anglo-Norman literature in the Anglo-Norman realm introduced literary trends from Continental Europe such as the chanson de geste. In the later medieval period a new form of English now known as Middle English evolved. This is the earliest form which is comprehensible to modern readers and listeners, albeit not easily.

The most significant Middle English author was the poet Geoffrey Chaucer who was active in the late 14th Century. His main works were The Canterbury Tales and Troilus and Criseyde. The multilingual audience for literature in the 14th century can be illustrated by the example of John Gower, who wrote in Latin, Middle English and Anglo-Norman. Religious literature, such as hagiographies enjoyed popularity.

Women writers such as Marie de France and Julian of Norwich were also active.

- Sir Gawain and the Green Knight by anonymous
- Morte d'Arthur by Sir Thomas Malory

Other Medieval Literatures

For a comparatively small country, Ireland has made a large contribution to world literature in all its branches.

The Irish literature that is best known outside the country is in English, but the Irish language also has the most significant body of written literature, both ancient and recent, in any Celtic language, in addition to a strong oral tradition of legends and poetry.

In Medieval Welsh literature the period before 1100 is known as the period of Y Cynfeirdd ("The earliest poets") or Yr Hengerdd ("The old poetry"). It roughly dates from the birth of the Welsh language until the arrival of the Normans in Wales towards the end of the eleventh century.

Geoffrey of Monmouth's Historia Regum Britanniae spread Celtic motifs to a wider audience.

The Jersey poet Wace is considered the founder of Jersey literature and contributed to the development of the Arthurian legend in British literature. His Brut showed the interest of Norman patrons in the mythologising of the new English territories of the Anglo-Norman realm. His Rou placed the Dukes of Normandy within an epic context.

Since at least the 14th century, poetry in English has been written in Ireland and by Irish writers abroad. The earliest poem in English by a Welsh poet dates from about 1470.

Among the earliest Lowland Scots literature is Barbour's Brus (14th century). Whyntoun's Kronykil and Blind Harry's Wallace (15th century) From the 13th century much literature based around the Royal Court in Edinburgh and the University of St. Andrews was produced by writers such as Henrysoun, Dunbar, Douglas and Lyndsay.

In the Cornish language Passhyon agan Arloedh (The Passion of our Lord), a poem of 259 eight-line verses written in 1375, is one of the earliest surviving works of Cornish literature. The most important work of literature surviving from the Middle Cornish period is An Ordinale Kernewek (The Cornish Ordinalia), a 9000-line religious drama composed around the year 1400. The longest single surviving work of Cornish literature is Bywnans

Meriasek (The Life of Meriasek), a play dated 1504, but probably copied from an earlier manuscript.

- Mabinogion
- Ulster Cycle
- Early English Jewish literature

Early Modern English Literature to 1660

The sonnet form and other Italian literary influences arrived in English literature. The sonnet was introduced into English by Thomas Wyatt in the early 16th century.

In the later 16th century English poetry was characterised by elaboration of language and extensive allusion to classical myths. The most important poets of this era include Edmund Spenser and Sir Philip Sidney.

The most important literary achievements of the English Renaissance were in drama. William Shakespeare wrote over thirty-five plays in several genres, including tragedy, comedy, history and romance. Other leading playwrights of the time included Ben Jonson, and Christopher Marlowe.

Elizabethan Theatre: At the Reformation the translation of liturgy and Bible into vernacular languages provided new literary models. The Anglican Book of Common Prayer and the Authorised Version of the Bible have been influential on the literatures of the islands. The major poets of the 17th century included John Donne and the other Metaphysical poets, and John Milton, the author of the religious epic Paradise Lost.

English Language Literature from 1660 to the Late 18th Century

The position of Poet Laureate was formalised in this period.

The early 18th century is known as the Augustan Age of English literature. The poetry of the time was highly formal, as exemplified by the works of Alexander Pope.

Although the documented history of Irish theatre began at least as early as 1601, the earliest Irish dramatists of note were William Congreve, one of the most interesting writers of Restoration comedies, and Oliver Goldsmith and Richard Brinsley Sheridan, who were two of the most successful playwrights on the London stage in the 18th century.

The English novel developed during the 18th century, partly in response to an expansion of the middle class reading public. One of the major early works in this genre was Robinson Crusoe by Daniel Defoe. The 18th century novel tended to be loosely structured and semi-comic. Major novelists of the middle and later part of the century included Henry Fielding, Laurence Sterne and Tobias Smollett, who was a great influence on Charles Dickens.

Although the epics of Celtic Ireland were written in prose and not verse, most people would probably consider that Irish fiction proper begins in the 18th century with the works of Jonathan Swift (especially Gulliver's Travels) and Oliver Goldsmith (especially The Vicar of Wakefield).

- First novel in English
- Cavalier poet

Non English-language Literatures from the 16th Century to the 19th Century

As the Norman nobles of Scotland assimilated to indigenous culture they commissioned Scots versions of popular continental romances, for example: Launcelot o the Laik and The Buik o Alexander. In the early 16th century, Gavin Douglas produced a Scots translation of the Aeneid. Chaucerian, classical and French literary language continued to influence Scots literature up until the Reformation. The Complaynt of Scotland shows the interplay of language and ideas between the kingdoms of Scotland and England in the years leading up to the Union of the Crowns.

The earliest datable text in Manx (preserved in 18th century manuscripts), a poetic history of the Isle of Man from the introduction of Christianity, dates to the 16th century at the latest.

The first book to be printed in Welsh was published in 1546. From the Reformation until the 19th century most literature in the Welsh language was religious in character.

The earliest surviving examples of Cornish prose are Pregothow Treger (The Tregear Homilies), a set of 66 sermons translated from English by John Tregear around 1555-1557.

The Book of Common Prayer and Bible were translated into Manx in the 17th and 18th centuries. A tradition of carvals, religious songs or carols, developed. Religious literature was common, but secular writing much rarer.

In Scotland, after the 17th century, anglicisation increased, though Lowland Scots was still spoken by the vast majority of the population. At the time, many of the oral ballads from the borders and the North East were written down. Writers of the period include Robert Sempill (c.1595-1665), Lady Wardlaw and Lady Grizel Baillie.

The first printed work in Manx dates from 1707: a translation of a Prayer Book catechism in English by Bishop Thomas Wilson.

In the Scots-speaking areas of Ulster there was traditionally a considerable demand for the work of Scottish poets, often in locally printed editions. Alexander Montgomerie's The Cherrie and the Slae in 1700, shortly over a decade later an edition of poems by Sir David Lindsay, nine printings of Allan Ramsay's The Gentle shepherd between 1743 and 1793, and an edition of Robert Burns' poetry in 1787, the same year as the Edinburgh edition, followed by reprints in 1789, 1793 and 1800. Among other Scottish poets published in Ulster were James Hogg and Robert Tannahill.

In the 18th century, Scottish writers such as Ramsay, Robert Fergusson, Robert Burns and Sir Walter Scott continued to use Lowland Scots. Scott introduced vernacular dialogue to his novels. The Habbie stanza was developed as a poetic form.

The first printed Jèrriais literature appears in the first newspapers following the introduction of the printing press at the end of the 18th century. The earliest identified dated example of printed poetry in Jèrriais is a fragment by Matchi L'Gé (Matthew Le Geyt 1777-1849) dated 1795.

Some 60 to 70 volumes of Ulster rhyming weaver poetry were published between 1750 and 1850, the peak being in the decades 1810 to 1840. These weaver poets, such as James Orr, looked to Scotland for their cultural and literary models and were not simple imitators but clearly inheritors of the same literary tradition following the same poetic and orthographic practices; it is not always immediately possible to distinguish traditional Scots writing from Scotland and Ulster.

The importance of translation in spreading the influence of English literature to other cultures of the islands can be exemplified by the abridged Manx version of Paradise Lost by John Milton published in 1796 by Thomas Christian. The influence also went the other way as Romanticism discovered inspiration in the literatures and legends of the Celtic countries of the islands. The Ossian hoax typifies the growth of this interest.

Increased literacy in rural and outlying areas and wider access to publishing through, for example, local newspapers encouraged regional literary development as the 19th century progressed. Some writers in lesser-used languages and dialects of the islands gained a literary following outside their native regions, for example William Barnes in Dorset, George Métivier (1790-1881) in Guernsey and Robert Pipon Marett in Jersey. George Métivier published Rimes Guernesiaises, a collection of poems in Dgèrnésiais and French in 1831.

The poems had first appeared in newspapers from 1813 onward. The first printed anthology of Jèrriais poetry, Rimes Jersiaises, was published in 1865.

Scots was used in the narrative by Ulster novelists such as W. G. Lyttle (1844-1896). Scots also regularly appeared in Ulster newspaper columns.

Scottish authors as Robert Louis Stevenson, William Alexander, George MacDonald and J. M. Barrie also wrote in Lowland Scots or used it in dialogue.

The first major novelist in the Welsh language was Daniel Owen, author of works such as Rhys Lewis (1885) and Enoc Huws (1891).

Edward Faragher (1831-1908) has been considered the last important native writer of Manx. He wrote poetry, reminiscences of his life as a fisherman, and translations of selected Aesop's Fables.

THE ANGLO-NORMAN PERIOD AND THE LATER MIDDLE AGES

With the Norman conquest of England, beginning in 1066, the Anglo-Saxon language rapidly diminished as a written literary language. The new aristocracy spoke French, and this became the standard language of courts, parliament, and polite society. As the invaders integrated, their language and literature mingled with that of the natives: the French dialect of the upper classes became Anglo-Norman, and Anglo-Saxon underwent a gradual transition into Middle English.

While Anglo-Norman or Latin was preferred for high culture, English literature by no means died out, and a number of important works illustrate the development of the language. Around the turn of the thirteenth century, Layamon wrote his Brut, based on Wace's twelfth century Anglo-Norman epic of the same name; Layamon's language is recognisably Middle English, though his prosody shows a strong Anglo-Saxon influence remaining. Other transitional works were preserved as popular entertainment, including a variety of romances and lyrics. With time, the English language regained prestige, and in 1362 it replaced French and Latin in Parliament and courts of law.

It was with the fourteenth century that major works of English literature began once again to appear; these include the so-called Pearl Poet's Pearl, Patience, Cleanness, and Sir Gawain and the Green Knight; Langland's political and religious allegory Piers Plowman; Gower's Confessio Amantis; and, of course, the works of Chaucer, the most highly regarded English poet of the Middle Ages, who was seen by his contemporaries as a successor to the great tradition of Virgil and Dante.

The reputation of Chaucer's successors in the 15th century has suffered in comparison with him, though Lydgate and Skelton are widely studied. However, the century really belongs to a group of remarkable Scottish writers. The rise of Scottish poetry began with the writing of The Kingis Quair by James I of Scotland. The main poets of this Scottish group were Robert Henryson, William Dunbar and Gavin Douglas. Henryson and Douglas introduced a note of almost savage satire, which may have owed something to the Gaelic bards, while Douglas' version of Virgil's Aeneid is one of the early monuments of Renaissance literary humanism in English.

THE RENAISSANCE IN ENGLAND

The Renaissance was slow in coming to England, with the generally accepted start date being around 1509. It is also generally accepted that the English Renaissance extended until the Restoration in 1660. However, a number of factors had prepared the way for the introduction of the new learning long before this start date. A number of medieval poets had, as already noted, shown an interest in the ideas of Aristotle and the writings of European Renaissance precursors such as Dante.

The introduction of movable-block printing by Caxton in 1474 provided the means for the more rapid dissemination of new or recently rediscovered writers and thinkers. Caxton also printed the works of Chaucer and Gower and these books helped establish the idea of a native poetic tradition that was linked to its European counterparts. In addition, the writings of English humanists like Thomas More and Thomas Elyot helped bring the ideas and attitudes associated with the new learning to an English audience.

Three other factors in the establishment of the English Renaissance were the Reformation, Counter Reformation, and the opening of the era of English naval power and overseas exploration and expansion. The establishment of the Church of England in 1535 accelerated the process of questioning the Catholic world-view that had previously dominated intellectual and artistic life. At the same time, long-distance sea voyages helped provide the stimulus and information that underpinned a new understanding of the nature of the universe which resulted in the theories of Nicolaus Copernicus and Johannes Kepler.

Early Renaissance Poetry

With a small number of exceptions, the early years of the 16th century are not particularly notable. The Douglas Aeneid was completed in 1513 and John Skelton wrote poems that were transitional between the late Medieval and Renaissance styles. The new king, Henry VIII, was something of a poet himself. The most significant English poet of this period was Thomas Wyatt, who was among the first poets to write sonnets in English.

THE ELIZABETHANS

The Elizabethan period (1558 to 1603) in poetry is characterised by a number of frequently overlapping developments. The introduction and adaptation of themes, models and verse forms from other European traditions and classical literature, the Elizabethan song tradition, the emergence of a courtly poetry often centered around the figure of the monarch and the growth of a verse-based drama are among the most important of these developments.

Elizabethan Song

A wide range of Elizabethan poets wrote songs, including Nicholas Grimald, Thomas Nashe and Robert Southwell. There are also a large number of extant anonymous songs from the period. Perhaps the greatest of all the songwriters was Thomas Campion. Campion is also notable because of his experiments with metres based on counting syllables rather than stresses. These quantitative metres were based on classical models and should be viewed as part of the wider Renaissance revival of Greek and Roman artistic methods.

The songs were generally printed either in miscellanies or anthologies such as Richard Tottel's 1557 Songs and Sonnets or in songbooks that included printed music to enable performance. These performances formed an integral part of both public and private entertainment. By the end of the 16th century, a new generation of composers, including John Dowland, William Byrd, Orlando Gibbons, Thomas Weelkes and Thomas Morley were helping to bring the art of Elizabethan song to an extremely high musical level.

Courtly Poetry

With the consolidation of Elizabeth's power, a genuine court sympathetic to poetry and the arts in general emerged. This encouraged the emergence of a poetry aimed at, and often set in, an idealised version of the courtly world.

Among the best known examples of this are Edmund Spenser's The Faerie Queene, which is effectively an extended hymn of praise to the queen, and Philip Sidney's Arcadia. This courtly trend can also be seen in Spenser's Shepheardes Calender. This poem marks the introduction into an English context of the classical pastoral, a mode of poetry that assumes an aristocratic audience with a certain kind of attitude to the land and peasants. The explorations of love found in the sonnets of William Shakespeare and the poetry of Walter Raleigh and others also implies a courtly audience.

Elizabethan verse Drama

Elizabethan verse drama is widely considered to be one of the major achievements of literature in English, and its most famous exponent, William Shakespeare, is revered as the greatest poet in the language. This drama, which served both as courtly masque and popular entertainment, deals with all the major themes of contemporary literature and life.

There are plays on European, classical, and religious themes reflecting the importance of humanism and the Reformation. There are also a number of plays dealing with English history that may be read as part of an effort to strengthen the British national myth and as artistic underpinnings for Elizabeth's resistance to the Spanish and other foreign threats. A number of the comic works for the stage also use bucolic themes connected with the pastoral genre.

In addition to Shakespeare, other notable dramatists of the period include Christopher Marlowe, Thomas Dekker and Ben Jonson.

CLASSICISM

Gavin Douglas' Aeneid, Thomas Campion's metrical experiments, and Spenser's Shepheardes Calender and plays like Shakespeare's Antony and Cleopatra are all examples of the influence of classicism on Elizabethan poetry. It remained common for poets of the period to write on themes from classical mythology; Shakespeare's Venus and Adonis and the Christopher Marlowe/ George Chapman Hero and Leander are examples of this kind of work. Translations of classical poetry also became more widespread, with the versions of Ovid's Metamorphoses by Arthur Golding (1565-7) and George Sandys (1626), and Chapman's translations of Homer's Iliad (1611) and Odyssey (c.1615), among the outstanding examples.

Jacobean and Caroline Poetry

English Renaissance poetry after the Elizabethan poetry can be seen as belonging to one of three strains; the Metaphysical poets, the Cavalier poets and the school of Spenser. However, the boundaries between these three groups are not always clear and an individual poet could write in more than one manner.

The Metaphysical Poets

The early 17th century saw the emergence of this group of poets who wrote in a witty, complicated style. The most famous of the Metaphysicals is probably John Donne. Others include George Herbert, Henry Vaughan, Andrew Marvell and Richard Crashaw. John Milton in his Comus falls into this group. The Metaphysical poets went out of favour in the 18th century but began to be read again in the Victorian era. Donne's reputation was finally fully restored by the approbation of T. S. Eliot in the early 20th century.

The Cavalier Poets

The Cavalier poets wrote in a lighter, more elegant and artificial style than the Metaphysical poets. Leading members of the group include Ben Jonson, Richard Lovelace, Robert Herrick, Edmund Waller, Thomas Carew and John Denham. The Cavalier poets can be seen as the forerunners of the major poets of the Augustan era, who admired them greatly.

The School of Spenser

The early 17th century also saw a group of poets who were interested in Giles and Phineas Fletcher. Although these poetsto John Milton's great mythic long poem, Paradise Lost.

The Restoration and 18th Century

It is perhaps ironic that Paradise Lost, a story of fallen pride, was the first major poem to appear in England after the Restoration. The court of Charles II had, in its years in France, learned a worldliness and sophistication that marked it as distinctively different from the monarchies that preceded the Republic. Even if Charles had wanted to reassert the divine right of kingship, the Protestantism and taste for power of the intervening years would have rendered it impossible.

Satire

It is hardly surprising that the world of fashion and scepticism that emerged encouraged the art of satire. All the major poets of the period, Samuel Butler, John Dryden, Alexander Pope and Samuel Johnson, and the Irish poet Jonathan Swift, wrote satirical verse. What is perhaps more surprising is that their satire was often written in defence of public order and the established church and government. However, writers such as Pope used their gift for satire to create scathing works responding to their detractors or to criticise what they saw as social atrocities perpetrated by the government.

Pope's "The Dunciad" is a satirical slaying of two of his literary adversaries (Lewis Theobald, and Colley Cibber in a later version), expressing the view that British society was falling apart morally, culturally, and intellectually.

18th Century Classicism

The 18th century is sometimes called the Augustan age, and contemporary admiration for the classical world extended to the poetry of the time. Not only did the poets aim for a polished high style in emulation of the Roman ideal, they also translated and imitated Greek and Latin verse. Dryden translated all the known works of Virgil, and Pope produced versions of the two Homeric epics. Horace and Juvenal were also widely translated and imitated, Horace most famously by John Wilmot, Earl of Rochester and Juvenal by Samuel Johnson's Vanity of Human Wishes.

Women Poets in the 18th Century

A number of women poets of note emerged during the period of the Restoration, including Aphra Behn, Margaret Cavendish, Mary Chudleigh, Anne Finch, Anne Killigrew, and Katherine Philips. Nevertheless, print publication by women poets was still relatively scarce when compared to that of men, though manuscript evidence indicates that many more women poets were practicing than was previously thought. Disapproval of feminine "forwardness," however, kept many out of print in the early part of the period, and even as the century progressed women authors still felt the need to justify their incursions into the public sphere by claiming economic necessity or the pressure of friends. Women writers were increasingly active in all genres throughout the eighteenth century, and by the 1790s women's poetry was flourishing. Notable poets later in the period include Anna Laetitia Barbauld, Joanna Baillie, Susanna Blamire, Felicia Hemans, Mary Leapor, Lady Mary Wortley Montagu, Hannah More, and Mary Robinson.

The Late 18th Century

Towards the end of the 18th century, poetry began to move away from the strict Augustan ideals and a new emphasis on sentiment and the feelings of the poet. This trend can perhaps be most clearly seen in the handling of nature, with a move away from poems about formal gardens and landscapes by urban poets and towards poems about nature as lived in. The leading exponents of this new trend include Thomas Gray, William Cowper, George Crabbe, Christopher Smart and Robert Burns as well as the Irish poet Oliver Goldsmith. These poets can be seen as paving the way for the Romantic movement.

The Romantic Movement

The last quarter of the 18th century was a time of social and political turbulence, with revolutions in the United States, France, Ireland and elsewhere. In Great Britain, movement for social change and a more inclusive sharing of power was also growing.

This was the backdrop against which the Romantic movement in English poetry emerged. The main poets of this movement were William Blake, William Wordsworth, Samuel Taylor Coleridge, Percy Bysshe Shelley, Lord Byron, and John Keats. The birth of English Romanticism is often dated to the publication in 1798 of Wordsworth and Coleridge's Lyrical Ballads. However, Blake had been publishing since the early 1780s. However, much of the focus on Blake only came about during the last century when Northrap Frye discussed his work in his book "The Anatomy of Criticism."

In poetry, the Romantic movement emphasised the creative expression of the individual and the need to find and formulate new forms of expression. The Romantics, with the partial exception of Byron, rejected the poetic ideals of the eighteenth century, and each of them returned to Milton for inspiration, though each drew something different from Milton. They also put a good deal of stress on their own originality. To the Romantics, the moment of creation was the most important in poetic expression and could not be repeated once it passed. Because of this new emphasis, poems that were not complete were nonetheless included in a poet's body of work such as Coleridge's "Kubla Khan" and "Christabel".

Additionally, the Romantic movement marked a shift in the use of language. Attempting to express the "language of the common man", Wordsworth and his fellow Romantic poets focused on employing poetic language for a wider audience, countering the mimetic, tightly constrained Neo-Classic poems (although it's important to note that the poet wrote first and foremost for his own creative, expression). In Shelley's "Defense of Poetry", he contends that poets are the "creators of language" and that the poet's job is to refresh language for their society.

The Romantics were not the only poets of note at this time. In the work of John Clare the late Augustan voice is blended with a peasant's first-hand knowledge to produce arguably some of the finest nature poetry in the English language. Another contemporary poet who does not fit into the Romantic group was Walter Savage Landor. Landor was a classicist whose poetry forms a link between the Augustans and Robert Browning, who much admired it.

THE ENGLISH LITERATURE AS A PART OF GENERAL MEDIEVAL EUROPEAN LITERATURE

One of the most striking general facts in the later Middle Ages is the uniformity of life in many of its aspects throughout all Western Europe. It was only during this period that the modern nations, acquiring national consciousness, began definitely to shape themselves out of the chaos which had followed the fall of the Roman Empire. The Roman Church, firmly established in every corner of every land, was the actual inheritor of much of the unifying power of the Roman government, and the feudal system everywhere gave to society the same political organization and ideals. In a truer sense, perhaps, than at any later time, Western Europe was one great brotherhood, thinking much the same thoughts, speaking in part the same speech, and actuated by the same beliefs. At least, the literature of the period, largely composed and copied by the great army of monks, exhibits everywhere a thorough uniformity in types and ideas.

We of the twentieth century should not allow ourselves to think vaguely of the Middle Ages as a benighted or shadowy period when life and the people who constituted it had scarcely anything in common with ourselves. In reality the men of the Middle Ages were moved by the same emotions and impulses as our own, and their lives presented the same incongruous mixture of nobility and baseness. Yet it is true that the externals of their existence were strikingly different from those of more recent times. In society the feudal system--lords with their serfs, towns struggling for municipal independence, kings and nobles doing, peaceably or with violence, very much what they pleased; a constant condition of public or private war; cities walled as a matter of course for protection against bands of robbers or hostile armies; the country still largely covered with forests, wildernesses, and fens; roads infested with brigands and so bad that travel was scarcely possible except on horseback; in private life, most of the modern comforts unknown, and the houses, even of the wealthy, so filthy and uncomfortable that all classes regularly, almost necessarily, spent most of the daylight hours in the open air; in industry no coal, factories, or large machinery, but in the towns guilds of workmen each turning out by hand his slow product of single articles; almost no education except for priests and monks, almost no conceptions of genuine science or history, but instead the abstract system of scholastic logic and philosophy, highly ingenious but highly fantastic; in religion no outward freedom of thought except for a few courageous spirits, but the arbitrary dictates of a despotic hierarchy, insisting on an ironbound creed which the remorseless process of time was steadily rendering more and more inadequate--this offers some slight suggestion of the conditions of life for several centuries, ending with the period with which we are now concerned.

In medieval literature likewise the modern student encounters much which seems at first sight grotesque. One of the most conspicuous examples is the pervasive use of allegory. The men of the Middle Ages often wrote, as we do, in direct terms and of simple things, but when they wished to rise above the commonplace they turned with a frequency which to-day appears astonishing to the devices of abstract personification and veiled meanings. No doubt this tendency was due in part to an idealizing dissatisfaction with the crudeness of their actual life (as well as to frequent inability to enter into the realm of deeper and finer thought without the aid of somewhat mechanical imagery); and no doubt it was greatly furthered also by the medieval passion for translating into elaborate and fantastic symbolism all the details of the Bible narratives. But from whatever cause, the tendency hardened into a ruling convention; thousands upon thousands of medieval manuscripts seem to declare that the world is a mirage of shadowy forms, or that it exists merely to body forth remote and highly surprising ideas.

Of all these countless allegories none was reiterated with more unwearied persistence than that of the Seven Deadly Sins (those sins which in the doctrine of the Church lead to spiritual death because they are wilfully committed). These sins are: Covetousness, Unchastity, Anger, Gluttony, Envy, Sloth, and, chief of all, Pride, the earliest of all, through which Lucifer was moved to his fatal rebellion against God, whence spring all human ills. Each of the seven, however, was interpreted as including so many related offences that among them they embraced nearly the whole range of possible wickedness. Personified, the Seven Sins in themselves almost dominate medieval literature, a sort of shadowy evil pantheon.

Moral and religious questions could scarcely be discussed without regard to them; and they maintain their commanding place even as late as in Spenser's 'Faerie Queene,' at the very end of the sixteenth century. To the Seven Sins were commonly opposed, but with much less emphasis, the Seven Cardinal Virtues, Faith, Hope, Charity (Love), Prudence, Temperance, Chastity, and Fortitude. Again, almost as prominent as the Seven Sins was the figure of Fortune with her revolving wheel, a goddess whom the violent vicissitudes and tragedies of life led the men of the Middle Ages, in spite of their Christianity, to bring over from classical literature and virtually to accept as a real divinity, with almost absolute control in human affairs. In the seventeenth century Shakspere's plays are full of allusions to her, but so for that matter is the everyday talk of all of us in the twentieth century.

LITERATURE IN THE THREE LANGUAGES

It is not to the purpose in a study like the present to give special attention to the literature written in England in Latin and French; we can speak only briefly of that composed in English. But in fact when the English had made its new beginning, about the year 1200, the same general forms flourished in all three languages, so that what is said in general of the English applies almost as much to the other two as well.

RELIGIOUS LITERATURE

We may virtually divide all the literature of the period, roughly, into (1) Religious and (2) Secular. But it must be observed that religious writings were far more important as literature during the Middle Ages than in more recent times, and the separation between religious and secular less distinct than at present. The forms of the religious literature were largely the same as in the previous period. There were songs, many of them addressed to the Virgin, some not only beautiful in their sincere and tender devotion, speaking for the finer spirits in an age of crudeness and violence, but occasionally beautiful as poetry. There were paraphrases of many parts of the Bible, lives of saints, in both verse and prose, and various other miscellaneous work. Perhaps worthy of special mention among single productions is the 'Cursor Mundi' (Surveyor of the World), an early fourteenth century poem of twenty-four thousand lines ('Paradise Lost' has less than eleven thousand), relating universal history from the beginning, on the basis of the Biblical narrative. Most important of all for their promise of the future, there were the germs of the modern drama in the form of the Church plays; but to these we shall give special attention in a later chapter.

SECULAR LITERATURE

In secular literature the variety was greater than in religious. We may begin by transcribing one or two of the songs, which, though not as numerous then as in some later periods, show that the great tradition of English secular lyric poetry reaches back from our own time to that of the Anglo-Saxons without a break. The best known of all is the 'Cuckoo Song,' of the thirteenth century, intended to be sung in harmony by four voices:

Sumer is icumen in; Lhude sing, cuccu! Groweth sed and bloweth med And springth the wde nu. Sing, cuccu! Awe bleteth after lomb, Lhouth after calve cu. Bulluc sterteth, bucke verteth; Murie sing, cuccu! Cuccu, cuccu, Wel singes thu, cuccu; Ne swik thu never nu.

Summer is come in; loud sing, cuckoo! Grows the seed and blooms the mead [meadow] and buds the wood anew. Sing, cuckoo! The ewe bleats for the lamb, lows for the calf the cow. The bullock gambols, the buck leaps; merrily sing, cuckoo! Cuckoo, cuckoo, well singest thou, cuckoo; cease thou never now.

The next is the first stanza of 'Alysoun' ('Fair Alice'):

Bytuene Mersh ant Averil, When spray beginnth to springe, The lutel foul hath hire wyl On hyre lud to synge. Ieh libbe in love-longinge For semlokest of alle thinge; He may me blisse bringe; Icham in hire baundoun. An hendy hap ichabbe ybent; Iehot from hevene it is me sent; From alle wymmen mi love is lent Ant lyht on Alysoun.

Between March and April, When the sprout begins to spring, The little bird has her desire In her tongue to sing. I live in love-longing For the fairest of all things; She may bring me bliss; I am at her mercy. A lucky lot I have secured; I think from heaven it is sent me; From all women my love is turned And is lighted on Alysoun.

There were also political and satirical songs and miscellaneous poems of various sorts, among them certain 'Bestiaries,' accounts of the supposed habits of animals, generally drawn originally from classical tradition, and most of them highly fantastic and allegorized in the interests of morality and religion. There was an abundance of extremely realistic coarse tales, hardly belonging to literature, in both prose and verse. The popular ballads of the fourteenth century we must reserve for later consideration. Most numerous of all the prose works, perhaps, were the Chronicles, which were produced generally in the monasteries and chiefly in the twelfth and thirteenth centuries, the greater part in Latin, some in French, and a few in rude English verse. Many of them were mere annals like the Anglo-Saxon Chronicle, but some were the lifelong works of men with genuine historical vision. Some dealt merely with the history of England, or a part of it, others with that of the entire world as it was known to medieval Europe. The majority will never be withdrawn from the obscurity of the manuscripts on which the patient care of their authors inscribed them; others have been printed in full and serve as the main basis for our knowledge of the events of the period.

THE ROMANCES

But the chief form of secular literature during the period, beginning in the middle of the twelfth century, was the romance, especially the metrical (verse) romance. The typical romances were the literary expression of chivalry.

They were composed by the professional minstrels, some of whom, as in Anglo-Saxon times, were richly supported and rewarded by kings and nobles, while others still wandered about the country, always welcome in the manor-houses. There, like Scott's Last Minstrel, they recited their sometimes almost endless works from memory, in the great halls or in the ladies' bowers, to the accompaniment of occasional strains on their harps. For two or three centuries the romances were to the lords and ladies, and to the wealthier citizens of the towns, much what novels are to the reading public of our own day.

By far the greater part of the romances current in England were written in French, whether by Normans or by French natives of the English provinces in France, and the English ones which have been preserved are mostly translations or imitations of French originals. The romances are extreme representatives of the whole class of literature of all times to which they have given the name. Frankly abandoning in the main the world of reality, they carry into that of idealized and glamorous fancy the chief interests of the medieval lords and ladies, namely, knightly exploits in war, and lovemaking. Love in the romances, also, retains all its courtly affectations, together with that worship of woman by man which in the twelfth century was exalted into a sentimental art by the poets of wealthy and luxurious Provence in Southern France. Side by side, again, with war and love, appears in the romances medieval religion, likewise conventionalized and childishly superstitious, but in some inadequate degree a mitigator of cruelty and a restrainer of lawless passion. Artistically, in some respects or all, the greater part of the romances are crude and immature.

Their usual main or only purpose is to hold attention by successions of marvellous adventures, natural or supernatural; of structure, therefore, they are often destitute; the characters are ordinarily mere types; and motivation is little considered. There were, however, exceptional authors, genuine artists, masters of meter and narrative, possessed by a true feeling for beauty; and in some of the romances the psychological analysis of love, in particular, is subtile and powerful, the direct precursor of one of the main developments in modern fiction.

The romances may very roughly be grouped into four great classes. First in time, perhaps, come those which are derived from the earlier French epics and in which love, if it appears at all, is subordinated to the military exploits of Charlemagne and his twelve peers in their wars against the Saracens. Second are the romances which, battered salvage from a greater past, retell in strangely altered romantic fashion the great stories of classical antiquity, mainly the achievements of Alexander the Great and the tragic fortunes of

Troy. Third come the Arthurian romances, and fourth those scattering miscellaneous ones which do not belong to the other classes, dealing, most of them, with native English heroes. Of these, two, 'King Horn' and 'Havelok,' spring direct from the common people and in both substance and expression reflect the hard reality of their lives, while 'Guy of Warwick' and 'Bevis of Hampton,' which are among the best known but most tedious of all the list, belong, in their original form, to the upper classes.

Of all the romances the Arthurian are by far the most important. They belong peculiarly to English literature, because they are based on traditions of British history, but they have assumed a very prominent place in the literature of the whole western world. Rich in varied characters and incidents to which a universal significance could be attached, in their own time they were the most popular works of their class; and living on vigorously after the others were forgotten, they have continued to form one of the chief quarries of literary material and one of the chief sources of inspiration for modern poets and romancers. It seems well worth while, therefore, to outline briefly their literary history.

The period in which their scene is nominally laid is that of the Anglo-Saxon conquest of Great Britain. Of the actual historical events of this period extremely little is known, and even the capital question whether such a person as Arthur ever really existed can never receive a definite answer. The only contemporary writer of the least importance is the Briton (priest or monk), Gildas, who in a violent Latin pamphlet of about the year 550 ('The Destruction and Conquest of Britain') denounces his countrymen for their sins and urges them to unite against the Saxons; and Gildas gives only the slightest sketch of what had actually happened. He tells how a British king (to whom later tradition assigns the name Vortigern) invited in the Anglo-Saxons as allies against the troublesome northern Scots and Picts, and how the Anglo-Saxons, victorious against these tribes, soon turned in furious conquest against the Britons themselves, until, under a certain Ambrosius Aurelianus, a man 'of Roman race,' the Britons successfully defended themselves and at last in the battle of Mount Badon checked the Saxon advance.

Next in order after Gildas, but not until about the year 800, appears a strangely jumbled document, last edited by a certain Nennius, and entitled 'Historia Britonum' (The History of the Britons), which adds to Gildas' outline traditions, natural and supernatural, which had meanwhile been growing up among the Britons (Welsh). It supplies the names of the earliest Saxon leaders, Hengist and Horsa (who also figure in the 'Anglo-Saxon Chronicle'), and narrates at length their treacherous dealings with Vortigern. Among other stories we find that of Vortigern's tower, where Gildas' Ambrosius appears as a boy of supernatural nature, destined to develop in the romances into the great magician Merlin. In Nennius' book occurs also the earliest mention of Arthur, who, in a comparatively sober passage, is said, some time after the days of Vortigern, to have 'fought against the Saxons, together with the kings of the Britons, but he himself was leader in the battles.' A list, also, is given of his twelve victories, ending with Mount Badon.

It is impossible to decide whether there is really any truth in this account of Nennius, or whether it springs wholly from the imagination of the Britons, attempting to solace themselves for their national overthrow; but it allows us to believe if we choose that sometime in the early sixth century there was a British leader of the name of Arthur, who by military genius rose to high command and for a while beat back the Saxon hordes. At most, however, it should be clearly realized, Arthur was probably only a local leader in some limited region, and, far from filling the splendid place which he occupies in the later romances, was but the hard-pressed captain of a few thousand barbarous and half-armed warriors.

For three hundred years longer the traditions about Arthur continued to develop among the Welsh people. The most important change which took place was Arthur's elevation to the position of chief hero of the British (Welsh) race and the subordination to him, as his followers, of all the other native heroes, most of whom had originally been gods. To Arthur himself certain divine attributes were added, such as his possession of magic weapons, among them the sword Excalibur. It also came to be passionately believed among the Welsh that he was not really dead but would some day return from the mysterious Other World to which he had withdrawn and reconquer the island for his people.

It was not until the twelfth century that these Arthurian traditions, the cherished heritage of the Welsh and their cousins, the Bretons across the English Channel in France, were suddenly adopted as the property of all Western Europe, so that Arthur became a universal Christian hero. This remarkable transformation, no doubt in some degree inevitable, was actually brought about chiefly through the instrumentality of a single man, a certain English archdeacon of Welsh descent, Geoffrey of Monmouth. Geoffrey, a literary and ecclesiastical adventurer looking about for a means of making himself famous, put forth about the year 1136, in Latin, a 'History of the Britons' from the earliest times to the seventh century, in which, imitating the form of the serious chronicles, he combined in cleverly impudent fashion all the adaptable miscellaneous material, fictitious, legendary, or traditional, which he found at hand. In dealing with Arthur, Geoffrey greatly enlarges on Gildas and Nennius; in part, no doubt, from his own invention, in part, perhaps, from Welsh tradition. He provides Arthur with a father, King Uther, makes of Arthur's wars against the Saxons only his youthful exploits, relates at length how Arthur conquered almost all of Western Europe, and adds to the earlier story the figures of Merlin, Guenevere, Modred, Gawain, Kay, and Bedivere. What is not least important, he gives to Arthur's reign much of the atmosphere of feudal chivalry which was that of the ruling class of his own age.

Geoffrey may or may not have intended his astonishing story to be seriously accepted, but in fact it was received with almost universal credence. For centuries it was incorporated in outline or in excerpts into almost all the sober chronicles, and what is of much more importance for literature, it was taken up and rehandled in various fashions by very numerous romancers. About twenty years after Geoffrey wrote, the French poet Wace, an English subject, paraphrased his entire 'History' in vivid, fluent, and diffuse verse. Wace imparts to the whole, in a thorough-going way, the manners of chivalry, and adds, among other things, a mention of the Round Table, which Geoffrey, somewhat chary of the supernatural, had chosen to omit, though it was one of the early elements of the Welsh tradition.

Other poets followed, chief among them the delightful Chretien of Troyes, all writing mostly of the exploits of single knights at Arthur's court, which they made over, probably, from scattering tales of Welsh and Breton mythology. To declare that most romantic heroes had been knights of Arthur's circle now became almost a matter of course. Prose romances also appeared, vast formless compilations, which gathered up into themselves story after story, according to the fancy of each successive editor. Greatest of the additions to the substance of the cycle was the story of the Holy Grail, originally an altogether independent legend. Important changes necessarily developed. Arthur himself, in many of the romances, was degraded from his position of the bravest knight to be the inactive figurehead of a brilliant court; and the only really historical element in the story, his struggle against the Saxons, was thrust far into the background, while all the emphasis was laid on the romantic achievements of the single knights.

6

The Nineteenth Century of Victorian Novel and Literature

At the same time Jane Austen was writing highly polished novels about the life of the landed gentry, seen from a woman's point of view, and wryly focused on practical social issues, especially marriage and money. Charles Dickens emerged on the literary scene in the 1830s, confirming the trend for serial publication. Dickens wrote vividly about London life and the struggles of the poor, but in a good-humoured fashion which was acceptable to readers of all classes. His early works such as the Pickwick Papers are masterpieces of comedy. Later his works became darker, without losing his genius for caricature.

It was in the Victorian era (1837-1901) that the novel became the leading form of literature in English. Most writers were now more concerned to meet the tastes of a large middle class reading public than to please aristocratic patrons. The best known works of the era include the emotionally powerful works of the Brontë sisters; the satire Vanity Fair by William Makepeace Thackeray and Anthony Trollope's insightful portrayals of the lives of the landowning and professional classes. George Eliot's novels are frequently held in the highest regard for their combination of high Victorian literary detail combined with an intellectual breadth that removes them from the narrow confines they often depict. An interest in rural matters and the changing social and economic situation of the countryside may be seen in the novels of Thomas Hardy and others. Literature for children was published during the Victorian period, some of which has become globally well-known, such as the work of Lewis Carroll.

VICTORIAN POETS

Leading poetic figures of the Victorian era included Alfred Tennyson,

Robert Browning (and his wife, Elizabeth Barrett Browning), and Matthew Arnold, whilst multi-disciplinary talents such as John Ruskin and Dante Gabriel Rossetti were also famous for their poetry.

Nonsense verse, such as by Edward Lear, taken with the work of Lewis Carroll, is regarded as a precursor of surrealism.

Ireland

In the 19th century, the Irish playwright Dion Boucicault was an extremely popular writer of comedies. However, it was in the last decade of the century that the Irish theatre finally came of age with the emergence of George Bernard Shaw and Oscar Wilde. All of these writers lived mainly in England and wrote in English.

The Celtic Revival (c. 1890), also known as the Irish Literary Revival, was begun by William Butler Yeats, Lady Gregory, John M. Synge, Sean O'Casey, James Joyce and others. The Revival stimulated new appreciation of traditional Irish literature. The movement also encouraged the creation of works written in the spirit of Irish culture, as distinct from English culture.

Wales

Anglo-Welsh literature is a term used to describe works written in the English language by Welsh writers, especially if they either have subject matter relating to Wales or (as in the case of Anglo-Welsh poetry in particular) are influenced by the Welsh language in terms of patterns of usage or syntax. It has been recognised as a distinctive entity only since the 20th century. The need for a separate identity for this kind of writing arose because of the parallel development of modern Welsh literature, i.e. literature in the Welsh language.

Scotland

The Kailyard school of Scottish writers presented an idealised version of society.

VICTORIAN POETRY

The Victorian era was a period of great political, social and economic change. The Empire recovered from the loss of the American colonies and entered a period of rapid expansion. This expansion, combined with increasing industrialisation and mechanisation, led to a prolonged period of economic growth. The Reform Act 1832 was the beginning of a process that would eventually lead to universal suffrage.

High Victorian Poetry

The major High Victorian poets were Alfred, Lord Tennyson, Robert Browning, Elizabeth Barrett Browning, Matthew Arnold and Gerard Manley Hopkins. Tennyson was, to some degree, the Spenser of the new age and his Idylls of the Kings can be read as a Victorian version of The Faerie Queen, that is as a poem that sets out to provide a mythic foundation to the idea of empire.

The Brownings spent much of their time out of England and explored European models and matter in much of their poetry. Robert Browning's great innovation was the dramatic monologue, which he used to its full extent in his long novel in verse, The Ring and the Book. Elizabeth Barrett Browning is perhaps best remembered for Sonnets from the Portuguese but her long poem Aurora Leigh is one of the classics of 19th century feminist literature.

Matthew Arnold was much influenced by Wordsworth, though his poem Dover Beach is often considered a precursor of the modernist revolution. Hopkins wrote in relative obscurity and his work was not published until after his death. His unusual style (involving what he called "sprung rhythm" and heavy reliance on rhyme and alliteration) had a considerable influence on many of the poets of the 1940s.

Pre-Raphaelites, Arts and Crafts, Aestheticism, and the "Yellow" 1890s

The Pre-Raphaelite Brotherhood was a mid-19th century arts movement dedicated to the reform of what they considered the sloppy Mannerist painting of the day. Although primarily concerned with the visual arts, two members, the brother and sister Dante Gabriel Rossetti and Christina Rossetti, were also poets of some ability. Their poetry shares many of the concerns of the painters; an interest in Medieval models, an almost obsessive attention to visual detail and an occasional tendency to lapse into whimsy. Dante Rossetti worked with, and had some influence on, the leading Arts and Crafts painter and poet William Morris. Morris shared the Pre-Raphaelite interest in the poetry of the European Middle Ages, to the point of producing some illuminated manuscript volumes of his work.

Towards the end of the century, English poets began to take an interest in French symbolism and Victorian poetry entered a decadent fin-de-siecle phase. Two groups of poets emerged, the Yellow Book poets who adhered to the tenets of Aestheticism, including Algernon Charles Swinburne, Oscar Wilde and Arthur Symons and the Rhymer's Club group that included Ernest Dowson, Lionel Johnson and W. B. Yeats.

NON ENGLISH LANGUAGE LITERATURES SINCE 1900

In the late 19th and early 20th century, Welsh literature began to reflect the way the Welsh language was increasingly becoming a political symbol. Two important literary nationalists were Saunders Lewis and Kate Roberts.

In the early 20th century in Scotland, a renaissance in the use of Lowland Scots occurred, its most vocal figure being Hugh MacDiarmid. Other contemporaries were Douglas Young, Sidney Goodsir Smith, Robert Garioch and Robert McLellan. However, the revival was largely limited to verse and other literature.

The end of the First World War saw a decline in the quantity of poetry published in Jèrriais and Dgèrnésiais in favour of short-story-like newspaper columns in prose, some being collected in book or booklet form-this being a common genre in the Norman mainland. The imported eisteddfod tradition in the Channel Islands encouraged recitation and performance, a tradition that continues today. The German military occupation of the Channel Islands 1940-1945 encouraged increased use of the vernacular languages among those who remained, but the German censorship permitted little original writing to be published. Within the restrictions, Les Chroniques de Jersey, the only surviving French language newspaper in the Islands, republished considerable quantities of older Jèrriais literature for purposes of morale and the assertion of identity. The post-Liberation social changes meant, however, that vernacular literature has never regained the situation it had enjoyed previously.

Sorley MacLean's work in Scottish Gaelic in the 1930s gave new value to modern literature in that language.

Highly anglicised Lowland Scots is often used in contemporary Scottish fiction, for example, the Edinburgh dialect of Lowland Scots in Trainspotting by Irvine Welsh. Edwin Morgan is the current Makar (Scottish national poet) and also produces translations of world literature.

Translations are an important feature of the literatures of the regional languages of the islands, for example: Contoyryssyn Ealish ayns Cheer ny Yindyssyn a Manx translation of Alice in Wonderland by Brian Stowell, published in 1990, or the 2004 Scots version of the Rubaiyat of Omar Khayyam by Rab Wilson. Alexander Hutchison has translated the poetry of Catullus into Scots, and in the 1980s Liz Lochhead produced a Scots translation of Tartuffe by Molière. Original literature continues to be promoted by organisations and institutions such as the Eisteddfod or the Mod. With the revival of Cornish there have been newer works written in the language. The bard Pol Hodge is an example of a poet writing in Cornish.

ENGLISH POETRY

The history of English poetry stretches from the middle of the 7th century to the present day. Over this period, English poets have written some of the most enduring poems in European culture, and the language and its poetry have spread around the globe. Consequently, the term English poetry is unavoidably ambiguous. It can mean poetry written in England, or poetry written in the English language.

The earliest surviving poetry from the area currently known as England was likely transmitted orally and then written down in versions that do not now survive; thus, dating the earliest poetry remains difficult and often controversial. The earliest surviving manuscripts date from the 10th century. Poetry written in Latin, Brythonic (a predecessor language of Welsh) and Old Irish survives which may date as early as the 6th century. The earliest surviving poetry written in Anglo-Saxon, the most direct predecessor of modern English, may have been composed as early as the seventh century.

With the growth of trade and the British Empire, the English language had been widely used outside England. In the twenty-first century, only a small percentage of the world's native English speakers live in England, and there is also a vast population of non-native speakers of English who are capable of writing poetry in the language. A number of major national poetries, including the American, Australian, New Zealand and Canadian poetry have emerged and developed. Since 1922, Irish poetry has also been increasingly viewed as a separate area of study. This article focuses on poetry written in English by poets born or spending a significant part of their lives in England. However, given the nature of the subject, this guideline has been applied with common sense, and reference is made to poetry in other languages or poets who are not primarily English where appropriate.

The Earliest English Poetry

The earliest known English poem is a hymn on the creation; Bede attributes this to Cædmon (fl. 658-680), who was, according to legend, an illiterate herdsman who produced extemporaneous poetry at a monastery at Whitby. This is generally taken as marking the beginning of Anglo-Saxon poetry.

Much of the poetry of the period is difficult to date, or even to arrange chronologically; for example, estimates for the date of the great epic Beowulf range from AD 608 right through to AD 1000, and there has never been anything even approaching a consensus. It is possible to identify certain key moments, however. The Dream of the Rood was written before circa AD 700, when excerpts were carved in runes on the Ruthwell Cross. Some poems on historical events, such as The Battle of Brunanburh (937) and the Battle of Maldon (991), appear to have been composed shortly after the events in question, and can be dated reasonably precisely in consequence.

By and large, however, Anglo-Saxon poetry is categorised by the manuscripts in which it survives, rather than its date of composition. The most important manuscripts are the four great poetical codices of the late tenth and early eleventh centuries, known as the Caedmon manuscript, the Vercelli Book, the Exeter Book, and the Beowulf manuscript.

While the poetry that has survived is limited in volume, it is wide in breadth. Beowulf is the only heroic epic to have survived in its entirety, but fragments of others such as Waldere and the Finnsburg Fragment show that it was not unique in its time. Other genres include much religious verse, from devotional works to biblical paraphrase; elegies such as The Wanderer, The Seafarer, and The Ruin (often taken to be a description of the ruins of Bath); and numerous proverbs, riddles, and charms.

With one notable exception (Rhyming Poem), Anglo-Saxon poetry depends on alliterative verse for its structure and any rhyme included is merely ornamental.

ENGLISH LANGUAGE LITERATURE SINCE 1900

The major lyric poet of the first decades of the 20th century was Thomas Hardy, who concentrated on poetry after the harsh response to his last novel, Jude the Obscure.

The most widely popular writer of the early years of the 20th century was arguably Rudyard Kipling, a highly versatile writer of novels, short stories and poems, often based on his experiences of British ruled India. Kipling was closely associated with imperialism and this has damaged his reputation in more recent times. From around 1910, the Modernist Movement began to influence English literature. Whereas their Victorian predecessors had usually been happy to cater to mainstream middle class taste, 20th century writers often felt alienated from it, and responded by writing more intellectually challenging works or by pushing the boundaries of acceptable content.

The major poets of this period included the American born T. S. Eliot and the Irishman William Butler Yeats. Free verse and other stylistic innovations came to the forefront in this era.

The experiences of the First World War were reflected in the work of war poets such as Wilfred Owen, Rupert Brooke, Isaac Rosenberg, Edmund Blunden and Siegfried Sassoon. Many writers turned away from patriotic and imperialist themes as a result of the war, notably Kipling.

Important novelists between the two World Wars included the Irish writer James Joyce, D.H. Lawrence and Virginia Woolf.

Joyce's increasingly complex works included Ulysses, an interpretation of the Odyssey set in Dublin, and culminated in the famously obscure Finnegans Wake. Lawrence wrote with understanding about the social life of the lower and middle classes, and the personal life of those who could not adapt to the social norms of his time. He attempted to explore human emotions more deeply than his contemporaries and challenged the boundaries of the acceptable treatment of sexual issues in works such as Lady Chatterley's Lover. Virginia Woolf was an influential feminist, and a major stylistic innovator associated with the stream of consciousness technique. Her novels included To the Lighthouse, Mrs Dalloway, and The Waves.

Novelists who wrote in a more traditional style, such as John Galsworthy and Arnold Bennett continued to receive great acclaim in the interwar period. At the same time the Georgian poets maintained a more conservative approach to poetry.

The leading poets of the middle and later 20th century included the traditionalist John Betjeman, Philip Larkin, Ted Hughes and the Northern Irish Catholic Seamus Heaney, who lived in the Republic of Ireland for much of his later life.

Major novelists of the middle and later 20th century included the satirist Evelyn Waugh, William Golding, Anthony Burgess, Grahame Greene and Iris Murdoch.

In drama, the drawing room plays of the post war period were challenged in the 1950s by the Angry Young Men, exemplified by as John Osborne's iconic play Look Back in Anger. Also in the 1950s, the bleak absurdist play Waiting for Godot, by the Southern Irish playwright Samuel Beckett profoundly affected British drama. The theatre of the absurd influenced playwrights of the later decades of the 20th century, including Harold Pinter, whose works are often characterized by menace or claustrophobia, and Tom Stoppard. Stoppard's works are however also notable for their high-spirited wit and the great range of intellectual issues which he tackles in different plays.

- Georgian poets

- Anthology of Twentieth-Century British and Irish Poetry
- British Poetry Revival
- Kitchen sink drama

THE FIRST THREE DECADES

The Victorian era continued into the early years of the 20th century and two figures emerged as the leading representative of the poetry of the old era to act as a bridge into the new. These were Yeats and Thomas Hardy. Yeats, although not a modernist, was to learn a lot from the new poetic movements that sprang up around him and adapted his writing to the new circumstances. Hardy was, in terms of technique at least, a more traditional figure and was to be a reference point for various anti-modernist reactions, especially from the 1950s onwards.

The Georgian Poets and World War I

The Georgian poets were the first major grouping of the post-Victorian era. Their work appeared in a series of five anthologies called Georgian Poetry which were published by Harold Monro and edited by Edward Marsh. The poets featured included Edmund Blunden, Rupert Brooke, Robert Graves, D. H. Lawrence, Walter de la Mare and Siegfried Sassoon. Their poetry represented something of a reaction to the decadence of the 1890s and tended towards the sentimental.

Brooke and Sassoon were to go on to win reputations as war poets and Lawrence quickly distanced himself from the group and was associated with the modernist movement. Other notable poets who wrote about the war include Isaac Rosenberg, Edward Thomas, Wilfred Owen, May Cannan and, from the home front, Hardy and Rudyard Kipling. Although many of these poets wrote socially-aware criticism of the war, most remained technically conservative and traditionalist.

Modernism

The early decades of the 20th century saw the United States begin to overtake the United Kingdom as the major economic power. In the world of poetry, this period also saw American writers at the forefront of avant-garde practices. Among the foremost of these poets were T.S. Eliot, H.D. and Ezra Pound, each of whom spent an important part of their writing lives in England. Pound's involvement with the Imagists marked the beginning of a revolution in the way poetry was written. English poets involved with this group included

D. H. Lawrence, Richard Aldington, T. E. Hulme, F. S. Flint, E. E. Cummings, Ford Madox Ford, Allen Upward and John Cournos. Eliot, particularly after the publication of The Waste Land, became a major figure and influence on other English poets.

In addition to these poets, other English modernists began to emerge. These included the London-Welsh poet and painter David Jones, whose first book, In Parenthesis, was one of the very few experimental poems to come out of World War I, the Scot Hugh MacDiarmid, Mina Loy and Basil Bunting.

The Thirties

The poets who began to emerge in the 1930s had two things in common; they had all been born too late to have any real experience of the pre-World War I world and they grew up in a period of social, economic and political turmoil. Perhaps as a consequence of these facts, themes of community, social (in)justice and war seem to dominate the poetry of the decade.

The poetic landscape of the decade was dominated by four poets; W. H. Auden, Stephen Spender, Cecil Day-Lewis and Louis MacNeice, although the last of these belongs at least as much to the history of Irish poetry. These poets were all, in their early days at least, politically active on the Left. Although they admired Eliot, they also represented a move away from the technical innovations of their modernist predecessors. A number of other, less enduring, poets also worked in the same vein. One of these was Michael Roberts, whose New Country anthology both introduced the group to a wider audience and gave them their name.

The 1930s also saw the emergence of a home-grown English surrealist poetry whose main exponents were David Gascoyne, Hugh Sykes Davies, George Barker, and Philip O'Connor. These poets turned to French models rather than either the New Country poets or English-language modernism, and their work was to prove of importance to later English experimental poets as it broadened the scope of the English avant-garde tradition.

John Betjeman and Stevie Smith, who were two of the most significant poets of this period, stood outside all schools and groups. Betjeman was a quietly ironic poet of Middle England with a fine command of a wide range of verse techniques. Smith was an entirely unclassifiable one-off voice.

The Forties

The 1940s opened with the United Kingdom at war and a new generation of war poets emerged in response. These included Keith Douglas, Alun Lewis,

Henry Reed and F.T. Prince. As with the poets of the First World War, the work of these writers can be seen as something of an interlude in the history of 20th century poetry. Technically, many of these war poets owed something to the 1930s poets, but their work grew out of the particular circumstances in which they found themselves living and fighting.

The main movement in post-war 1940s poetry was the New Romantic group that included Dylan Thomas, George Barker, W. S. Graham, Kathleen Raine, Henry Treece and J. F. Hendry. These writers saw themselves as in revolt against the classicism of the New Country poets. They turned to such models as Gerard Manley Hopkins, Arthur Rimbaud and Hart Crane and the word play of James Joyce. Thomas, in particular, helped Anglo-Welsh poetry to emerge as a recognisable force.

Other significant poets to emerge in the 1940s include Lawrence Durrell, Bernard Spencer, Roy Fuller, Norman Nicholson, Vernon Watkins, R. S. Thomas and Norman McCaig. These last four poets represent a trend towards regionalism and poets writing about their native areas; Watkins and Thomas in Wales, Nicholson in Cumberland and MacCaig in Scotland.

The Fifties

The 1950s were dominated by three groups of poets, The Movement, The Group and a number of poets that gathered around the label Extremist Art.

The Movement poets as a group came to public notice in Robert Conquest's 1955 anthology New Lines. The core of the group consisted of Philip Larkin, Elizabeth Jennings, D. J. Enright, Kingsley Amis, Thom Gunn and Donald Davie. They were identified with a hostility to modernism and internationalism, and looked to Hardy as a model. However, both Davie and Gunn later moved away from this position.

As befits their name, the Group were much more formally a group of poets, meeting for weekly discussions under the chairmanship of Philip Hobsbaum and Edward Lucie-Smith. Other Group poets included Martin Bell, Peter Porter, Peter Redgrove, George MacBeth and David Wevill. Hobsbaum spent some time teaching in Belfast, where he was a formative influence on the emerging Northern Ireland poets including Seamus Heaney.

The term Extremist Art was first used by the poet A. Alvarez to describe the work of the American poet Sylvia Plath. Other poets associated with this group included Plath's one-time husband Ted Hughes, Francis Berry and Jon Silkin. These poets are sometimes compared with the Expressionist German school.

A number of young poets working in what might be termed a modernist vein also started publishing during this decade. These included Charles Tomlinson, Gael Turnbull, Roy Fisher and Bob Cobbing. These poets can now be seen as forerunners of some of the major developments during the following two decades.

The 1960s and 1970s

In the early part of the 1960s, the centre of gravity of mainstream poetry moved to Ireland, with the emergence of Seamus Heaney, Tom Paulin, Paul Muldoon and others. In England, the most cohesive groupings can, in retrospect, be seen to cluster around what might loosely be called the modernist tradition and draw on American as well as indigenous models.

The British Poetry Revival was a wide-reaching collection of groupings and subgroupings that embraces performance, sound and concrete poetry as well as the legacy of Pound, Jones, MacDiarmid, Loy and Bunting, the Objectivist poets, the Beats and the Black Mountain poets, among others. Leading poets associated with this movement include J. H. Prynne, Eric Mottram, Tom Raworth, Denise Riley and Lee Harwood.

The Mersey Beat poets were Adrian Henri, Brian Patten and Roger McGough. Their work was a self-conscious attempt at creating an English equivalent to the Beats. Many of their poems were written in protest against the established social order and, particularly, the threat of nuclear war. Although not actually a Mersey Beat poet, Adrian Mitchell is often associated with the group in critical discussion. Contemporary poet Steve Turner has also been compared with them.

PERIOD OF ENGLISH DRAMA

Drama was introduced to England from Europe by the Romans, and auditoriums were constructed across the country for this purpose. By the medieval period, the mummers' plays had developed, a form of early street theatre associated with the Morris dance, concentrating on themes such as Saint George and the Dragon and Robin Hood. These were folk tales re-telling old stories, and the actors travelled from town to town performing these for their audiences in return for money and hospitality. The medieval mystery plays and morality plays, which dealt with Christian themes, were performed at religious festivals.

The period known as the English Renaissance, approximately 1500-1660, saw a flowering of the drama and all the arts. The most famous example of the mystery play, Everyman, and the two candidates for the earliest comedy in English Nicholas Udall's Ralph Roister Doister and the anonymous Gammer Gurton's Needle, all belong to the 16th century.

During the reign of Elizabeth I in the late 16th and early 17th century, a London-centred culture that was both courtly and popular produced great poetry and drama. Perhaps the most famous playwright in the world, William Shakespeare from Stratford-upon-Avon, wrote plays that are still performed in theatres across the world to this day. He was himself an actor and deeply involved in the running of the theatre company that performed his plays. Other important playwrights of this period include Christopher Marlowe, Ben Jonson, and John Webster. Various types of plays were popular. Ben Jonson, for example, was often engaged to write courtly masques, ornate plays where the actors wore masks. The three types that seem most often studied today are the histories, the comedies, and the tragedies. Most playwrights tended to specialise in one or another of these, but Shakespeare is remarkable in that he produced all three types. His 38 plays include tragedies such as Hamlet (1603), Othello (1604), and King Lear (1605); comedies such as A Midsummer Night's Dream (1594-96) and Twelfth Night (1602); and history plays such as Henry IV, part 1-2. Some have hypothesized that the English Renaissance paved the way for the sudden dominance of drama in English society, arguing that the questioning mode popular during this time was best served by the competing characters in the plays of the Elizabethan dramatists.

During the Interregnum 1649-1660, English theatres were kept closed by the Puritans for religious and ideological reasons. When the London theatres opened again with the Restoration of the monarchy in 1660, they flourished under the personal interest and support of Charles II. Wide and socially mixed audiences were attracted by topical writing and by the introduction of the first professional actresses (in Shakespeare's time, all female roles had been played by boys). New genres of the Restoration were heroic drama, pathetic drama, and Restoration comedy.

Notable heroic tragedies of this period include John Dryden's All for Love (1677) and (Aureng-Zebe) (1675), and Thomas Otway's Venice Preserved (1682). The Restoration plays that have best retained the interest of producers and audiences today are the comedies, such as George Etherege's The Man of Mode (1676), William Wycherley's The Country Wife (1676), John Vanbrugh's The Relapse (1696), and William Congreve's The Way of the World (1700). This period saw the first professional woman playwright, Aphra Behn, author of many comedies including The Rover (1677). Restoration comedy is famous or notorious for its sexual explicitness, a quality encouraged by Charles II (1660-1685) personally and by the rakish aristocratic ethos of his court.

In the 18th century, the highbrow and provocative Restoration comedy lost favour, to be replaced by sentimental comedy, domestic tragedy such as George Lillo's The London Merchant (1731), and by an overwhelming interest in Italian opera. Popular entertainment became more dominant in this period than ever before. Fair-booth burlesque and musical entertainment, the ancestors of the English music hall, flourished at the expense of legitimate English drama, which went into a long period of decline. By the early 19th century, the drama was no longer represented by stage plays at all, but by closet drama, plays written to be privately read in a "closet" (a small domestic room).

A change came in the later 19th century with the plays on the London stage by the Irishmen George Bernard Shaw and Oscar Wilde and the Norwegian Henrik Ibsen, all of whom influenced domestic English drama and vitalised it again.

Postmodernism had a pround effect on English Drama in the latter half of the 20th Century. This can be seen particularly in the work of Samuel Beckett (most notably in Waiting for Godot), who in turn influenced writers such as Harold Pinter and Tom Stoppard.

Today the West End of London has a large number of theatres, particularly centred around Shaftesbury Avenue. A prolific writer of music for musicals of the 20th century, Andrew Lloyd Webber, has dominated the West End for a number of years, and his works have travelled to Broadway in New York and around the world, as well as being turned into film.

The Royal Shakespeare Company operates out of Stratford-upon-Avon, producing mainly but not exclusively Shakespeare's plays.

PERIOD OF ENGLISH NOVEL

Early Novels in English

Romantic Novels: The Romantic period saw the first flowering of the English novel. The Romantic and the Gothic novel are closely related; both imagined almost-supernatural forces operating in nature or directing human fate. Just as William Wordsworth and other poets were integral to the growth of English Romanticism, so Mary Shelley, and Ann Radcliffe were key to the sudden popularity of the Gothic novel.

It is equally important to recognize, however, the role that the contemporary reader played in the history of the English novel. For many years, novels were considered light reading for young, single women. Novels written with this in mind often contained sometimes heavy moral instruction, and, like earlier English literature, attempted to provide an example of the correct kind of conduct.

Jane Austen was a key novelist of this period.

Victorian Novels

The novel first began to dominate English literature during the Victorian era. Most Victorian novels were long and closely wrought, full of intricate language, but the dominant feature of Victorian novels might be their verisimilitude, that is, their close representation to the real social life of the age. This social life was largely informed by the development of the emerging middle class and the manners and expectations of this class, as opposed to the aristocrat forms dominating previous ages.

For the first time in English history, female authors assumed a central role. The English novel was defined, to a large extent, by the works of Charlotte Brontë, Elizabeth Gaskell, and George Eliot.

None of this should imply that the Victorian novel was not diverse; it was, extraordinarly so. Emily Brontë and Charles Dickens wrote in very different styles and addressed altogether different themes. Key to Victorian style is the concept of the authorial intrusion and the address to the reader. For example, the author might interrupt her narrative to pass judgment on a character, or pity or praise another, while later seeming to exclaim "Dear Reader!" and inform or remind the reader of some other relevant fact.

Serial Novels

Most novels of the Victorian period were published in serial form; that is, individual chapters or sections appearing in subsequent journal issues. As such, demand was high for each new appearance of the novel to introduce some new element, whether it be a plot twist or a new character, so as to maintain the reader's interest. During this time, authors were paid by the word, which tended to create wordy prose. In part for these reasons, Victorian novels are made up of a variety of plots and a large number of characters, appearing and reappearing as events dictate.

7

French Revolution and English Literature

SOCIAL RESULTS OF THE CONQUEST

In most respects, or all, the Norman conquest accomplished precisely that racial rejuvenation of which, as we have seen, Anglo-Saxon England stood in need. For the Normans brought with them from France the zest for joy and beauty and dignified and stately ceremony in which the Anglo-Saxon temperament was poor--they brought the love of light-hearted song and chivalrous sports, of rich clothing, of finely-painted manuscripts, of noble architecture in cathedrals and palaces, of formal religious ritual, and of the pomp and display of all elaborate pageantry. In the outcome they largely reshaped the heavy mass of Anglo-Saxon life into forms of grace and beauty and brightened its duller surface with varied and brilliant colors.

For the Anglo-Saxons themselves, however, the Conquest meant at first little else than that bitterest and most complete of all national disasters, hopeless subjection to a tyrannical and contemptuous foe. The Normans were not heathen, as the 'Danes' had been, and they were too few in number to wish to supplant the conquered people; but they imposed themselves, both politically and socially, as stern and absolute masters. King William confirmed in their possessions the few Saxon nobles and lesser land-owners who accepted his rule and did not later revolt; but both pledges and interest compelled him to bestow most of the estates of the kingdom, together with the widows of their former holders, on his own nobles and the great motley throng of turbulent fighters who had made up his invading army.

In the lordships and manors, therefore, and likewise in the great places of the Church, were established knights and nobles, the secular ones holding in feudal tenure from the king or his immediate great vassals, and each supported in turn by Norman men-at-arms; and to them were subjected as serfs, workers bound to the land, the greater part of the Saxon population. As visible signs of the changed order appeared here and there throughout the country massive and gloomy castles of stone, and in the larger cities, in place of the simple Anglo-Saxon churches, cathedrals lofty and magnificent beyond all Anglo-Saxon dreams. What sufferings, at the worst, the Normans inflicted on the Saxons is indicated in a famous passage of the 'Anglo-Saxon Chronicle,' an entry seventy years subsequent to the Conquest, of which the least distressing part may be thus paraphrased:

'They filled the land full of castles. They compelled the wretched men of the land to build their castles and wore them out with hard labor. When the castles were made they filled them with devils and evil men. Then they took all those whom they thought to have any property, both by night and by day, both men and women, and put them in prison for gold and silver, and tormented them with tortures that cannot be told; for never were any martyrs so tormented as these were.'

THE UNION OF THE RACES AND LANGUAGES

That their own race and identity were destined to be absorbed in those of the Anglo-Saxons could never have occurred to any of the Normans who stood with William at Hastings, and scarcely to any of their children. Yet this result was predetermined by the stubborn tenacity and numerical superiority of the conquered people and by the easy adaptability of the Norman temperament. Racially, and to a less extent socially, intermarriage did its work, and that within a very few generations. Little by little, also, Norman contempt and Saxon hatred were softened into tolerance, and at last even into a sentiment of national unity. This sentiment was finally to be confirmed by the loss of Normandy and other French possessions of the Norman-English kings in the thirteenth century, a loss which transformed England from a province of the Norman Continental empire and of a foreign nobility into an independent country, and further by the wars ('The Hundred Years' War') which England-Norman nobility and Saxon yeomen fighting together--carried on in France in the fourteenth century.

In language and literature the most general immediate result of the Conquest was to make of England a trilingual country, where Latin, French, and Anglo-Saxon were spoken separately side by side. With Latin, the tongue of the Church and of scholars, the Norman clergy were much more thoroughly familiar than the Saxon priests had been; and the introduction of the richer

Latin culture resulted, in the latter half of the twelfth century, at the court of Henry II, in a brilliant outburst of Latin literature. In England, as well as in the rest of Western Europe, Latin long continued to be the language of religious and learned writing--down to the sixteenth century or even later.

French, that dialect of it which was spoken by the Normans--Anglo-French (English-French) it has naturally come to be called--was of course introduced by the Conquest as the language of the governing and upper social class, and in it also during the next three or four centuries a considerable body of literature was produced.

Anglo-Saxon, which we may now term English, remained inevitably as the language of the subject race, but their literature was at first crushed down into insignificance. Ballads celebrating the resistance of scattered Saxons to their oppressors no doubt circulated widely on the lips of the people, but English writing of the more formal sorts, almost absolutely ceased for more than a century, to make a new beginning about the year 1200. In the interval the 'Anglo-Saxon Chronicle' is the only important document, and even this, continued at the monastery of Peterboro, comes to an end in 1154, in the midst of the terrible anarchy of Stephen's reign.

It must not be supposed, notwithstanding, that the Normans, however much they despised the English language and literature, made any effort to destroy it. On the other hand, gradual union of the two languages was no less inevitable than that of the races themselves. From, the very first the need of communication, with their subjects must have rendered it necessary for the Normans to acquire some knowledge of the English language; and the children of mixed parentage of course learned it from their mothers.

The use of French continued in the upper strata of society, in the few children's schools that existed, and in the law courts, for something like three centuries, maintaining itself so long partly because French was then the polite language of Western Europe. But the dead pressure of English was increasingly strong, and by the end of the fourteenth century and of Chaucer's life French had chiefly given way to it even at Court.

As we have already implied, however, the English which triumphed was in fact English-French--English was enabled to triumph partly because it had now largely absorbed the French. For the first one hundred or one hundred and fifty years, it seems, the two languages remained for the most part pretty clearly distinct, but in the thirteenth and fourteenth centuries English, abandoning its first aloofness, rapidly took into itself a large part of the French (originally Latin) vocabulary; and under the influence of the French it carried much farther the process of dropping its own comparatively complicated grammatical inflections--a process which had already gained much momentum even before the Conquest. This absorption of the French was most fortunate for English. To the Anglo-Saxon vocabulary--vigorous, but harsh, limited in extent, and lacking in fine discriminations and power of abstract expression, was now added nearly the whole wealth of French, with its fullness, flexibility, and grace. As a direct consequence the resulting language, modern English, is the richest and most varied instrument of expression ever developed at any time by any race.

THE RESULT FOR POETRY

For poetry the fusion meant even more than for prose. The metrical system, which begins to appear in the thirteenth century and comes to perfection a century and a half later in Chaucer's poems combined what may fairly be called the better features of both the systems from which it was compounded. We have seen that Anglo-Saxon verse depended on regular stress of a definite number of quantitatively long syllables in each line and on alliteration; that it allowed much variation in the number of unstressed syllables; and that it was without rime.

French verse, on the other hand, had rime (or assonance) and carefully preserved identity in the total number of syllables in corresponding lines, but it was uncertain as regarded the number of clearly stressed ones. The derived English system adopted from the French (1) rime and (2) identical line-length, and retained from the Anglo-Saxon (3) regularity of stress. (4) It largely abandoned the Anglo-Saxon regard for quantity and (5) it retained alliteration not as a basic principle but as an (extremely useful) subordinate device. This metrical system, thus shaped, has provided the indispensable formal basis for making English poetry admittedly the greatest in the modern world.

THE NORMANS

The Normans who conquered England were originally members of the same stock as the 'Danes' who had harried and conquered it in the preceding centuries--the ancestors of both were bands of Baltic and North Sea pirates who merely happened to emigrate in different directions; and a little farther back the Normans were close cousins, in the general Germanic family, of the Anglo-Saxons themselves. The exploits of this whole race of Norse sea-kings make one of the most remarkable chapters in the history of medieval Europe. In the ninth and tenth centuries they mercilessly ravaged all the coasts not only of the West but of all Europe from the Rhine to the Adriatic. 'From the fury of the Norsemen, good Lord, deliver us!' was a regular part of the litany of the unhappy French.

They settled Iceland and Greenland and prematurely discovered America; they established themselves as the ruling aristocracy in Russia, and as the imperial body-guard and chief bulwark of the Byzantine empire at Constantinople; and in the eleventh century they conquered southern Italy and Sicily, whence in the first crusade they pressed on with unabated vigor to Asia Minor. Those bands of them with whom we are here concerned, and who became known distinctively as Normans, fastened themselves as settlers, early in the eleventh century, on the northern shore of France, and in return for their acceptance of Christianity and acknowledgment of the nominal feudal sovereignty of the French king were recognized as rightful possessors of the large province which thus came to bear the name of Normandy. Here by intermarriage with the native women they rapidly developed into a race which while retaining all their original courage and enterprise took on also, together with the French language, the French intellectual brilliancy and flexibility and in manners became the chief exponent of medieval chivalry.

The different elements contributed to the modern English character by the latest stocks which have been united in it have been indicated by Matthew Arnold in a famous passage ('On the Study of Celtic Literature'): 'The Germanic [Anglo-Saxon and 'Danish'] genius has steadiness as its main basis, with commonness and humdrum for its defect, fidelity to nature for its excellence. The Norman genius, talent for affairs as its main basis, with strenuousness and clear rapidity for its excellence, hardness and insolence for its defect.' The Germanic (Anglo-Saxon and 'Danish') element explains, then, why uneducated Englishmen of all times have been thick-headed, unpleasantly self-assertive, and unimaginative, but sturdy fighters; and the Norman strain why upper-class Englishmen have been self-contained, inclined to snobbishness, but vigorously aggressive and persevering, among the best conquerors, organizers, and administrators in the history of the world.

THE ENGLISH DIALECTS

The study of the literature of the period is further complicated by the division of English into dialects. The Norman Conquest put a stop to the progress of the West-Saxon dialect toward complete supremacy, restoring the dialects of the other parts of the island to their former positions of equal authority. The actual result was the development of three groups of dialects, the Southern, Midland (divided into East and West) and Northern, all differing among themselves in forms and even in vocabulary. Literary activity when it recommenced was about equally distributed among the three, and for three centuries it was doubtful which of them would finally win the first place.

In the outcome success fell to the East Midland dialect, partly through the influence of London, which under the Norman kings replaced Winchester as the capital city and seat of the Court and Parliament, and partly through the influence of the two Universities, Oxford and Cambridge, which gradually grew up during the twelfth and thirteenth centuries and attracted students from all parts of the country. This victory of the East Midland form was marked by, though it was not in any large degree due to, the appearance in the fourteenth century of the first great modern English poet, Chaucer. To the present day, however, the three dialects, and subdivisions of them, are easily distinguishable in colloquial use; the common idiom of such regions as Yorkshire and Cornwall is decidedly different from that of London or indeed any other part of the country.

ENGLISH LITERATURE FROM THE DEATH OF POPE TO THE FRENCH REVOLUTION

Pope's example continued potent for fifty years after his death. Especially was this so in satiric and didactic poetry. Not only Dr. Johnson's adaptations from *Juvenal*, London, 1738, and the *Vanity of Human Wishes*, 1749, but Gifford's *Baviad*, 1791, and *Maeviad*, 1795, and Byron's *English Bards and Scotch Reviewers*, 1809, were in the verse and manner of Pope. In Johnson's *Lives of the Poets*, 1781, Dryden and Pope are treated as the two greatest English poets. But long before this a revolution in literary taste had begun, a movement which is variously described as The Return to Nature, or The Rise of the New Romantic School.

For nearly a hundred years poetry had dealt with manners and the life of towns, the gay, prosaic life of Congreve or of Pope. The sole concession to the life of nature was the old pastoral, which, in the hands of cockneys, like Pope and Ambrose Philips, who merely repeated stock descriptions at second or third hand, became even more artificial than a *Beggar's Opera* or a *Rape of the Lock*. These, at least, were true to their environment, and were natural, just *because* they were artificial. But the *Seasons* of James Thomson, published in installments from 1726-30, had opened a new field. Their theme was the English landscape, as varied by the changes of the year, and they were written by a true lover and observer of nature. Mark Akenside's *Pleasures of Imagination*,

1744, published the year of Pope's death, was written like the *Seasons,* in blank verse; and although its language had much of the formal, didactic cast of the Queen Anne poets, it pointed unmistakably in the new direction. Thomson had painted the soft beauties of a highly cultivated land—lawns, gardens, forest-preserves, orchards, and sheep-walks. But now a fresh note was struck in the literature, not of England alone, but of Germany and France—romanticism, the chief element in which was a love of the wild. Poets turned from the lameness of modern existence to savage nature and the heroic simplicity of life among primitive tribes. In France, Rousseau introduced the idea of the natural man, following his instincts in disregard of social conventions.

In Germany Bodmer published, in 1753, the first edition of the old German epic, the *Nibelungen Lied.* Works of a similar tendency in England were the odes of William Collins and Thomas Gray, published between 1747-57, especially Collins's *Ode on the Superstitions of the Highlands,* and Gray's*Bard,* a pindaric, in which the last survivor of the Welsh bards invokes vengeance on Edward I., the destroyer of his guild. Gray and Mason, his friend and editor, made translations from the ancient Welsh and Norse poetry.

Thomas Percy's *Reliques of Ancient English Poetry,* 1765, aroused a taste for old ballads. Richard Hurd's *Letters on Chivalry and Romance,* Thomas Warton's *History of English Poetry,* 1774-78, Tyrwhitt's critical edition of Chaucer, and Horace Walpole's Gothic romance, the *Castle of Otranto,* 1765, stimulated this awakened interest in the picturesque aspects of feudal life, and contributed to the fondness for supernatural and mediaeval subjects. James Beattie's *Minstrel,* 1771, described the educating influence of Scottish mountain scenery upon the genius of a young poet. But the most remarkable instances of this passion for wild nature and the romantic past were the *Poems of Ossian* and Thomas Chatterton's literary forgeries.

In 1762 James Macpherson published the first installment of what professed to be a translation of the poems of Ossian, a Gaelic bard, whom tradition placed in the 3d century. Macpherson said that he made his version—including two complete epics, *Fingal* and *Temora,* from Gaelic MSS., which he had collected in the Scottish Highlands. A fierce controversy at once sprang up over the genuineness of these remains. Macpherson was challenged to produce his originals, and when, many years after, he published the Gaelic text, it was asserted that this was nothing but a translation of his own English into modern Gaelic. Of the MSS. which he professed to have found not a scrap remained: the Gaelic text was printed from transcriptions in Macpherson's handwriting or in that of his secretaries.

But whether these poems were the work of Ossian or of Macpherson, they made a deep impression upon the time. Napoleon admired them greatly, and Goethe inserted passages from the "Songs of Selma" in his *Sorrows of Werther*. Macpherson composed—or translated—them in an abrupt, rhapsodical prose, resembling the English version of Job or of the prophecies of Isaiah. They filled the minds of their readers with images of vague sublimity and desolation; the mountain torrent, the mist on the hills, the ghosts of heroes half seen by the setting moon, the thistle in the ruined courts of chieftains, the grass whistling on the windy heath, the gray rock by the blue stream of Lutha, and the cliffs of sea-surrounded Gormal.

"A tale of the times of old!"

"Why, thou wanderer unseen! Thou bender of the thistle of Lora; why, thou breeze of the valley, hast thou left mine ear? I hear no distant roar of streams! No sound of the harp from the rock! Come, thou huntress of Lutha, Malvina, call back his soul to the bard. I look forward to Lochlin of lakes, to the dark billowy bay of U-thorno, where Fingal descends from Ocean, from the roar of winds. Few are the heroes of Morven in a land unknown."

Thomas Chatterton, who died by his own hand in 1770, at the age of seventeen, is one of the most wonderful examples of precocity in the history of literature. His father had been sexton of the ancient Church of St. Mary Redcliff, in Bristol, and the boy's sensitive imagination took the stamp of his surroundings. He taught himself to read from a black-letter Bible. He drew charcoal sketches of churches, castles, knightly tombs, and heraldic blazonry. When only eleven years old, he began the fabrication of documents in prose and verse, which he ascribed to a fictitious Thomas Rowley, a secular priest at Bristol in the 15th century. Chatterton pretended to have found these among the contents of an old chest in the muniment room of St. Mary Redcliff's. The Rowley poems included two tragedies, *Aella* and*Goddwyn*, two cantos of a long poem on the *Battle of Hastings*, and a number of ballads and minor pieces.

Chatterton had no precise knowledge of early English, or even of Chaucer. His method of working was as follows: He made himself a manuscript glossary of the words marked as archaic in Bailey's and Kersey's English dictionaries, composed his poems first in modern language, and then turned them into ancient spelling, and substituted here and there the old words in his glossary for their modern equivalents. Naturally he made many mistakes, and though Horace Walpole, to whom he sent some of his pieces, was unable to detect the forgery, his friends, Gray and Mason, to whom he submitted them, at once pronounced them spurious.

Nevertheless there was a controversy over Rowley, hardly less obstinate than that over Ossian, a controversy made possible only by the then almost universal ignorance of the forms, scansion, and vocabulary of early English poetry. Chatterton's poems are of little value in themselves, but they are the record of an industry and imitative quickness, marvelous in a mere child, and they show how, with the instinct of genius, he threw himself into the main literary current of his time.

Discarding the couplet of Pope, the poets now went back for models to the Elizabethan writers. Thomas Warton published, in 1753, his *Observations on the Faerie Queene*. Beattie's *Minstrel*, Thomson's*Castle of Indolence*, William Shenstone's *Schoolmistress*, and John Dyer's *Fleece*, were all written in the Spenserian stanza. Shenstone gave a partly humorous effect to his poem by imitating Spenser's archaisms, and Thomson reproduced in many passages the copious harmony and luxuriant imagery of the *Faerie Queene*. The *Fleece* was a poem on English wool-growing, after the fashion of Vergil's*Georgics*. The subject was unfortunate, for, as Dr. Johnson said, it is impossible to make poetry out of serges and druggets. Dyer's *Grongar Hill*, which mingles reflection with natural description in the manner of Gray's *Elegy written in a Country Churchyard*, was composed in the octosyllabic verse of Milton's *L'Allegro* and *Il Penseroso*.

Milton's minor poems, which had hitherto been neglected, exercised a great influence on Collins and Gray. Collins's *Ode to Simplicity* was written in the stanza of Milton's *Nativity*, and his exquisite unrimed *Ode to Evening* was a study in versification, after Milton's translation of Horace's *Ode to Pyrrha*, in the original meters.

Shakespeare began to to be studied more reverently: numerous critical editions of his plays were issued, and Garrick restored his pure text to the stage. Collins was an enthusiastic student of Shakespeare, and one of his sweetest poems, the *Dirge in Cymbeline*, was inspired by the tragedy of *Cymbeline*.

The verse of Gray, Collins, and the Warton brothers, abounds in verbal reminiscences of Shakespeare; but their genius was not allied to his, being exclusively lyrical, and not at all dramatic. The Muse of this romantic school was Fancy rather than Passion. A thoughtful melancholy, a gentle, scholarly pensiveness, the spirit of Milton's *Il Penseroso*, pervades their poetry. Gray was a fastidious scholar, who produced very little, but that little of the finest quality. His famous *Elegy*, expressing a meditative mood in language of the choicest perfection, is the representative poem of the second half of the 18th century, as the *Rape of the Lock* is of the first. The romanticists were quietists, and their scenery is characteristic.

They loved solitude and evening, the twilight vale, the mossy hermitage, ruins, glens, and caves. Their style was elegant and academic, retaining a little of the stilted poetic diction of their classical forerunners. Personification and periphrasis were their favourite mannerisms: Collins's Odes were largely addressed to abstractions, such as Fear, Pity, Liberty, Mercy, and Simplicity. A poet in their dialect was always a "bard;" a countryman was "the untutored swain," and a woman was a "nymph" or "the fair," just as in Dryden and Pope. Thomson is perpetually mindful of Vergil, and afraid to speak simply. He uses too many Latin epithets, like *amusive* and *precipitant,* and calls a fish-line

"The floating line snatched from the hoary steed."

They left much for Cowper and Wordsworth to do in the way of infusing the new blood of a strong, racy English into our exhausted poetic diction. Their poetry is impersonal, bookish, literary. It lacks emotional force, except now and then in Gray's immortal *Elegy,* in his *Ode on a Distant Prospect of Eton College,* in Collins's lines, *On the Death of Thomson,* and his little ode beginning,"How sleep the brave?"

The new school did not lack critical expounders of its principles and practice. Joseph Warton published, in 1756, the first volume of his *Essay on the Genius and Writings of Pope,* an elaborate review of Pope's writings *seriatim,* doing him certainly full justice, but ranking him below Shakespeare, Spenser, and Milton. "Wit and satire," wrote Warton,"are transitory and perishable, but nature and passion are eternal.... He stuck to describing modern manners; but those manners, because they are familiar, artificial, and polished, are, in their very nature, unfit for any lofty effort of the Muse.

Whatever poetical enthusiasm he actually possessed he withheld and stifled. Surely it is no narrow and niggardly encomium to say, he is the great Poet of Reason, the first of Ethical authors in verse." Warton illustrated his critical positions by quoting freely not only from Spenser and Milton, but from recent poets, like Thomson, Gray, Collins, and Dyer. He testified that the Seasons had "been very instrumental in diffusing a general taste for the beauties of nature and landscape."

It was symptomatic of the change in literary taste that the natural or English school of landscape gardening now began to displace the French and Dutch fashion of clipped hedges, regular parterres, etc., and that Gothic architecture came into repute. Horace Walpole was a virtuoso in Gothic art, and in his castle, at Strawberry Hill, he made a collection of ancient armor, illuminated MSS., and bric-a-brac of all kinds. Gray had been Walpole's traveling companion in France and Italy, and the two had quarreled and separated, but were afterward reconciled. From Walpole's private printing-press, at Strawberry Hill, Gray's two "sister odes," the *Bard* and the *Progress of Poesy*, were first printed, in 1757. Both Gray and Walpole were good correspondents, and their printed letters are among the most delightful literature of the kind.

The central figure among the English men of letters of that generation was Samuel Johnson (1709-84), whose memory has been preserved less by his own writings than by James Boswell's famous *Life of Johnson*, published in 1791. Boswell was a Scotch laird and advocate, who first met Johnson in London, when the latter was fifty-four years old. Boswell was not a very wise or witty person, but he reverenced the worth and intellect which shone through his subject's uncouth exterior.

He followed him about, note-book in hand, bore all his snubbings patiently, and made the best biography ever written. It is related that the doctor once said that if he thought Boswell meant to write *his* life, he should prevent it by taking *Boswell's*. And yet Johnson's own writings and this biography of him have changed places in relative importance so completely, that Carlyle predicted that the former would soon be reduced to notes on the latter; and Macaulay said that the man who was known to his contemporaries as a great writer was known to posterity as an agreeable companion.

Johnson was one of those rugged, eccentric, self-developed characters, so common among the English. He was the son of a Lichfield book-seller, and after a course at Oxford, which was cut short by poverty, and an unsuccessful career as a school-master, he had come up to London, in 1737, where he supported himself for many years as a book-seller's hack. Gradually his great learning and abilities, his ready social wit and powers as a talker, caused his company to be sought at the tables of those whom he called "the great."

He was a clubbable man, and he drew about him at the tavern a group of the most distinguished intellects of the time, Edmund Burke, the orator and statesman, Oliver Goldsmith, Sir Joshua Reynolds, the portrait painter, and David Garrick, the great actor, who had been a pupil in Johnson's school, near Lichfield. Johnson was the typical John Bull of the last century. His oddities, virtues, and prejudices were thoroughly English. He hated Frenchmen, Scotchmen, and Americans, and had a cockneyish attachment to London. He was a high Tory, and an orthodox churchman; he loved a lord in the abstract, and yet he asserted a sturdy independence against any lord in particular.

He was deeply religious, but had an abiding fear of death. He was burly in person, and slovenly in dress, his shirt-frill always covered with snuff. He was a great diner out, an inordinate tea-drinker, and a voracious and untidy feeder. An inherited scrofula, which often took the form of hypochondria and threatened to affect his brain, deprived him of control over the muscles of his face.

Boswell describes how his features worked, how he snorted, grunted, whistled, and rolled about in his chair when getting ready to speak. He records his minutest traits, such as his habit of pocketing the orange peels at the club, and his superstitious way of touching all the posts between his house and the Mitre Tavern, going back to do it, if he skipped one by chance. Though bearish in his manners and arrogant in dispute, especially when talking "for victory," Johnson had a large and tender heart. He loved his ugly, old wife—twenty-one years his senior—and he had his house full of unfortunates—a blind woman, an invalid surgeon, a destitute widow, a negro servant—whom he supported for many years, and bore with all their ill-humours patiently.

Among Johnson's numerous writings the ones best entitled to remembrance are, perhaps, his *Dictionary of the English Language,* 1755; his moral tale, *Rasselas,* 1759; the introduction to his *Edition of Shakespeare,* 1765; and his *Lives of the Poets,* 1781. Johnson wrote a sonorous, cadenced prose, full of big Latin words and balanced clauses. Here is a sentence, for example, from his *Visit to the Hebrides*: "We were now treading that illustrious island which was once the luminary of the Caledonian regions, whence savage clans and roving barbarians derived the benefits of knowledge and the blessings of religion. To abstract the mind from all local emotion would be impossible, if it were endeavored, and would be foolish, if it were possible." The difference between his colloquial style and his book style is well illustrated in the instance cited by Macaulay.

Speaking of Villier's *Rehearsal,* Johnson said,"It has not wit enough to keep it sweet;" then paused and added—translating English into Johnsonese—"it has not vitality sufficient to preserve it from putrefaction." There is more of this in Johnson's *Rambler* and *Idler papers* than in his latest work, the *Lives of the Poets.* In this he showed himself a sound and judicious critic, though with decided limitations. His understanding was solid, but he was a thorough classicist, and his taste in poetry was formed on Pope.

He was unjust to Milton and to his own contemporaries, Gray, Collins, Shenstone, and Dyer. He had no sense of the higher and subtler graces of romantic poetry, and he had a comical indifference to the "beauties of nature." When Boswell once ventured to remark that poor Scotland had, at least, some "noble, wild prospects," the doctor replied that the noblest prospect a Scotchman ever saw was the road that led to London.

The English novel of real life had its origin at this time. Books like De Foe's *Robinson Crusoe, Captain Singleton, Journal of the Plague,* etc., were tales of incident and adventure rather than novels. The novel deals primarily with character and with the interaction of characters upon one another, as developed by a regular plot. The first English novelist, in the modern sense of the word, was Samuel Richardson, a printer, who began authorship in his fiftieth year with his *Pamela,* the story of a young servant girl, who resisted the seductions of her master, and finally, as the reward of her virtue, became his wife.

Clarissa Harlowe, 1748, was the tragical history of a high spirited young lady, who being driven from home by her family, because she refused to marry the suitor selected for her, fell into the toils of Lovelace, an accomplished rake. After struggling heroically against every form of artifice and violence, she was at last drugged and ruined. She died of a broken heart, and Lovelace, borne down by remorse, was killed in a duel by a cousin of Clarissa. Sir *Charles Grandison,* 1753, was Richardson's portrait of an ideal fine gentleman, whose stately doïngs fill eight volumes, but who seems to the modern reader a bore and a prig. All of these novels were written in the form of letters passing between the characters, a method which fitted Richardson's subjective cast of mind. He knew little of life, but he identified himself intensely with his principal character and produced a strong effect by minute, accumulated touches.

Clarissa Harlowe is his masterpiece, though even in that the situation is painfully prolonged, the heroine's virtue is self-conscious and rhetorical, and there is something almost ludicrously unnatural in the copiousness with which she pours herself out in gushing epistles to her female correspondent at the very moment when she is beset with dangers, persecuted, agonized, and driven nearly mad. In Richardson's novels appears, for the first time, that sentimentalism which now began to infect European literature. *Pamela* was translated into French and German, and fell in with that current of popular feeling which found fullest expression in Rousseau's *Nouvelle Heloise,* 1759, and Goethe's *Leiden des Jungen Werther,* which set all the world a-weeping in 1774.

Coleridge said that to pass from Richardson's books to those of Henry Fielding was like going into the fresh air from a close room heated by stoves. Richardson, it has been affirmed, knew *man,* but Fielding knew *men.* The latter's first novel, *Joseph Andrews,* 1742, was begun as a travesty of *Pamela.*

The hero, a brother of Pamela, was a young footman in the employ of Lady Booby, from whom his virtue suffered a like assault to that made upon Pamela's by her master. This reversal of the natural situation was in itself full of laughable possibilities, had the book gone on simply as a burlesque. But the exuberance of Fielding's genius led him beyond his original design. This hero, leaving Lady Booby's service, goes traveling with good Parson Adams, and is soon engaged in a series of comical and rather boisterous adventures.

Fielding had seen life, and his characters were painted from the life with a bold, free hand. He was a gentleman by birth, and had made acquaintance with society and the town in 1727, when he was a handsome, stalwart young fellow, with high animal spirits and a great appetite for pleasure. He soon ran himself into debt and began writing for the stage; married, and spent his wife's fortune, living for awhile in much splendor as a country gentleman, and afterward in a reduced condition as a rural justice with a salary of 500 pounds of "the dirtiest money on earth." Fielding's masterpiece was *Tom Jones,* 1749, and it remains one of the best of English novels.

Its hero is very much after Fielding's own heart, wild, spendthrift, warm-hearted, forgiving, and greatly in need of forgiveness. The same type of character, with the lines deepened, re-appears in Captain Booth, in *Amelia,* 1751, the heroine of which is a portrait of Fielding's wife. With Tom Jones is contrasted Blifil, the embodiment of meanness, hypocrisy, and cowardice. Sophia Western, the heroine, is one of Fielding's most admirable creations.

For the regulated morality of Richardson, with its somewhat old-grannified air, Fielding substituted instinct. His virtuous characters are virtuous by impulse only, and his ideal of character is manliness. In *Jonathan Wild* the hero is a highwayman. This novel is ironical, a sort of prose mock-heroic, and is one of the strongest, though certainly the least pleasing, of Fielding's writings.

Tobias Smollett was an inferior Fielding with a difference. He was a Scotch ship-surgeon and had spent some time in the West Indies. He introduced into fiction the now familiar figure of the British tar, in the persons of Tom Bowling and Commodore Trunnion, as Fielding had introduced, in Squire Western, the equally national type of the hard-swearing, deep-drinking, fox-hunting Tory squire.

Both Fielding and Smollett were of the hearty British "beef-and-beer" school; their novels are downright, energetic, coarse, and high-blooded; low life, physical life, runs riot through their pages—tavern brawls, the breaking of pates, and the off-hand courtship of country wenches. Smollett's books, such as *Roderick Random,* 1748, *Peregrine Pickle,* 1751, and *Ferdinand Count*

Fathom, 1752, were more purely stories of broadly comic adventure than Fielding's. The latter's view of life was by no means idyllic; but with Smollett this English realism ran into vulgarity and a hard Scotch literalness, and character was pushed to caricature. "The generous wine of Fielding," says Taine,"in Smollett's hands becomes brandy of the dram-shop." A partial exception to this is to be found in his last and best novel, *Humphrey Clinker,* 1770. The influence of Cervantes and of the French novelist, Le Sage, who finished his *Adventures of Gil Blas* in 1735, are very perceptible in Smollett.

A genius of much finer mold was Lawrence Sterne, the author of *Tristram Shandy,* 1759-67, and the *Sentimental Journey,* 1768. *Tristram Shandy* is hardly a novel: the story merely serves to hold together a number of characters, such as Uncle Toby and Corporal Trim, conceived with rare subtlety and originality.

Sterne's chosen province was the whimsical, and his great model was Rabelais. His books are full of digressions, breaks, surprises, innuendoes, double meanings, mystifications, and all manner of odd turns. Coleridge and Carlyle unite in pronouncing him a great humorist.

Thackeray says that he was only a great jester. Humour is the laughter of the heart, and Sterne's pathos is closely interwoven with his humour. He was the foremost of English sentimentalists, and he had that taint of insincerity which distinguishes sentimentalism from genuine sentiment, like Goldsmith's, for example. Sterne, in life, was selfish, heartless, and untrue. A clergyman, his worldliness and vanity and the indecency of his writings were a scandal to the Church, though his sermons were both witty and affecting.

He enjoyed the titilation of his own emotions, and he had practiced so long at detecting the latent pathos that lies in the expression of dumb things and of poor, patient animals, that he could summon the tear of sensibility at the thought of a discarded postchaise, a dead donkey, a starling in a cage, or of Uncle Toby putting a house fly out of the window, and saying,"There is room enough in the world for thee and me." It is a high proof of his cleverness that he generally succeeds in raising the desired feeling in his readers even from such trivial occasions. He was a minute philosopher, his philosophy was kindly, and he taught the delicate art of making much out of little.

Less coarse than Fielding, he is far more corrupt. Fielding goes bluntly to the point; Sterne lingers among the temptations and suspends the expectation to tease and excite it. Forbidden fruit had a relish for him, and his pages seduce. He is full of good sayings, both tender and witty. It was Sterne, for example, who wrote,"God tempers the wind to the shorn lamb."

A very different writer was Oliver Goldsmith, whose *Vicar of Wakefield,* 1766, was the earliest, and is still one of the best, novels of domestic and rural life. The book, like its author, was thoroughly Irish, full of bulls and inconsistencies. Very improbable things happened in it with a cheerful defiance of logic. But its characters are true to nature, drawn with an idyllic sweetness and purity, and with touches of a most loving humour.

Its hero, Dr. Primrose, was painted after Goldsmith's father, a poor clergyman of the English Church in Ireland, and the original, likewise, of the country parson in Goldsmith's *Deserted Village,* 1770, who was "passing rich on forty pounds a year." This poem, though written in the fashionable couplet of Pope, and even containing a few verses contributed by Dr. Johnson—so that it was not at all in line with the work of the romanticists—did, perhaps, as much as any thing of Gray or of Collins to recall English poetry to the simplicity and freshness of country life.

Except for the comedies of Sheridan and Goldsmith, and, perhaps, a few other plays, the stage had now utterly declined. The novel, which is dramatic in essence, though not in form, began to take its place, and to represent life, though less intensely, yet more minutely, than the theater could do. In the novelists of the 18th century, the life of the people, as distinguished from "society" or the upper classes, began to invade literature. Richardson was distinctly a bourgeois writer, and his contemporaries—Fielding, Smollett, Sterne, and Goldsmith—ranged over a wide variety of ranks and conditions.

This is one thing which distinguishes the literature of the second half of the 18th century from that of the first, as well as in some degree from that of all previous centuries. Among the authors of this generation whose writings belonged to other departments of thought than pure literature may be mentioned, in passing, the great historian, Edward Gibbon, whose *Decline and Fall of the Roman Empire* was published from 1776-88, and Edmund Burke, whose political speeches and pamphlets possess a true literary quality. The romantic poets had addressed the imagination rather than the heart.

It was reserved for two men—a contrast to one another in almost every respect—to bring once more into British song a strong individual feeling, and with it a new warmth and directness of speech.

These were William Cowper (1731-1800) and Robert Burns (1759-96). Cowper spoke out of his own life experience, his agony, his love, his worship and despair; and straightway the varnish that had glittered over all our poetry since the time of Dryden melted away. Cowper had scribbled verses when he was a young law student at the Middle Temple in London, and he had contributed to the *Olney Hymns,* published in 1779 by his friend and pastor, the Rev. John Newton; but he only began to write poetry in earnest when he was nearly fifty years old.

In 1782, the date of his first volume, he said, in a letter to a friend, that he had read but one English poet during the past twenty years. Perhaps, therefore, of all English poets of equal culture, Cowper owed the least impulse to books and the most to the need of uttering his inmost thoughts and feelings. Cowper had a most unhappy life. As a child, he was shy, sensitive, and sickly, and suffered much from bullying and fagging at a school whither he was sent after his mother's death. This happened when he was six years old; and in his affecting lines written *On Receipt of My Mother's Picture,* he speaks of himself as a

"Wretch even then, life's journey just begun."

In 1763 he became insane and was sent to an asylum, where he spent a year. Judicious treatment restored him to sanity, but he came out a broken man and remained for the rest of his life an invalid, unfitted for any active occupation. His disease took the form of religious melancholy.

He had two recurrences of madness, and both times made attempts upon his life. At Huntingdon, and afterward at Olney, in Buckinghamshire, he found a home with the Unwin family, whose kindness did all which the most soothing and delicate care could do to heal his wounded spirit. His two poems *To Mary Unwin,* together with the lines on his mother's picture, were almost the first examples of deep and tender sentiment in the lyrical poetry of the last century. Cowper found relief from the black thoughts that beset him only in an ordered round of quiet household occupations.

He corresponded indefatigably, took long walks through the neighbourhood, read, sang, and conversed with Mrs. Unwin and his friend, Lady Austin; and amused himself with carpentry, gardening, and raising pets, especially hares, of which gentle animals he grew very fond. All these simple tastes, in which he found for a time a refuge and a sheltered happiness, are reflected in his best poem, *The Task,* 1785. Cowper is the poet of the family affections, of domestic life, and rural retirement; the laureate of the fireside, the tea-table, the evening lamp, the garden, the green-house, and the rabbit-coop. He draws with elegance and precision a chair, a clock, a harpsichord, a barometer, a piece of needle-work.

But Cowper was an out-door as well as an in-door man. The Olney landscape was tame, a fat, agricultural region, where the sluggish Ouse wound between plowed fields and the horizon was bounded by low hills. Nevertheless

Cowper's natural descriptions are at once more distinct and more imaginative than Thomson's. *The Task* reflects, also, the new philanthropic spirit, the enthusiasm of humanity, the feeling of the brotherhood of men to which Rousseau had given expression in France and which issued in the French Revolution.

In England this was the time of Wilberforce, the antislavery agitator; of Whitefield, the eloquent revival preacher; of John and Charles Wesley, and of the Evangelical and Methodist movements which gave new life to the English Church. John Newton, the curate of Olney and the keeper of Cowper's conscience, was one of the leaders of the Evangelicals; and Cowper's first volume of *Table Talk* and other poems, 1782, written under Newton's inspiration, was a series of sermons in verse, somewhat intolerant of all worldly enjoyments, such as hunting, dancing, and theaters.

"God made the country and man made the town," he wrote. He was a moralizing poet, and his morality was sometimes that of the invalid and the recluse. Byron called him a "coddled poet." And, indeed, there is a suspicion of gruel and dressing-gowns about him. He lived much among women, and his sufferings had refined him to a feminine delicacy. But there is no sickliness in his poetry, and he retained a charming playful humour—displayed in his excellent comic ballad, *John Gilpin*; and Mrs. Browning has sung of him,

"How when one by one sweet sounds and wandering lights departed

He bore no less a loving face, because so broken-hearted."

At the close of the year 1786 a young Scotchman, named Samuel Rose, called upon Cowper at Olney, and left with him a small volume, which had appeared at Edinburgh during the past summer, entitled*Poems chiefly in the Scottish Dialect, by Robert Burns*. Cowper read the book through twice, and, though somewhat bothered by the dialect, pronounced it a "very extraordinary production."

This momentary flash, as of an electric spark, marks the contact not only of the two chief British poets of their generation, but of two literatures. Scotch poets, like Thomson and Beattie, had written in Southern English, and, as Carlyle said, *in vacuo*, that is, with nothing specially national in their work. Burns's sweet though rugged Doric first secured the vernacular poetry of his country a hearing beyond the border. He had, to be sure, a whole literature of popular songs and ballads behind him, and his immediate models were Allan Ramsay and Robert Ferguson; but these remained provincial, while Burns became universal. He was born in Ayrshire, on the banks of "bonny Doon," in a clay biggin not far from "Alloway's auld haunted kirk," the scene of the witch dance in *Tam O'Shanter*. His father was a hard-headed, God-fearing tenant farmer, whose life and that of his sons was a harsh struggle with poverty.

The crops failed; the landlord pressed for his rent; for weeks at a time the family tasted no meat; yet this life of toil was lightened by love and homely pleasures. In the *Cotter's Saturday Night*, Burns has drawn a beautiful picture of his parents' household, the rest that came at the week's end, and the family worship about the "wee bit ingle, blinkin' bonnily." Robert was handsome, wild, and witty.

He was universally susceptible, and his first songs, like his last, were of "the lasses." His head had been stuffed, in boyhood, with "tales and songs concerning devils, ghosts, fairies, brownies, witches, warlocks, spunkies, kelpies, elf-candles, dead-lights," etc., told him by one Jenny Wilson, an old woman who lived in the family. His ear was full of ancient Scottish tunes, and as soon as he fell in love he began to make poetry as naturally as a bird sings.

He composed his verses while following the plow or working in the stack-yard; or, at evening, balancing on two legs of his chair and watching the light of a peat fire play over the reeky walls of the cottage. Burns's love songs are in many keys, ranging from strains of the most pure and exalted passion, like *Ae Fond Kiss* and *To Mary in Heaven*, to such loose ditties as *When Januar' Winds* and *Green Grow the Rashes O*.

Burns liked a glass almost as well as a lass, and at Mauchline, where he carried on a farm with his brother Gilbert, after their father's death, he began to seek a questionable relief from the pressure of daily toil and unkind fates, in the convivialities of the tavern. There, among the wits of the Mauchline Club, farmers' sons, shepherds from the uplands, and the smugglers who swarmed over the west coast, he would discuss politics and farming, recite his verses, and join in the singing and ranting, while

"Bousin o'er the nappy,
And gettin' fou and unco happy."

To these experiences we owe not only those excellent drinking songs, *John Barleycorn* and *Willie Brewed a Peck o' Maut*, but the headlong fun of *Tam O'Shanter*, and the visions, grotesquely terrible, of *Death and Dr. Hornbook*, and the dramatic humour of the *Jolly Beggars*. Cowper had celebrated "the cup which cheers but not inebriates." Burns sang the praises of *Scotch Drink*. Cowper was a stranger to Burns's high animal spirits, and his robust enjoyment of life. He had affections, but no passions.

At Mauchline, Burns, whose irregularities did not escape the censure of the kirk, became involved, through his friendship with Gavin Hamilton, in the controversy between the Old Light and New Light clergy. His *Holy Fair, Holy Tulzie, Two Herds, Holy Willie's Prayer,* and *Address to the Unco Gude,* are satires against bigotry and hypocrisy. But in spite of the rollicking profanity of his language, and the violence of his rebound against the austere religion of Scotland, Burns was at bottom deeply impressible by religious ideas, as may be seen from his *Prayer under the Pressure of Violent Anguish,* and *Prayer in Prospect of Death.*

His farm turned out a failure, and he was on the eve of sailing for Jamaica, when the favour with which his volume of poems was received, stayed his departure, and turned his steps to Edinburgh. There the peasant poet was lionized for a winter season by the learned and polite society of the Scotch capital, with results in the end not altogether favourable to Burns's best interests.

For when society finally turned the cold shoulder on him, he had to go back to farming again, carrying with him a bitter sense of injustice and neglect. He leased a farm in Ellisland, in 1788, and some friends procured his appointment as exciseman for his district. But poverty, disappointment, irregular habits, and broken health clouded his last years, and brought him to an untimely death at the age of thirty-seven. He continued, however, to pour forth songs of unequaled sweetness and force. "The man sank," said Coleridge,"but the poet was bright to the last."

Burns is the best of British song-writers. His songs are singable; they are not merely lyrical poems. They were meant to be sung, and they are sung. They were mostly set to old Scottish airs, and sometimes they were built up from ancient fragments of anonymous, popular poetry, a chorus, or stanza, or even a single line. Such are, for example, *Auld Lang Syne, My Heart's in the Highlands,* and *Landlady, Count the Lawin.* Burns had a great, warm heart. His sins were sins of passion, and sprang from the same generous soil that nourished his impulsive virtues.

His elementary qualities as a poet were sincerity, a healthy openness to all impressions of the beautiful, and a sympathy which embraced men, animals, and the dumb objects of nature. His tenderness towards flowers and the brute creation may be read in his lines *To a Mountain Daisy, To a Mouse,* and *The Auld Farmer's New Year's Morning Salutation to his Auld Mare Maggie.* Next after love and good fellowship, patriotism is the most frequent motive of his song. Of his national anthem, *Scots wha hae wi' Wallace bled,* Carlyle said: "So long as there is warm blood in the heart of Scotchman, or man, it will move in fierce thrills under this war ode." Burns's politics were a singular mixture of sentimental toryism with practical democracy. A romantic glamour was thrown over the fortunes of the exiled Stuarts, and to have been "out" in '45 with the Young Pretender was a popular thing in parts of Scotland. To this purely poetic loyalty may be attributed such Jacobite ballads of Burns as *Over the Water to Charlie.*

But his sobre convictions were on the side of liberty and human brotherhood, and are expressed in the *Twa Dogs*, the *First Epistle to Davie*, and *A Man's a Man for a' that.* His sympathy with the Revolution led him to send four pieces of ordnance, taken from a captured smuggler, as a present to the French Convention, a piece of bravado which got him into difficulties with his superiors in the excise. The poetry which Burns wrote, not in dialect, but in the classical English, is in the stilted manner of his century, and his prose correspondence betrays his lack of culture by his constant lapse into rhetorical affectation and fine writing.

LAGHAMON'S 'BRUT'

Thus it had come about that Arthur, originally the national hero of the Welsh, and the deadly foe of the English, was adopted, as a Christian champion, not only for one of the medieval Nine Worthies of all history, but for the special glory of the English race itself. In that light he figures in the first important work in which native English reemerges after the Norman Conquest, the 'Brut' (Chronicle) wherein, about the year 1200, Laghamon paraphrased Wace's paraphrase of Geoffrey.

Laghamon was a humble parish priest in Worcestershire, and his thirty-two thousand half-lines, in which he imperfectly follows the Anglo-Saxon alliterative meter, are rather crude; though they are by no means dull, rather are often strong with the old-time Anglo-Saxon fighting spirit. In language also the poem is almost purely Saxon; occasionally it admits the French device of rime, but it is said to exhibit, all told, fewer than a hundred words of French origin. Expanding throughout on Wace's version, Laghamon adds some minor features; but English was not yet ready to take a place beside French and Latin with the reading class, and the poem exercised no influence on the development of the Arthurian story or on English literature.

SIR GAWAIN AND THE GREEN KNIGHT

We can make special mention of only one other romance, which all students should read in modern translation, namely, 'Sir Gawain (pronounced

Gaw'-wain) and the Green Knight.' This is the brief and carefully constructed work of an unknown but very real poetic artist, who lived a century and more later than Laghamon and probably a little earlier than Chaucer. The story consists of two old folk-tales, here finely united in the form of an Arthurian romance and so treated as to bring out all the better side of knightly feeling, with which the author is in charming sympathy. Like many other medieval writings, this one is preserved by mere chance in a single manuscript, which contains also three slightly shorter religious poems (of a thousand or two lines apiece), all possibly by the same author as the romance. One of them in particular, 'The Pearl,' is a narrative of much fine feeling, which may well have come from so true a gentleman as he. The dialect is that of the Northwest Midland, scarcely more intelligible to modern readers than Anglo-Saxon, but it indicates that the author belonged to the same border region between England and Wales from which came also Geoffrey of Monmouth and Laghamon, a region where Saxon and Norman elements were mingled with Celtic fancy and delicacy of temperament. The meter, also, is interesting--the Anglo-Saxon unrimed alliterative verse, but divided into long stanzas of irregular length, each ending in a 'bob' of five short riming lines.

'Sir Gawain and the Green Knight' may very fittingly bring to a close our hasty survey of the entire Norman-French period, a period mainly of formation, which has left no literary work of great and permanent fame, but in which, after all, there were some sincere and talented writers, who have fallen into forgetfulness rather through the untoward accidents of time than from lack of genuine merit in themselves.

8

The Victorian Period Literature

GENERAL CONDITIONS

The last completed period of English literature, almost coincident in extent with the reign of the queen whose name it bears (Victoria, queen 1837-1901), stands nearly beside The Elizabethan period in the significance and interest of its work. The Elizabethan literature to be sure, in its imaginative and spiritual enthusiasm, is the expression of a period more profoundly great than the Victorian; but the Victorian literature speaks for an age which witnessed incomparably greater changes than any that had gone before in all the conditions of life--material comforts, scientific knowledge, and, absolutely speaking, in intellectual and spiritual enlightenment. Moreover, to twentieth century students the Victorian literature makes a specially strong appeal because it is in part the literature of our own time and its ideas and point of view are in large measure ours. We must begin by glancing briefly at some of the general determining changes and conditions to which reference has just been made, and we may naturally begin with the merely material ones.

Before the accession of Queen Victoria the 'industrial revolution,' the vast development of manufacturing made possible in the latter part of the eighteenth century by the introduction of coal and the steam engine, had rendered England the richest nation in the world, and the movement continued with steadily accelerating momentum throughout the period. Hand in hand with it went the increase of population from less than thirteen millions in England in 1825 to nearly three times as many at the end of the period. The introduction of the steam railway and the steamship, at the beginning of the period, in place of the lumbering stagecoach and the sailing vessel, broke up the old stagnant and stationary habits of life and increased the amount of travel at least a thousand times.

The discovery of the electric telegraph in 1844 brought almost every important part of Europe, and eventually of the world, nearer to every town dweller than the nearest county had been in the eighteenth century; and the development of the modern newspaper out of the few feeble sheets of 1825 (dailies and weeklies in London, only weeklies elsewhere), carried full accounts of the doings of the whole world, in place of long-delayed fragmentary rumors, to every door within a few hours. No less striking was the progress in public health and the increase in human happiness due to the enormous advance in the sciences of medicine, surgery, and hygiene. Indeed these sciences in their modern form virtually began with the discovery of the facts of bacteriology about 1860, and the use of antiseptics fifteen years later, and not much earlier began the effective opposition to the frightful epidemics which had formerly been supposed to be dependent only on the will of Providence.

Political and social progress, though less astonishing, was substantial. In 1830 England, nominally a monarchy, was in reality a plutocracy of about a hundred thousand men--landed nobles, gentry, and wealthy merchants--whose privileges dated back to fifteenth century conditions. The first Reform Bill, of 1832, forced on Parliament by popular pressure, extended the right of voting to men of the 'middle class,' and the subsequent bills of 1867 and 1885 made it universal for men. Meanwhile the House of Commons slowly asserted itself against the hereditary House of Lords, and thus England became perhaps the most truly democratic of the great nations of the world. At the beginning of the period the social condition of the great body of the population was extremely bad. Laborers in factories and mines and on farms were largely in a state of virtual though not nominal slavery, living, many of them, in unspeakable moral and physical conditions.

Little by little improvement came, partly by the passage of laws, partly by the growth of trades-unions. The substitution in the middle of the century of free-trade for protection through the passage of the 'Corn-Laws' afforded much relief by lowering the price of food. Socialism, taking shape as a definite movement in the middle of the century, became one to be reckoned with before its close, though the majority of the more well-to-do classes failed to understand even then the growing necessity for far-reaching economic and social changes. Humanitarian consciousness, however, gained greatly during the period. The middle and upper classes awoke to some extent to their duty to the poor, and sympathetic benevolent effort, both organized and informal, increased very largely in amount and intelligence. Popular education, too, which in 1830 had no connection with the State and was in every respect very incomplete, was developed and finally made compulsory as regards the rudiments.

Still more permanently significant, perhaps, was the transformation of the former conceptions of the nature and meaning of the world and life, through the discoveries of science. Geology and astronomy now gradually compelled all thinking people to realize the unthinkable duration of the cosmic processes and the comparative littleness of our earth in the vast extent of the universe. Absolutely revolutionary for almost all lines if thought was the gradual adoption by almost all thinkers of the theory of Evolution, which, partly formulated by Lamarck early in the century, received definite statement in 1859 in Charles Darwin's 'Origin of Species.' The great modification in the externals of religious belief thus brought about was confirmed also by the growth of the science of historical criticism.

This movement of religious change was met in its early stages by the very interesting reactionary 'Oxford' or 'Tractarian' Movement, which asserted the supreme authority of the Church and its traditional doctrines. The most important figure in this movement, who connects it definitely with literature, was John Henry Newman (1801-90), author of the hymn 'Lead, Kindly Light,' a man of winning personality and great literary skill. For fifteen years, as vicar of the Oxford University Church, Newman was a great spiritual force in the English communion, but the series of 'Tracts for the Times' to which he largely contributed, ending in 1841 in the famous Tract 90, tell the story of his gradual progress toward Rome.

Thereafter as an avowed Roman Catholic and head of a monastic establishment Newman showed himself a formidable controversialist, especially in a literary encounter with the clergyman-novelist Charles Kingsley which led to Newman's famous 'Apologia pro Vita Sua' (Apology for My Life), one of the secondary literary masterpieces of the century.

His services to the Catholic Church were recognized in 1879 by his appointment as a Cardinal. More than one of the influences thus hastily surveyed combine in creating the moral, social, and intellectual strenuousness which is one of the main marks of the literature of the period. More conspicuously than ever before the majority of the great writers, not least the poets and novelists, were impelled not merely by the emotional or dramatic creative impulse but by the sense of a message for their age which should broaden the vision and elevate the ideals of the masses of their fellows. The literature of the period, therefore, lacks the disinterested and joyous spontaneity of, for example, the Elizabethan period, and its mood is far more complex than that of the partly socially-minded pseudo-classicists.

While all the new influences were manifesting themselves in Victorian literature they did not, of course, supersede the great general inherited tendencies. This literature is in the main romantic. On the social side this should be evident; the Victorian social humanitarianism is merely the developed form of the eighteenth century romantic democratic impulse. On the esthetic side the romantic traits are also present, though not so aggressively as in the previous period; with romantic vigor the Victorian literature often combines exquisite classical finish; indeed, it is so eclectic and composite that all the definite older terms take on new and less sharply contrasting meanings when applied to it.

So long a period naturally falls into sub-divisions; during its middle part in particular, progress and triumphant romanticism, not yet largely attacked by scientific scepticism, had created a prevailing atmosphere of somewhat passive sentiment and optimism both in society and in literature which has given to the adjective 'mid-Victorian' a very definite denotation. The adjective and its period are commonly spoken of with contempt in our own day by those persons who pride themselves on their complete sophistication and superiority to all intellectual and emotional weakness. But during the 'mid-Victorian' years, there was also a comparative healthiness in the lives of the well-to-do classes and in literature which had never before been equalled and which may finally prove no less praiseworthy than the rather self-conscious freedom and unrestraint of the early twentieth century.

The most important literature of the whole period falls under the three heads of essays, poetry, and prose fiction, which we may best consider in that order.

ALFRED TENNYSON

In poetry, apart from the drama, the Victorian period is the greatest in English literature. Its most representative, though not its greatest, poet is Alfred Tennyson. Tennyson, the fourth of a large family of children, was born in Somersby, Lincolnshire, in 1809. That year, as it happened, is distinguished by the birth of a large number of eminent men, among them Gladstone, Darwin, and Lincoln. Tennyson's father was a clergyman, holding his appointments from a member of the landed gentry; his mother was peculiarly gentle and benevolent. From childhood the poet, though physically strong, was moody and given to solitary dreaming; from early childhood also he composed poetry, and when he was seventeen he and one of his elder brothers brought out a volume of verse, immature, but of distinct poetic feeling and promise.

The next year they entered Trinity College, Cambridge, where Tennyson, too reserved for public prominence, nevertheless developed greatly through association with a gifted group of students. Called home by the fatal illness of his father shortly before his four year's were completed, he decided, as Milton had done, and as Browning was even then doing, to devote himself to his art; but, like Milton, he equipped himself, now and throughout his life, by hard and systematic study of many of the chief branches of knowledge, including the sciences. His next twenty years were filled with difficulty and sorrow.

Two volumes of poems which he published in 1830 and 1832 were greeted by the critics with their usual harshness, which deeply wounded his sensitive spirit and checked his further publication for ten years; though the second of these volumes contains some pieces which, in their later, revised, form, are among his chief lyric triumphs. In 1833 his warm friend Arthur Hallam, a young man of extraordinary promise, who was engaged, moreover, to one of Tennyson's sisters, died suddenly without warning. Tennyson's grief, at first overwhelming, was long a main factor in his life and during many years found slow artistic expression in 'In Memoriam' and other poems. A few years later came another deep sorrow. Tennyson formed an engagement of marriage with Miss Emily Sellwood, but his lack of worldly prospects led her relatives to cancel it.

Tennyson now spent much of his time in London, on terms of friendship with many literary men, including Carlyle, who almost made an exception in his favor from his general fanatical contempt for poetry. In 1842 Tennyson published two volumes of poems, including the earlier ones revised; he here won an undoubted popular success and was accepted by the best judges as the chief living productive English poet. Disaster followed in the shape of an unfortunate financial venture which for a time reduced his family to serious straits and drove him with shattered nerves to a sanitarium. Soon, however, he received from the government as a recognition of his poetic achievement a permanent annual pension of two hundred pounds, and in 1847 he published the strange but delightful 'Princess.' The year 1850 marked the decisive turning point of his career. He was enabled to renew his engagement and be married; the publication of 'In Memoriam' established him permanently in a position of such popularity as few living poets have ever enjoyed; and on the death of Wordsworth he was appointed Poet Laureate.

The prosperity of the remaining half of his life was a full recompense for his earlier struggles, though it is marked by few notable external events. Always a lover of the sea, he soon took up his residence in the Isle of Wight.

His production of poetry was steady, and its variety great. The largest of all his single achievements was the famous series of 'Idylls of the King,' which formed a part of his occupation for many years. In much of his later work there is a marked change from his earlier elaborate decorativeness to a style of vigorous strength. At the age of sixty-five, fearful that he had not yet done enough to insure his fame, he gave a remarkable demonstration of poetic vitality by striking out into the to him new field of poetic drama.

His important works here are the three tragedies in which he aimed to complete the series of Shakspere's chronicle-history plays; but he lacked the power of dramatic action, and the result is rather three fine poems than successful plays. In 1883, after having twice refused a baronetcy, he, to the regret of his more democratic friends, accepted a peerage (barony). Tennyson disliked external show, but he was always intensely loyal to the institutions of England, he felt that literature was being honored in his person, and he was willing to secure a position of honor for his son, who had long rendered him devoted service.

He died quietly in 1892, at the age of eighty-three, and was buried in Westminster Abbey beside Browning, who had found a resting-place there three years earlier. His personal character, despite some youthful morbidness, was unusually delightful, marked by courage, honesty, sympathy, and straightforward manliness. He had a fine voice and took undisguised pleasure in reading his poems aloud. The chief traits of his poetry in form and substance may be suggested in a brief summary.

1. Most characteristic, perhaps, is his exquisite artistry (in which he learned much from Keats). His appreciation for sensuous beauty, especially color, is acute; his command of poetic phraseology is unsurpassed; he suggests shades of, feeling and elusive aspiration with, marvelously subtile power; his descriptions are magnificently beautiful, often with much detail; and his melody is often the perfection of sweetness. Add the truth and tenderness of his emotion, and it results that he is one of the finest and most moving of lyric poets. Nor is all this beauty vague and unsubstantial. Not only was he the most careful of English poets, revising his works with almost unprecedented pains, but his scientific habit of mind insists on the greatest accuracy; in his allusions to Nature he often introduces scientific facts in a way thitherto unparalleled, and sometimes even only doubtfully poetic.

   The influence of the classic literatures on his style and expression was great; no poet combines more harmoniously classic perfection and romantic feeling.

2. The variety of his poetic forms is probably greater than that of any other English poet. In summary catalogue may be named: lyrics, both delicate and stirring; ballads; romantic dreams and fancies; descriptive poems; sentimental reveries, and idyls; long narratives, in which he displays perfect narrative skill; delightfully realistic character-sketches, some of them in dialect; dramas; and meditative poems, long and short, on religious, ethical, and social questions. In almost all these forms he has produced numerous masterpieces.
3. His chief deficiency is in the dramatic quality. No one can present more finely than he moods (often carefully set in a harmoniously appropriate background of external nature) or characters in stationary position; and there is splendid spirit in his narrative passages of vigorous action. Nevertheless his genius and the atmosphere of his poems are generally dreamy, romantic, and aloof from actual life. A brilliant critic has caustically observed that he 'withdraws from the turmoil of the real universe into the fortress of his own mind, and beats the enemy in toy battles with toy soldiers.' He never succeeded in presenting to the satisfaction of most good critics a vigorous man in vigorous action.
4. The ideas of his poetry are noble and on the whole clear. He was an independent thinker, though not an innovator, a conservative liberal, and was so widely popular because he expressed in frank but reverent fashion the moderately advanced convictions of his time. His social ideals, in which he is intensely interested, are those of Victorian humanitarianism. He hopes ardently for a steady amelioration of the condition of the masses, proceeding toward a time when all men shall have real opportunity for full development; and freedom is one of his chief watchwords. But with typical English conservatism he believes that progress must be gradual, and that it should be controlled by order, loyalty, and reverence. Like a true Englishman, also, he is sure that the institutions of England are the best in the world, so that he is a strong supporter of the monarchy and the hereditary aristocracy. In religion, his inherited belief, rooted in his deepest fibers, early found itself confronted by the discoveries of modern science, which at first seemed to him to proclaim that the universe is much what it seemed to the young Carlyle, a remorseless monster, 'red in tooth and claw,' scarcely thinkable as the work of a Christian God who cares for man.

Tennyson was too sincere to evade the issue, and after years of inner struggle he arrived at a positive faith in the central principles of Christianity, broadly interpreted, though it was avowedly a faith based on instinct and emotional need rather than on unassailable reasoning. His somewhat timid disposition, moreover, never allowed him to enunciate his conclusions with anything like the buoyant aggressiveness of his contemporary, Robert Browning. How greatly science had influenced his point of view appears in the conception which is central in his later poetry, namely that the forces of the universe are governed by unchanging Law, through which God works. The best final expression of his spirit is the lyric 'Crossing the Bar,' which every one knows and which at his own request is printed last in all editions of his works.

JOHN RUSKIN

Among the other great Victorian writers the most obvious disciple of Carlyle in his opposition to the materialism of modern life is John Ruskin. But Ruskin is much more than any man's disciple; and he also contrasts strongly with Carlyle, first because a large part of his life was devoted to the study of Art--he is the single great art-critic in English Literature--and also because he is one of the great preachers of that nineteenth century humanitarianism at which Carlyle was wont to sneer.

Ruskin's parents were Scotch, but his father, a man of artistic tastes, was established as a wine-merchant in London and had amassed a fortune before the boy's birth in 1819. The atmosphere of the household was sternly Puritan, and Ruskin was brought up under rigid discipline, especially by his mother, who gave him most of his early education. He read, wrote, and drew precociously; his knowledge of the Bible, in which his mother's training was relentlessly thorough, of Scott, Pope, and Homer, dates from his fifth or sixth year. For many years during his boyhood he accompanied his parents on long annual driving trips through Great Britain and parts of Europe, especially the Alps. By these experiences his inborn passion for the beautiful and the grand in Nature and Art was early developed. During seven years he was at Oxford, where his mother lived with him and watched over him; until her death in his fifty-second year she always continued to treat him like a child, an attitude to which, habit and affection led him to submit with a matter-of-course docility that his usual wilfulness and his later fame render at first sight astonishing. At Oxford, as throughout his life, he showed himself brilliant but not a close or careful student, and he was at that time theologically too rigid a Puritan to be interested in the Oxford Movement, then in its most intense stage.

His career as a writer began immediately after he left the University. It falls naturally into two parts, the first of about twenty years, when he was concerned almost altogether with Art, chiefly Painting and Architecture; and the second somewhat longer, when he was intensely absorbed in the problems of society and strenuously working as a social reformer. From the outset, however, he was actuated by an ardent didactic purpose; he wrote of Art in order to awake men's spiritual natures to a joyful delight in the Beautiful and thus to lead, them to God, its Author.

The particular external direction of Ruskin's work in Art was given, as usual, more or less by accident. His own practice in water-color drawing led him as a mere youth to a devoted admiration for the landscape paintings of the contemporary artist J.M.W. Turner. Turner, a romantic revolutionist against the eighteenth century theory of the grand style, was then little appreciated; and when Ruskin left the University he began, with characteristic enthusiasm, an article on 'Modern Painters,' designed to demonstrate Turner's superiority to all possible rivals. Even the first part of this work expanded itself into a volume, published in 1843, when Ruskin was only twenty-four; and at intervals during the next seventeen years he issued four additional volumes, the result of prolonged study both of Nature and of almost all the great paintings in Europe.

The completed book is a discursive treatise, the various volumes necessarily written from more or less different view-points, on many of the main aspects, general and technical, of all art, literary as well as pictorial. For Ruskin held, and brilliantly demonstrated, that the underlying principles of all the Fine Arts are identical, and 'Modern Painters' contains some of the most famous and suggestive passages of general literary criticism ever written, for example those on The Pathetic Fallacy and The Grand Style. Still further, to Ruskin morality and religion are inseparable from Art, so that he deals searchingly, if incidentally, with those subjects as well. Among his fundamental principles are the ideas that a beneficent God has created the world and its beauty directly for man's use and pleasure; that all true art and all true life are service of God and should be filled with a spirit of reverence; that art should reveal truth; and that really great and good art can spring only from noble natures and a sound national life.

The style of the book is as notable as the substance. It is eloquent with Ruskin's enthusiastic admiration for Beauty and with his magnificent romantic rhetoric (largely the result, according to his own testimony, of his mother's exacting drill in the Bible), which here and elsewhere make him one of the greatest of all masters of gorgeous description and of fervid exhortation. The book displays fully, too, another of his chief traits, an intolerant dogmatism, violently contemptuous of any judgments but his own. On the religious side, especially, Ruskin's Protestantism is narrow, and even bigoted, but it softens as the book proceeds (and decidedly more in his later years). With all its faults, 'Modern Painters' is probably the greatest book ever written on Art and is an immense storehouse, of noble material, and suggestion.

In the intervals of this work Ruskin published others less comprehensive, two of which are of the first importance. 'The Seven Lamps of Architecture' argues that great art, as the supreme expression of life, is the result of seven moral and religious principles, Sacrifice, Truth, Power, and the like. 'The Stones of Venice' is an, impassioned exposition of the beauty of Venetian Gothic architecture, and here as always Ruskin expresses his vehement preference for the Gothic art of the Middle Ages as contrasted with the less original and as it seems to him less sincere style of the Renaissance.

The publication of the last volume of 'Modern Painters' in 1860 roughly marks the end of Ruskin's first period. Several influences had by this time begun to sadden him. More than ten years before, with his usual filial meekness, he had obeyed his parents in marrying a lady who proved uncongenial and who after a few years was divorced from him. Meanwhile acquaintance with Carlyle had combined with experience to convince him of the comparative ineffectualness of mere art-criticism as a social and religious force. He had come to feel with increasing indignation that the modern industrial system, the materialistic political economy founded on it, and the whole modern organization of society reduce the mass of men to a state of intellectual, social, and religious squalor and blindness, and that while they continue in this condition it is of little use to talk to them about Beauty.

He believed that some of the first steps in the necessary redemptive process must be the education of the poor and a return to what he conceived (certainly with much exaggeration) to have been the conditions of medieval labor, when each craftsman was not a mere machine but an intelligent and original artistic creator; but the underlying essential was to free industry from the spirit of selfish money-getting and permeate it with Christian sympathy and respect for man as man. The ugliness of modern life in its wretched city tenements and its hideous factories Ruskin would have utterly destroyed, substituting such a beautiful background (attractive homes and surroundings) as would help to develop spiritual beauty. With his customary vigor Ruskin proceeded henceforth to devote himself to the enunciation, and so far as possible the realization of these beliefs, first by delivering lectures and writing books. He was met, like all reformers, with a storm of protest, but most of his ideas gradually became the accepted principles of social theory. Among his works dealing with these subjects may be named 'Unto This Last,' 'Munera

Pulveris' (The Rewards of the Dust--an attack on materialistic political economy), and 'Fors Clavigera' (Fortune the Key-Bearer), the latter a series of letters to workingmen extending over many years. To 1865 belongs his most widely-read book, 'Sesame and Lilies,' three lectures on the spiritual meaning of great literature in contrast to materialism, the glory of womanhood, and the mysterious significance of life.

From the death of his mother in 1871 Ruskin began to devote his large inherited fortune to 'St. George's Guild,' a series of industrial and social experiments in which with lavish generosity he attempted to put his theories into practical operation. All these experiments, as regards direct results, ended in failure, though their general influence was great. Among other movements now everywhere taken for granted 'social settlements' are a result of his efforts.

All this activity had not caused Ruskin altogether to abandon the teaching of art to the members of the more well-to-do classes, and beginning in 1870 he held for three or four triennial terms the newly-established professorship of Art at Oxford and gave to it much hard labor. But this interest was now clearly secondary in his mind.

Ruskin's temper was always romantically high-strung, excitable, and irritable. His intense moral fervor, his multifarious activities, and his disappointments were also constant strains on his nervous force. In 1872, further, he was rejected in marriage by a young girl for whom he had formed a deep attachment and who on her death-bed, three years later, refused, with strange cruelty, to see him. In 1878 his health temporarily failed, and a few years later he retired to the home, 'Brantwood,' at Coniston in the Lake Region, which he had bought on the death of his mother. Here his mind gradually gave way, but intermittently, so that he was still able to compose 'Praterita' (The Past), a delightful autobiography. He died in 1900.

Ruskin, like Carlyle, was a strange compound of genius, nobility, and unreasonableness, but as time goes on his dogmatism and violence may well be more and more forgotten, while his idealism, his penetrating interpretation of art and life, his fruitful work for a more tolerable social order, and his magnificent mastery of style and description assure him a permanent place in the history of English literature and of civilization.

MATTHEW ARNOLD

Contemporary with Carlyle and Ruskin and fully worthy to rank with them stands still a third great preacher of social and spiritual regeneration,

Matthew Arnold, whose personality and message, however, were very different from theirs and who was also one of the chief Victorian poets. Arnold was born in 1822, the son--and this is decidedly significant--of the Dr. Thomas Arnold who later became the famous headmaster of Rugby School and did more than any other man of the century to elevate the tone of English school life. Matthew Arnold proceeded from Rugby to Oxford (Balliol College), where he took the prize for original poetry and distinguished himself as a student. This was the period of the Oxford Movement, and Arnold was much impressed by Newman's fervor and charm, but was already too rationalistic in thought to sympathize with his views.

After graduation Arnold taught Greek for a short time at Rugby and then became private secretary to Lord Lansdoune, who was minister of public instruction. Four years later, in 1851, Arnold was appointed an inspector of schools, a position which he held almost to the end of his life and in which he labored very hard and faithfully, partly at the expense of his creative work. His life was marked by few striking outward events. His marriage and home were happy. Up to 1867 his literary production consisted chiefly of poetry, very carefully composed and very limited in amount, and for two five-year terms, from 1857 to 1867, he held the Professorship of Poetry at Oxford.

At the expiration of his second term he did not seek for reappointment, because he did not care to arouse the opposition of Gladstone--then a power in public affairs--and stir up religious controversy. His retirement from this position virtually marks the very distinct change from the first to the second main period of his career. For with deliberate self-sacrifice he now turned from poetry to prose essays, because he felt that through the latter medium he could render what seemed to him a more necessary public service. With characteristic self-confidence, and obeying his inherited tendency to didacticism, he appointed himself, in effect, a critic of English national life, beliefs, and taste, and set out to instruct the public in matters of literature, social relations, politics and religion. In many essays, published separately or in periodicals, he persevered in this task until his death in 1888.

As a poet Arnold is generally admitted to rank among the Victorians next after Tennyson and Browning. The criticism, partly true, that he was not designed by Nature to be a poet but made himself one by hard work rests on his intensely, and at the outset coldly, intellectual and moral temperament. He himself, in modified Puritan spirit, defined poetry as a criticism of life; his mind was philosophic; and in his own verse, inspired by Greek poetry, by Goethe and Wordsworth, he realized his definition. In his work, therefore, delicate melody and sensuous beauty were at first much less conspicuous than a high moral sense, though after the first the elements of external beauty greatly developed, often to the finest effect.

In form and spirit his poetry is one of the very best later reflections of that of Greece, dominated by thought, dignified, and polished with the utmost care. 'Sohrab and Rustum,' his most ambitious and greatest single poem, is a very close and admirable imitation of 'The Iliad.' Yet, as the almost intolerable pathos of 'Sohrab and Rustum' witnesses, Arnold is not by any means deficient, any more than the Greek poets were, in emotion. He affords, in fact, a striking example of classical form and spirit united with the deep, self-conscious, meditative feeling of modern Romanticism.

In substance Arnold's poetry is the expression of his long and tragic spiritual struggle. To him religion, understood as a reverent devotion to Divine things, was the most important element in life, and his love of pure truth was absolute; but he held that modern knowledge had entirely disproved the whole dogmatic and doctrinal scheme of historic Christianity and that a new spiritual revelation was necessary. To his Romantic nature, however, mere knowledge and mere modern science, which their followers were so confidently exalting, appeared by no means adequate to the purpose; rather they seemed to him largely futile, because they did not stimulate the emotions and so minister to the spiritual life.

Further, the restless stirrings of his age, beginning to arouse itself from the social lethargy of centuries, appeared to him pitifully unintelligent and devoid of results. He found all modern life, as he says in 'The Scholar-Gypsy,' a 'strange disease,' in which men hurry wildly about in a mad activity which they mistake for achievement. In Romantic melancholy he looked wistfully back by contrast to periods when 'life was fresh and young' and could express itself vigorously and with no torturing introspection. The exaggerated pessimism in this part of his outcry is explained by his own statement, that he lived in a transition time, when the old faith was (as he held) dead, and the new one (partly realized in our own generation) as yet 'powerless to be born.'

Arnold's poetry, therefore, is to be viewed as largely the expression, monotonous but often poignantly beautiful, of a temporary mood of questioning protest. But if his conclusion is not positive, it is at least not weakly despairing. Each man, he insists, should diligently preserve and guard in intellectual and moral integrity the fortress of his own soul, into which, when necessary, he can retire in serene and stoical resignation, determined to endure and to 'see life steadily and see it whole.' Unless the man himself proves traitor, the littlenesses of life are powerless to conquer him. In fact, the invincible courage of the thoroughly disciplined spirit in the midst of doubt and external discouragement has never been, more nobly expressed than by Arnold in such poems as 'Palladium' and (from a different point of view) 'The Last Word.'

There is a striking contrast (largely expressing an actual change of spirit and point of view) between the manner of Arnold's poetry and that of his prose. In the latter he entirely abandons the querulous note and assumes instead a tone of easy assurance, jaunty and delightfully satirical. Increasing maturity had taught him that merely to sit regarding the past was useless and that he himself had a definite doctrine, worthy of being preached with all aggressiveness.

We have already said that his essays fall into four classes, literary, social, religious, and political, though they cannot always be sharply distinguished. As a literary critic he is uneven, and, as elsewhere, sometimes superficial, but his fine appreciation and generally clear vision make him refreshingly stimulating. His point of view is unusually broad, his chief general purpose being to free English taste from its insularity, to give it sympathetic acquaintance with the peculiar excellences of other literatures. Some of his essays, like those on 'The Function of Criticism at the Present Time,' 'Wordsworth,' and 'Byron,' are among the best in English, while his 'Essays on Translating Homer' present the most famous existing interpretation of the spirit and style of the great Greek epics.

In his social essays, of which the most important form the volume entitled 'Culture and Anarchy,' he continues in his own way the attacks of Carlyle and Ruskin. Contemporary English life seems to him a moral chaos of physical misery and of the selfish, unenlightened, violent expression of untrained wills. He too looks with pitying contempt on the material achievements of science and the Liberal party as being mere 'machinery,' means to an end, which men mistakenly worship as though it possessed a real value in itself. He divides English society into three classes:

1. The Aristocracy, whom he nick-names 'The Barbarians,' because, like the Germanic tribes who overthrew the Roman Empire, they vigorously assert their own privileges and live in the external life rather than in the life of the spirit.
2. The Middle Class, which includes the bulk of the nation. For them he borrows from German criticism the name 'Philistines,' enemies of the chosen people, and he finds their prevailing traits to be intellectual and spiritual narrowness and a fatal and superficial satisfaction with mere activity and material prosperity.

3. 'The Populace,' the 'vast raw and half-developed residuum.' For them Arnold had sincere theoretical sympathy (though his temperament made it impossible for him to enter into the same sort of personal sympathy with them as did Ruskin); but their whole environment and conception of life seemed to him hideous. With his usual uncomplimentary frankness Arnold summarily described the three groups as 'a materialized upper class, a vulgarized middle class, and a brutalized lower class.'

For the cure of these evils Arnold's proposed remedy was Culture, which he defined as a knowledge of the best that has been thought and done in the world and a desire to make the best ideas prevail. Evidently this Culture is not a mere knowledge of books, unrelated to the rest of life. It has indeed for its basis a very wide range of knowledge, acquired by intellectual processes, but this knowledge alone Arnold readily admitted to be 'machinery.'

The real purpose and main part of Culture is the training, broadening, and refining of the whole spirit, including the emotions as well as the intellect, into sympathy with all the highest ideals, and therefore into inward peace and satisfaction. Thus Culture is not indolently selfish, but is forever exerting itself to 'make the best ideas'--which Arnold also defined as 'reason and the will, of God'--'prevail.'

Arnold felt strongly that a main obstacle to Culture was religious narrowness. He held that the English people had been too much occupied with the 'Hebraic' ideal of the Old Testament, the interest in morality or right conduct, and though he agreed that this properly makes three quarters of life, he insisted that it should be joined with the Hellenic (Greek) ideal of a perfectly rounded nature. He found the essence of Hellenism expressed in a phrase which he took from Swift, 'Sweetness and Light,' interpreting Sweetness to mean the love of Beauty, material and spiritual, and Light, unbiased intelligence; and he urged that these forces be allowed to have the freest play.

He vigorously attacked the Dissenting denominations, because he believed them to be a conspicuous embodiment of Philistine lack of Sweetness and Light, with an unlovely insistence on unimportant external details and a fatal blindness to the meaning of real beauty and real spirituality. Though he himself was without a theological creed, he was, and held that every Englishman should be, a devoted adherent of the English Church, as a beautiful, dignified, and national expression of essential religion, and therefore a very important influence for Culture.

Toward democracy Arnold took, not Carlyle's attitude of definite opposition, but one of questioning scrutiny. He found that one actual tendency of modern democracy was to 'let people do as they liked,' which, given the crude violence of the Populace, naturally resulted in lawlessness and therefore threatened anarchy.

Culture, on the other hand, includes the strict discipline of the will and the sacrifice of one's own impulses for the good of all, which means respect for Law and devotion to the State.

Existing democracy, therefore, he attacked with unsparing irony, but he did not condemn its principle. One critic has said that 'his ideal of a State can best be described as an Educated Democracy, working by Collectivism in Government, Religion and Social Order.' But in his own writings he scarcely gives expression to so definite a conception.

Arnold's doctrine, of course, was not perfectly comprehensive nor free from prejudices; but none could be essentially more useful for his generation or ours. We may readily grant that it is, in one sense or another, a doctrine for chosen spirits, but if history makes anything clear it is that chosen spirits are the necessary instruments of all progress and therefore the chief hope of society.

The differences between Arnold's teaching and that of his two great contemporaries are probably now clear. All three are occupied with the pressing necessity of regenerating society.

Carlyle would accomplish this end by means of great individual characters inspired by confidence in the spiritual life and dominating their times by moral strength; Ruskin would accomplish it by humanizing social conditions and spiritualizing and refining all men's natures through devotion to the principles of moral Right and esthetic Beauty; Arnold would leaven the crude mass of society, so far as possible, by permeating it with all the myriad influences of spiritual, moral, and esthetic culture. All three, of course, like every enlightened reformer, are aiming at ideal conditions which can be actually realized only in the distant future.

Arnold's style is one of the most charming features of his work. Clear, direct, and elegant, it reflects most attractively his own high breeding; but it is also eminently forceful, and marked by very skilful emphasis and reiteration. One of his favorite devices is a pretense of great humility, which is only a shelter from which he shoots forth incessant and pitiless volleys of ironical raillery, light and innocent in appearance, but irresistible in aim and penetrating power. He has none of the gorgeousness of Ruskin or the titanic strength of Carlyle, but he can be finely eloquent, and he is certainly one of the masters of polished effectiveness.

ELIZABETH BARRETT BROWNING AND ROBERT BROWNING

Robert Browning, Tennyson's chief poetic contemporary, stands in striking artistic contrast to Tennyson--a contrast which perhaps serves to enhance the reputation of both. Browning's life, if not his poetry, must naturally be considered in connection with that of Elizabeth Barrett Browning, with whom he was united in what appears the most ideal marriage of two important writers in the history of literature.

Elizabeth Barrett, the daughter of a country gentleman of Herefordshire (the region of the Malvern Hills and of 'Piers Plowman'), was born in 1806. She was naturally both healthy and intellectually precocious; the writing of verse and outdoor life divided all her early life, and at seventeen she published, a volume of immature poems. At fifteen, however, her health was impaired by an accident which happened as she was saddling her pony, and at thirty, after a removal of the family to London, it completely failed. From that time on for ten years she was an invalid, confined often to her bed and generally to her chamber, sometimes apparently at the point of death. Nevertheless she kept on with persistent courage and energy at her study and writing. The appearance of her poems in two volumes in 1844 gave her a place among the chief living poets and led to her acquaintance with Browning.

Browning was born in a London suburb in 1812 (the same year with Dickens), of very mixed ancestry, which may partly explain the very diverse traits in his nature and poetry. His father, a man of artistic and cultured tastes, held a subordinate though honorable position in the Bank of England. The son inherited a strong instinct for all the fine arts, and though he composed verses before he could write, seemed for years more likely to become a musician than a poet. His formal schooling was irregular, but he early began to acquire from his father's large and strangely-assorted library the vast fund of information which astonishes the reader of his poetry, and he too lived a healthy out-of-door life.

His parents being Dissenters, the universities were not open to him, and when he was seventeen his father somewhat reluctantly consented to his own unhesitating choice of poetry as a profession. For seventeen years more he continued in his father's home, living a normal life among his friends, writing continuously, and gradually acquiring a reputation among some good critics, but making very little impression on the public. Some of his best short poems date from these years, such as 'My Last Duchess' and 'The Bishop Orders His Tomb'; but his chief effort went into a series of seven or eight poetic dramas, of which 'Pippa Passes' is best known and least dramatic. They are noble poetry, but display in marked degree the psychological subtilety which in part of his poetry demands unusually close attention from the reader.

In one of the pieces in her volumes of 1844 Elizabeth Barrett mentioned Browning, among other poets, with generous praise. This led to a correspondence between the two, and soon to a courtship, in which Browning's earnestness finally overcame Miss Barrett's scrupulous hesitation to lay upon him (as she felt) the burden of her invalidism. Indeed her invalidism at last helped to turn the scales in Browning's favor, for the physicians had declared that Miss Barrett's life depended on removal to a warmer climate, but to this her father, a well-intentioned but strangely selfish man, absolutely refused to consent. The record of the courtship is given in Mrs. Browning's 'Sonnets from the Portuguese' (a whimsical title, suggested by Mrs.

Browning's childhood nickname, 'The Little Portuguese'), which is one of the finest of English sonnet-sequences. The marriage, necessarily clandestine, took place in 1846; Mrs. Browning's father thenceforth treated her as one dead, but the removal from her morbid surroundings largely restored her health for the remaining fifteen years of her life. During these fifteen years the two poets resided chiefly in various cities of Italy, with a nominal home in Florence, and Mrs. Browning had an inherited income which sufficed for their support until their poetry became profitable. Their chief works during this period were Mrs. Browning's 'Aurora Leigh' (1856), a long 'poetic novel' in blank verse dealing with the relative claims of Art and Social Service and with woman's place in the world; and Browning's most important single publication, his two volumes of 'Men and Women' (1855), containing fifty poems, many of them among his very best.

Mrs. Browning was passionately interested in the Italian struggle for independence against Austrian tyranny, and her sudden death in 1861 seems to have been hastened by that of the Italian statesman Cavour. Browning, at first inconsolable, soon returned with his son to London, where he again made his home, for the rest of his life. Henceforth he published much poetry, for the most part long pieces of subtile psychological and spiritual analysis. In 1868-9 he brought out his characteristic masterpiece, 'The Ring and the Book,' a huge psychological epic, which proved the tardy turning point in his reputation. People might not understand the poem, but they could not disregard it, the author became famous, almost popular, and a Browning cult arose, marked by the spread of Browning societies in both England and America. Browning enjoyed his success for twenty years and died quietly in 1889 at the home of his son in Venice.

Browning earnestly reciprocated his wife's loyal devotion and seemed really to believe, as he often insisted, that her poetry was of a higher order than his own. Her achievement, indeed, was generally overestimated, in her own day and later, but it is now recognized that she is scarcely a really great artist. Her intense emotion, her fine Christian idealism, and her very wide reading give her real power; her womanly tenderness is admirable; and the breadth of her interests and sometimes the clearness of her judgment are notable; but her secluded life of ill-health rendered her often sentimental, high-strung, and even hysterical.

She has in her the impulses and material of great poetry, but circumstances and her temperament combined to deny her the patient self-discipline necessary for the best results. She writes vehemently to assert the often-neglected rights of women and children or to denounce negro slavery and all oppression; and sometimes, as when in 'The Cry of the Children' she revealed the hideousness of child-labor in the factories, she is genuine and irresistible; but more frequently she produces highly romantic or mystical imaginary narrations (often in medieval settings). She not seldom mistakes enthusiasm or indignation for artistic inspiration, and she is repeatedly and inexcusably careless in meter and rime. Perhaps her most satisfactory poems, aside from those above mentioned, are 'The Vision of Poets' and 'The Rime of the Duchess May.'

In considering the poetry of Robert Browning the inevitable first general point is the nearly complete contrast with Tennyson. For the melody and exquisite beauty of phrase and description which make so large a part of Tennyson's charm, Browning cares very little; his chief merits as an artist lie mostly where Tennyson is least strong; and he is a much more independent and original thinker than Tennyson. This will become more evident in a survey of his main characteristics.

1. Browning is the most thoroughly vigorous and dramatic of all great poets who employ other forms than the actual drama. Of his hundreds of poems the great majority set before the reader a glimpse of actual life and human personalities--an action, a situation, characters, or a character--in the clearest and most vivid possible way. Sometimes the poem is a ringing narration of a fine exploit, like 'How They Brought the Good News'; sometimes it is quieter and more reflective. Whatever the style, however, in the great majority of cases Browning employs the form which without having actually invented it he developed into an instrument of thitherto unsuspected power, namely the dramatic monolog in which a character discusses his situation or life or some central part or incident, of it, under circumstances which reveal with

wonderful completeness its significance and his own essential character. To portray and interpret life in this way, to give his readers a sudden vivid understanding of its main forces and conditions in representative moments, may be called the first obvious purpose, or perhaps rather instinct, of Browning and his poetry. The dramatic economy of space which he generally attains in his monologs is marvelous. In 'My Last Duchess' sixty lines suffice to etch into our memories with incredible completeness and clearness two striking characters, an interesting situation, and the whole of a life's tragedy.

2. Despite his power over external details it is in the human characters, as the really significant and permanent elements of life, that Browning is chiefly interested; indeed he once declared directly that the only thing that seemed to him worth while was the study of souls. The number and range of characters that he has portrayed are unprecedented, and so are the keenness, intenseness, and subtilety of the analysis. Andrea del Sarto, Fra Lippo Lippi, Cleon, Karshish, Balaustion, and many scores of others, make of his poems a great gallery of portraits unsurpassed in interest by those of any author whatever except Shakspere. It is little qualification of his achievement to add that all his persons are somewhat colored by his own personality and point of view, or that in his later poetry he often splits hairs very ingeniously in his effort to understand and present sympathetically the motives of all characters, even the worst. These are merely some of the secondary aspects of his peculiar genius. Browning's favorite heroes and heroines, it should be added, are men and women much like himself, of strong will and decisive power of action, able to take the lead vigorously and unconventionally and to play controlling parts in the drama of life.

3. The frequent comparative difficulty of Browning's poetry arises in large part first from the subtilety of his thought and second from the obscurity of his subject-matter and his fondness for out-of-the-way characters. It is increased by his disregard of the difference between his own extraordinary mental power and agility on the one hand and on the other the capacity of the average person, a disregard which leads him to take much for granted that most readers are obliged to study out with no small amount of labor. Moreover Browning was hasty in composition, corrected his work little, if at all, and was downright careless in such details as sentence structure. But the difficulty arising from these various eccentricities occurs chiefly in his longer poems, and often serves mainly as a mental stimulus. Equally striking, perhaps, is his frequent grotesqueness in choice of subject and

in treatment, which seems to result chiefly from his wish to portray the world as it actually is, keeping in close touch with genuine everyday reality; partly also from his instinct to break away from placid and fiberless conventionality.

4. Browning is decidedly one of those who hold the poet to be a teacher, and much, indeed most, of his poetry is occupied rather directly with the questions of religion and the deeper meanings of life. Taken all together, that is, his poetry constitutes a very extended statement of his philosophy of life. The foundation of his whole theory is a confident and aggressive optimism. He believes, partly on the basis of intellectual reasoning, but mainly on what seems to him the convincing testimony of instinct, that the universe is controlled by a loving God, who has made life primarily a thing of happiness for man. Man should accept life with gratitude and enjoy to the full all its possibilities. Evil exists only to demonstrate the value of Good and to develop character, which can be produced only by hard and sincere struggle. Unlike Tennyson, therefore, Browning has full confidence in present reality--he believes that life on earth is predominantly good.

   Nevertheless earthly life is evidently incomplete in itself, and the central law of existence is Progress, which gives assurance of a future life where man may develop the spiritual nature which on earth seems to have its beginning and distinguishes man from the brutes. This future life, however, is probably not one but many, a long succession of lives, the earlier ones not so very different, perhaps, from the present one on earth; and even the worst souls, commencing the next life, perhaps, as a result of their failure here, at a spiritual stage lower than the present one, must ultimately pass through all stages of the spiritual process, and come to stand with all the others near the perfection of God himself. This whole theory, which, because later thought has largely adopted it from Browning, seems much less original to-day than when he first propounded it, is stated and reiterated in his poems with a dynamic idealizing power which, whether or not one assents to it in details, renders it magnificently stimulating. It is rather fully expressed as a whole, in two of Browning's best known and finest poems, 'Rabbi ben Ezra,' and 'Abt Vogler.' Some critics, it should be added, however, feel that Browning is too often and too insistently a teacher in his poetry and that his art would have gained if he had introduced his philosophy much more incidentally.

5. In his social theory Browning differs not only from Tennyson but from the prevailing thought of his age, differs in that his emphasis is

individualistic. Like all the other Victorians he dwells on the importance of individual devotion to the service of others, but he believes that the chief results of such effort must be in the development of the individual's character, not greatly in the actual betterment of the world. The world, indeed, as it appears to him, is a place of probation and we cannot expect ever to make it over very radically; the important thing is that the individual soul shall use it to help him on his 'lone way' to heaven. Browning, accordingly, takes almost no interest in the specific social and political questions of his day, a fact which certainly will not operate against the permanence of his fame. More detrimental, no doubt, aside from the actual faults which we have mentioned, will be his rather extravagant Romanticism--the vehemence of his passion and his insistence on the supreme value of emotion. With these characteristics classically minded critics have always been highly impatient, and they will no doubt prevent him from ultimately taking a place beside Shakspere and the serene Milton; but they will not seriously interfere, we may be certain, with his recognition as one of the very great English poets.

ROSSETTI AND THE PRE-RAPHAELITE MOVEMENT

Many of the secondary Victorian poets must here be passed by, but several of them are too important to be dismissed without at least brief notice. The middle of the century is marked by a new Romantic impulse, the Pre-Raphaelite Movement, which begins with Dante Gabriel Rossetti. Rossetti was born in London in 1828. His father was an Italian, a liberal refugee from the outrageous government of Naples, and his mother was also half Italian. The household, though poor, was a center for other Italian exiles, but this early and tempestuous political atmosphere created in the poet, by reaction, a lifelong aversion for politics. His desultory education was mostly in the lines of painting and the Italian and English poets. His own practice in poetry began as early as is usual with poets, and before he was nineteen, by a special inspiration, he wrote his best and most famous poem, 'The Blessed Damosel.' In the school of the Royal Academy of Painting, in 1848, he met William Holman Hunt and John E. Millais, and the three formed the Pre-Raphaelite Brotherhood, in which Rossetti, whose disposition throughout his life was extremely self-assertive, or even domineering, took the lead.

The purpose of the Brotherhood was to restore to painting and literature the qualities which the three enthusiasts found in the fifteenth century Italian painters, those who just preceded Raphael. Rossetti and his friends did not decry the noble idealism of Raphael himself, but they felt that in trying to follow his grand style the art of their own time had become too abstract and conventional. They wished to renew emphasis on serious emotion, imagination, individuality, and fidelity to truth; and in doing so they gave special attention to elaboration of details in a fashion distinctly reminiscent of medievalism. Their work had much, also, of medieval mysticism and symbolism. Besides painting pictures they published a very short-lived periodical, 'The Germ,' containing both literary material and drawings. Ruskin, now arriving at fame and influence, wrote vigorously in their favor, and though the Brotherhood did not last long as an organization, it has exerted a great influence on subsequent painting.

Rossetti's impulses were generous, but his habits were eccentric and selfish, and his life unfortunate. His engagement with Miss Eleanor Siddal, a milliner's apprentice (whose face appears in many of his pictures), was prolonged by his lack of means for nine years; further, he was an agnostic, while she held a simple religious faith, and she was carrying on a losing struggle with tuberculosis. Sixteen months after their marriage she died, and on a morbid impulse of remorse for inconsiderateness in his treatment of her Rossetti buried his poems, still unpublished, in her coffin. After some years, however, he was persuaded to disinter and publish them. Meanwhile he had formed friendships with the slightly younger artists William Morris and Edward Burne-Jones, and they established a company for the manufacture of furniture and other articles, to be made beautiful as well as useful, and thus to aid in spreading the esthetic sense among the English people.

After some years Rossetti and Burne-Jones withdrew from the enterprise, leaving it to Morris. Rossetti continued all his life to produce both poetry and paintings. His pictures are among the best and most gorgeous products of recent romantic art--'Dante's Dream,' 'Beata Beatrix,' 'The Blessed Damosel,' and many others. During his later years he earned a large income, and he lived in a large house in Cheyne Row, Chelsea (near Carlyle), where for a while, as long as his irregular habits permitted, the novelist George Meredith and the poet Swinburne were also inmates. He gradually grew more morbid, and became a rather pitiful victim of insomnia, the drug chloral, and spiritualistic delusions about his wife. He died in 1882.

Rossetti's poetry is absolutely unlike that of any other English poet, and the difference is clearly due in large part to his Italian race and his painter's instinct. He has, in the didactic sense, absolutely no religious, moral, or social interests; he is an artist almost purely for art's sake, writing to give beautiful embodiment to moods, experiences, and striking moments. If it is true of

Tennyson, however, that he stands aloof from actual life, this is far truer of Rossetti. His world is a vague and languid region of enchantment, full of whispering winds, indistinct forms of personified abstractions, and the murmur of hidden streams; its landscape sometimes bright, sometimes shadowy, but always delicate, exquisitely arranged for luxurious decorative effect. In his ballad-romances, to be sure, such as, 'The King's Tragedy,' there is much dramatic vigor; yet there is still more of medieval weirdness.

Rossetti, like Dante, has much of spiritual mysticism, and his interest centers in the inner rather than the outer life; but his method, that of a painter and a southern Italian, is always highly sensuous. His melody is superb and depends partly on a highly Latinized vocabulary, archaic pronunciations, and a delicate genius in sound-modulation, the effect being heightened also by frequent alliteration and masterly use of refrains. 'Sister Helen,' obviously influenced by the popular ballad 'Edward, Edward,' derives much of its tremendous tragic power from the refrain, and in the use of this device is perhaps the most effective poem in the world. Rossetti is especially facile also with the sonnet. His sonnet sequence, 'The House of Life,' one of the most notable in English, exalts earthly Love as the central force in the world and in rather fragmentary fashion traces the tragic influence of Change in both life and love.

WILLIAM MORRIS

William Morris, a man of remarkable versatility and tremendous energy, which expressed themselves in poetry and many other ways, was the son of a prosperous banker, and was born in London in 1834. At Oxford in 1853-55 he became interested in medieval life and art, was stimulated by the poetry of Mrs. Browning and Tennyson, became a friend of Burne-Jones, wrote verse and prose, and was a member of a group called 'The Brotherhood,' while a little later published for a year a monthly magazine not unlike 'The Germ.' He apprenticed himself to an architect, but at the same time also practised several decorative arts, such as woodcarving, illuminating manuscripts, and designing furniture, stained glass and embroidery.

Together with Burne-Jones, moreover, he became an enthusiastic pupil of Rossetti in painting. His first volume of verse, 'The Defence of Guinevere and Other Poems,' put forth in 1858, shows the influence of Rossetti and Pre-Raphaelitism, but it mainly gives vivid presentation to the spirit of fourteenth-century French chivalry. In 1861 came the foundation of the decorative-art firm of Morris and Co., which after some years grew into a large business, continued to be Morris' main occupation to the end of his life, and has exercised a great influence, both in England and elsewhere, on the beautifying of the surroundings of domestic life.

Meanwhile Morris had turned to the writing of long narrative poems, which he composed with remarkable fluency. The most important is the series of versions of Greek and Norse myths and legends which appeared in 1868-70 as 'The Earthly Paradise.' Shortly after this he became especially interested in Icelandic literature and published versions of some of its stories; notably one of the Siegfried tale, 'Sigurd the Volsung.' In the decade from 1880 to 1890 he devoted most of his energy to work for the Socialist party, of which he became a leader. His ideals were largely identical with those of Ruskin; in particular he wished to restore (or create) in the lives of workingmen conditions which should make of each of them an independent artist. The practical result of his experience was bitter disappointment, he was deposed from his leadership, finally abandoned the party, and returned to art and literature. He now published a succession of prose romances largely inspired by the Icelandic sagas and composed in a strange half-archaic style. He also established the 'Kelmscott Press,' which he made famous for its production of elaborate artistic editions of great books. He died in 1896.

Morris' shorter poems are strikingly dramatic and picturesque, and his longer narrations are remarkably facile and often highly pleasing. His facility, however, is his undoing. He sometimes wrote as much as eight hundred lines in a day, and he once declared: 'If a chap can't compose an epic poem while he's weaving tapestry, he had better shut up; he'll never do any good at all.' In reading his work one always feels that there is the material of greatness, but perhaps nothing that he wrote is strictly great. His prose will certainly prove less permanent than his verse.

SWINBURNE

A younger disciple of the Pre-Raphaelite Movement but also a strongly original artist was Algernon Charles Swinburne. Born in 1837 into a wealthy family, the son of an admiral, he devoted himself throughout his life wholly to poetry, and his career was almost altogether devoid of external incident. After passing through Eton and Oxford he began as author at twenty-three by publishing two plays imitative of Shakspere. Five years later he put forth 'Atalanta in Calydon,' a tragedy not only drawn from Greek heroic legend, but composed in the ancient Greek manner, with long dialogs and choruses. These two volumes express the two intensely vigorous forces which were strangely combined in his nature; for while no man has ever been a more violent romanticist than Swinburne, yet, as one critic has said, 'All the romantic riot in his blood clamored for Greek severity and Greek restraint.'

During the next fifteen years he was partly occupied with a huge poetic trilogy in blank verse on Mary Queen of Scots, and from time to time he wrote other dramas and much prose criticism, the latter largely in praise of the Elizabethan dramatists and always wildly extravagant in tone. He produced also some long narrative poems, of which the chief is 'Tristram of Lyonesse.' His chief importance, however, is as a lyric poet, and his lyric production was large. His earlier poems in this category are for the most part highly objectionable in substance or sentiment, but he gradually worked into a better vein. He was a friend of George Meredith, Burne-Jones, Morris, Rossetti (to whom he loyally devoted himself for years), and the painter Whistler. He died in 1909.

Swinburne carried his radicalism into all lines. Though an ardently patriotic Englishman, he was an extreme republican; and many of his poems are dedicated to the cause of Italian independence or to liberty in general. The significance of his thought, however, is less than that of any other English poet who can in any sense be called great; his poetry is notable chiefly for its artistry, especially for its magnificent melody. Indeed, it has been cleverly said that he offers us an elaborate service of gold and silver, but with little on it except salt and pepper. In his case, however, the mere external beauty and power often seem their own complete and satisfying justification. His command of different meters is marvelous; he uses twice as many as Browning, who is perhaps second to him in this respect, and his most characteristic ones are those of gloriously rapid anapestic lines with complicated rime-schemes.

Others of his distinctive traits are lavish alliteration, rich sensuousness, grandiose vagueness of thought and expression, a great sweep of imagination, and a corresponding love of vastness and desolation. He makes much decorative use of Biblical imagery and of vague abstract personifications--in general creates an atmosphere similar to that of Rossetti. Somewhat as in the case of Morris, his fluency is almost fatal--he sometimes pours out his melodious but vague emotion in forgetfulness of all proportion and restraint. From the intellectual and spiritual point of view he is nearly negligible, but as a musician in words he has no superior, not even Shelley.

9

Victorian Imperialism Poets and Literature

Great Britain during Victoria's reign was not just a powerful island nation. It was the center of a global empire that fostered British contact with a wide variety of other cultures, though the exchange was usually an uneven one. By the end of the nineteenth century, nearly one-quarter of the earth's land surface was part of the British Empire, and more than 400 million people were governed from Great Britain, however nominally. An incomplete list of British colonies and quasi-colonies in 1901 would include Australia, British Guiana (now Guyana), Brunei, Canada, Cyprus, Egypt, Gambia, the Gold Coast (Ghana), Hong Kong, British India (now Bangladesh, India, Myanmar, Pakistan, Sri Lanka), Ireland, Kenya, Malawi, the Malay States (Malaysia), Malta, Mauritius, New Zealand, Nigeria, Sierra Leone, Singapore, Somaliland (Somalia), South Africa, the Sudan, Rhodesia (Zimbabwe), and Trinidad and Tobago. Queen Victoria's far-flung empire was a truly heterogenous entity, governed by heterogenous practices.

It included Crown Colonies like Jamaica, ruled from Britain, and protectorates like Uganda, which had relinquished only partial sovereignty to Britain. Ireland was a sort of internal colony whose demands for home rule were alternately entertained and discounted. India had started the century under the control of the East India Company, but was directly ruled from Britain after the 1857 Indian Mutiny (the first Indian war of independence), and Victoria was crowned Empress of India in 1877. Colonies like Canada and Australia with substantial European populations had become virtually self-governing by the end of the century and were increasingly considered near-equal partners in the imperial project. By contrast, colonies and protectorates with large indigenous populations like Sierra Leone, or with large transplanted populations of ex-slaves and non-European laborers like Trinidad, would not gain autonomy until the twentieth century.

As Joseph Chamberlain notes in The True Conception of Empire, the catastrophic loss of the American colonies had given rise to a certain disenchantment with empire-building. But despite a relative lack of interest in the British imperial project during the early nineteenth century, the Empire continued to grow, acquiring a number of new territories as well as greatly expanding its colonies in Canada and Australia and steadily pushing its way across the Indian subcontinent. A far more rapid expansion took place between 1870 and 1900, three decades that witnessed a new attitude towards and practice of empire-building known as the new imperialism and which would continue until World War I.

During this period Britain was involved in fierce competition for new territories with its European rivals, particularly in Africa. It was becoming increasingly invested, imaginatively and ideologically, in the idea of empire. It found itself more and more dependent on a global economy and committed to finding (and forcing) new trading partners, including what we might call virtual colonies, nations that were not officially part of the Empire but were economically enthrall to powerful Great Britain. All of these motives helped fuel the new imperialism. British expansion was not allowed to progress unchallenged-the Empire went to war with the Ashanti, the Zulus, and the Boers, to name a few, and critics like J. J. Thomas and John Atkinson Hobson denounced imperialism as a corrupt and debasing enterprise-but it progressed at an astonishing pace nonetheless.

The distinction between imperialism and colonialism is difficult to pin down, because the two activities can seem indistinguishable at times. Roughly speaking, imperialism involves the claiming and exploiting of territories outside of ones own national boundaries for a variety of motives.

For instance, Great Britain seized territories in order to increase its own holdings and enhance its prestige, to secure trade routes, to obtain raw materials such as sugar, spices, tea, tin, and rubber, and to procure a market for its own goods. Colonialism involves the settling of those territories and the transformation-the Victorians would have said reformation-of the social structure, culture, government, and economy of the people found there. Thomas Babington Macaulay's "Minute on Indian Education" gives us a good sense of this kind of interventionist colonialism at work.

The Empire did not found colonies in all of its possessions, nor were colony populations necessarily interested in anglicizing the indigenous peoples they shared space with, as is clear from Anthony Trollope's dismissive assessment of the Australian aborigines.

But in general Great Britain was able to justify its expansion into other peoples lands by claiming a civilizing mission based on its own moral, racial, and national superiority. As we see from the selections by Edward Tylor and Benjamin Kidd, late-Victorian science sought to prove that non-Europeans were less evolved, biologically and culturally, and thus unable properly to govern themselves or develop their own territories. Other writers like W. Winwood Reade and Richard Marsh described the imperfectly evolved colonial subjects as fearsome cannibals and beasts, hardly human at all. Thus they were patently in need of taming, and taking on this job was "The White Man's Burden" in Rudyard Kiplings famous phrase.

THE MODERN PERIOD OF PROGRESS AND UNREST

When Victoria became queen, in 1837, English literature seemed to have entered upon a period of lean years, in marked contrast with the poetic fruitfulness of the romantic age which we have just studied. Coleridge, Shelley, Keats, Byron, and Scott had passed away, and it seemed as if there were no writers in England to fill their places. Wordsworth had written, in 1835,

Like clouds that rake, the mountain summits,
Or waves that own no curbing hand,
How fast has brother followed brother,
From sunshine to the sunless land!

In these lines is reflected the sorrowful spirit of a literary man of the early nineteenth century who remembered the glory that had passed away from the earth. But the leanness of these first years is more apparent than real. Keats and Shelley were dead, it is true, but already there had appeared three disciples of these poets who were destined to be far more widely, read than were their masters. Tennyson had been publishing poetry since 1827, his first poems appearing almost simultaneously with the last work of Byron, Shelley, and Keats; but it was not until 1842, with the publication of his collected poems, in two volumes, that England recognized in him one of her great literary leaders. So also Elizabeth Barrett had been writing since 1820, but not till twenty years later did her poems become deservedly popular; and Browning had published his Pauline in 1833, but it was not until 1846, when he published the last of the series called Bells and Pomegranates, that the reading public began to appreciate his power and originality. Moreover, even as romanticism seemed passing away, a group of great prose writers--Dickens, Thackeray, Carlyle, and Ruskin--had already begun to proclaim the literary glory of a new age, which now seems to rank only just below the Elizabethan and the Romantic periods.

HISTORICAL SUMMARY

Amid the multitude of social and political forces of this great age, four things stand out clearly. First, the long struggle of the Anglo-Saxons for personal liberty is definitely settled, and democracy becomes the established order of the day. The king, who appeared in an age of popular weakness and ignorance, and the peers, who came with the Normans in triumph, are both stripped of their power and left as figureheads of a past civilization. The last vestige of personal government and of the divine right of rulers disappears; the House of Commons becomes the ruling power in England; and a series of new reform bills rapidly extend the suffrage, until the whole body of English people choose for themselves the men who shall represent them.

Second, because it is an age of democracy, it is an age of popular education, of religious tolerance, of growing brotherhood, and of profound social unrest. The slaves had been freed in 1833; but in the middle of the century England awoke to the fact that slaves are not necessarily negroes, stolen in Africa to be sold like cattle in the market place, but that multitudes of men, women, and little children in the mines and factories were victims of a more terrible industrial and social slavery. To free these slaves also, the unwilling victims of our unnatural competitive methods, has been the growing purpose of the Victorian Age until the present day.

Third, because it is an age of democracy and education, it is an age of comparative peace. England begins to think less of the pomp and false glitter of fighting, and more of its moral evils, as the nation realizes that it is the common people who bear the burden and the sorrow and the poverty of war, while the privileged classes reap most of the financial and political rewards. Moreover, with the growth of trade and of friendly foreign relations, it becomes evident that the social equality for which England was contending at home belongs to the whole race of men; that brotherhood is universal, not insular; that a question of justice is never settled by fighting; and that war is generally unmitigated horror and barbarism. Tennyson, who came of age when the great Reform Bill occupied attention, expresses the ideals of the Liberals of his day who proposed to spread the gospel of peace,

Till the war-drum throbb'd no longer, and the battle-flags were furled
In the Parliament of Man, the Federation of the world.

Fourth, the Victorian Age is especially remarkable because of its rapid progress in all the arts and sciences and in mechanical inventions. A glance at any record of the industrial achievements of the nineteenth century will show how vast they are, and it is unnecessary to repeat here the list of the inventions, from spinning looms to steamboats, and from matches to electric lights. All these material things, as well as the growth of education, have their influence upon the life of a people, and it is inevitable that they should react upon its prose and poetry; though as yet we are too much absorbed in our sciences and mechanics to determine accurately their influence upon literature. When these new things shall by long use have became familiar as country roads, or have been replaced by newer and better things, then they also will have their associations and memories, and a poem on the railroads may be as suggestive as Wordsworth's sonnet on Westminster Bridge; and the busy, practical workingmen who to-day throng our streets and factories may seem, to a future and greater age, as quaint and poetical as to us seem the slow toilers of the Middle Ages.

LITERARY CHARACTERISTICS

When one is interested enough to trace the genealogy of Victoria he finds, to his surprise, that in her veins flowed the blood both of William the Conqueror and of Cerdic, the first Saxon king of England; and this seems to be symbolic of the literature of her age, which embraces the whole realm of Saxon and Norman life,--the strength and ideals of the one, and the culture and refinement of the other. The romantic revival had done its work, and England entered upon a new free period, in which every form of literature, from pure romance to gross realism, struggled for expression. At this day it is obviously impossible to judge the age as a whole; but we are getting far enough away from the early half of it to notice certain definite characteristics. First, though the age produced many poets, and two who deserve to rank among the greatest, nevertheless this is emphatically an age of prose. And since the number of readers has increased a thousandfold with the spread of popular education, it is the age of the newspaper, the magazine, and the modern novel,--the first two being the story of the world's daily life, and the last our pleasantest form of literary entertainment, as well as our most successful method of presenting modern problems and modern ideals.

The novel in this age fills a place which the drama held in the days of Elizabeth; and never before, in any age or language, has the novel appeared in such numbers and in such perfection.

Moral Purpose

The second marked characteristic of the age is that literature, both in prose and in poetry, seems to depart from the purely artistic standard, of art for art's sake, and to be actuated by a definite moral purpose Tennyson,

Browning, Carlyle, Ruskin,--who and what were these men if not the teachers of England, not vaguely but definitely, with superb faith in their message, and with the conscious moral purpose to uplift and to instruct? Even the novel breaks away from Scott's romantic influence, and first studies life as it is, and then points out what life may and ought to be. Whether we read the fun and sentiment of Dickens, the social miniatures of Thackeray, or the psychological studies of George Eliot, we find in almost every case a definite purpose to sweep away error and to reveal the underlying truth of human life. So the novel sought to do for society in this age precisely what Lyell and Darwin sought to do for science, that is, to find the truth, and to show how it might be used to uplift humanity. Perhaps for this reason the Victorian Age is emphatically an age of realism rather than of romance,--not the realism of Zola and Ibsen, but a deeper realism which strives to tell the whole truth, showing moral and physical diseases as they are, but holding up health and hope as the normal conditions of humanity.

It is somewhat customary to speak of this age as an age of doubt and pessimism, following the new conception of man and of the universe which was formulated by science under the name of involution. It is spoken of also as a prosaic age, lacking in great ideals.

Both these criticisms seem to be the result of judging a large thing when we are too close to it to get its true proportions, just as Cologne Cathedral, one of the world's most perfect structures, seems to be a shapeless pile of stone when we stand too close beneath its mighty walls and buttresses. Tennyson's immature work, like that of the minor poets, is sometimes in a doubtful or despairing strain; but his In Memoriam is like the rainbow after storm; and Browning seems better to express the spirit of his age in the strong, manly faith of "Rabbi Ben Ezra," and in the courageous optimism of all his poetry. Stedman's Victorian Anthology is, on the whole, a most inspiring book of poetry. It would be hard to collect more varied cheer from any age. And the great essayists, like Macaulay, Carlyle, Ruskin, and the great novelists, like Dickens, Thackeray, George Eliot, generally leave us with a larger charity and with a deeper faith in our humanity.

So also the judgment that this age is too practical for great ideals may be only a description of the husk that hides a very full ear of corn. It is well to remember that Spenser and Sidney judged their own age (which we now consider to be the greatest in our literary history) to be altogether given over to materialism, and to be incapable of literary greatness. Just as time has made us smile at their blindness, so the next century may correct our judgment of this as a material age, and looking upon the enormous growth of charity and brotherhood among us, and at the literature which expresses our faith in men, may judge the Victorian Age to be, on the whole, the noblest and most inspiring in the history of the world.

OTHER VICTORIA POETS

Among the other Victorian poets, three, at least, must be mentioned. Arthur Hugh Clough (1819-1861), tutor at Oxford and later examiner in the government education office, expresses the spiritual doubt and struggle of the period in noble poems similar to those of Matthew Arnold, whose fine elegy 'Thyrsis' commemorates him. Edward Fitzgerald (1809-1883), Irish by birth, an eccentric though kind-hearted recluse, and a friend of Tennyson, is known solely for his masterly paraphrase (1859) of some of the Quatrains of the skeptical eleventh-century Persian astronomer-poet Omar Khayyam. The similarity of temper between the medieval oriental scholar and the questioning phase of the Victorian period is striking (though the spirit of Fitzgerald's verse is no doubt as much his own as Omar's), and no poetry is more poignantly beautiful than the best of this.

Christina Rossetti (1830-94), the sister of Dante Gabriel Rossetti, lived in London with her mother in the greatest seclusion, occupied with an ascetic devotion to the English Church, with her poetry, and with the composition, secondarily, of prose articles and short stories. Her poetry is limited almost entirely to the lyrical expression of her spiritual experiences, much of it is explicitly religious, and all of it is religious in feeling. It is tinged with the Pre-Raphaelite mystic medievalism; and a quiet and most affecting sadness is its dominant trait; but the power and beauty of a certain small part of it perhaps entitle her to be called the chief of English poetesses.

THE EARLIER SECONDARY NOVELISTS

To Scott's position of unquestioned supremacy among romancers and novelists Charles Dickens succeeded almost immediately on Scott's death, but certain secondary early Victorian novelists may be considered before him. In the lives of two of these, Bulwer-Lytton and Benjamin Disraeli, there are interesting parallels. Both were prominent in politics, both began writing as young men before the commencement of the Victorian period, and both ended their literary work only fifty years later. Edward Bulwer, later created Sir Edward Bulwer-Lytton, and finally raised to the peerage as Lord Lytton (1803-1873), was almost incredibly fluent and versatile. Much of his life a member of Parliament and for a while of the government, he was a vigorous pamphleteer.

His sixty or more really literary works are of great variety; perhaps the best known of them are his second novel, the trifling 'Pelham' (1828), which inaugurated a class of so-called 'dandy' novels, giving sympathetic presentation to the more frivolous social life of the 'upper' class, and the historical romances 'The Last Days of Pompeii' (1834) and 'Harold' (1843). In spite of his real ability, Bulwer was a poser and sentimentalist, characteristics for which he was vigorously ridiculed by Thackeray.

Benjamin Disraeli, later Earl of Beaconsfield (1804-1881), a much less prolific writer, was by birth a Jew. His immature earliest novel, 'Vivian Grey' (1826), deals, somewhat more sensibly, with the same social class as Bulwer's 'Pelham.' In his novels of this period, as in his dress and manner, he deliberately attitudinized, a fact which in part reflected a certain shallowness of character, in part was a device to attract attention for the sake of his political ambition. After winning his way into Parliament he wrote in 1844-7 three political novels,' Coningsby,' 'Sybil,' and 'Tancred,' which set forth his Tory creed of opposition to the dominance of middle-class Liberalism. For twenty-five years after this he was absorbed in the leadership of his party, and he at last became Prime Minister. In later life he so far returned to literature as to write two additional novels.

Vastly different was the life and work of Charlotte Bronte (1816-1855). Miss Bronte, a product and embodiment of the strictest religious sense of duty, somewhat tempered by the liberalizing tendency of the time, was the daughter of the rector of a small and bleak Yorkshire village, Haworth, where she was brought up in poverty. The two of her sisters who reached maturity, Emily and Anne, both still more short-lived than she, also wrote novels, and Emily produced some lyrics which strikingly express the stern, defiant will that characterized all the children of the family. Their lives were pitifully bare, hard, and morbid, scarcely varied or enlivened except by a year which Charlotte and Emily spent when Charlotte was twenty-six in a private school in Brussels, followed on Charlotte's part by a return to the same school for a year as teacher. In 1847 Charlotte's novel 'Jane Eyre' (pronounced like the word 'air') won a great success. Her three later novels are less significant. In 1854 she was married to one of her father's curates, a Mr. Nicholls, a sincere but narrow-minded man. She was happy in the marriage, but died within a few months, worn out by the unremitting physical and moral strain of forty years.

The significance of 'Jane Eyre' can be suggested by calling it the last striking expression of extravagant Romanticism, partly Byronic, but grafted on the stern Bronte moral sense. One of its two main theses is the assertion of the supreme authority of religious duty, but it vehemently insists also on the right of the individual conscience to judge of duty for itself, in spite of conventional opinion, and, difficult as this may be to understand to-day, it was denounced at the time as irreligious. The Romanticism appears further in the volcanic but sometimes melodramatic power of the love story, where the heroine is a somewhat idealized double of the authoress and where the imperfect portrayal of the hero reflects the limitations of Miss Bronte's own experience.

Miss Bronte is the subject of one of the most delightfully sympathetic of all biographies, written by Mrs. Elizabeth Cleghorn Gaskell. Mrs. Gaskell was authoress also of many stories, long and short, of which the best known is 'Cranford' (1853), a charming portrayal of the quaint life of a secluded village.

WILLIAM M. THACKERAY

Dickens' chief rival for fame during his later lifetime and afterward was Thackeray, who presents a strong contrast with him, both as man and as writer.

Thackeray, the son of an East India Company official, was born at Calcutta in 1811. His father died while he was a child and he was taken to England for his education; he was a student in the Charterhouse School and then for a year at Cambridge. Next, on the Continent, he studied drawing, and though his unmethodical and somewhat idle habits prevented him from ever really mastering the technique of the art, his real knack for it enabled him later on to illustrate his own books in a semi-grotesque but effective fashion. Desultory study of the law was interrupted when he came of age by the inheritance of a comfortable fortune, which he managed to lose within a year or two by gambling, speculations, and an unsuccessful effort at carrying on a newspaper. Real application to newspaper and magazine writing secured him after four years a place on 'Eraser's Magazine,' and he was married. Not long after, his wife became insane, but his warm affection for his daughters gave him throughout his life genuine domestic happiness.

For ten years Thackeray's production was mainly in the line of satirical humorous and picaresque fiction, none of it of the first rank. During this period he chiefly attacked current vices, snobbishness, and sentimentality, which latter quality, Thackeray's special aversion, he found rampant in contemporary life and literature, including the novels of Dickens. The appearance of his masterpiece, 'Vanity Fair' (the allegorical title taken from a famous incident in 'Pilgrim's Progress'), in 'Fraser's Magazine' in 1847-8 (the year before Dickens' 'David Copperfield') brought him sudden fame and made him a social lion. Within the next ten years he produced his other important novels, of which the best are 'Pendennis,' 'Henry Esmond,' and 'The Newcomes,' and also his charming essays (first delivered as lectures) on the eighteenth century in England, namely 'English Humorists,' and 'The Four Georges.' All his novels except 'Henry Esmond' were published serially, and he generally delayed composing each instalment until the latest possible moment, working reluctantly except under the stress of immediate compulsion. He was for three years, at its commencement, editor of 'The Cornhill Magazine.' He died in 1863 at the age of fifty-two, of heart failure.

The great contrast between Dickens and Thackeray results chiefly from the predominance in Thackeray of the critical intellectual quality and of the somewhat fastidious instinct of the man of society and of the world which Dickens so conspicuously lacked. As a man Thackeray was at home and at ease only among people of formal good breeding; he shrank from direct contact with the common people; in spite of his assaults on the frivolity and vice of fashionable society, he was fond of it; his spirit was very keenly analytical; and he would have been chagrined by nothing more than by seeming to allow his emotion to get the better of his judgment.

His novels seem to many readers cynical, because he scrutinizes almost every character and every group with impartial vigor, dragging forth every fault and every weakness into the light. On the title page of 'Vanity Fair' he proclaims that it is a novel without a hero; and here, as in some of his lesser works, most of the characters are either altogether bad or worthless and the others very largely weak or absurd, so that the impression of human life which the reader apparently ought to carry away is that of a hopeless chaos of selfishness, hypocrisy, and futility. One word, which has often been applied to Thackeray, best expresses his attitude--disillusionment. The last sentences of 'Vanity Fair' are characteristic: 'Oh! Vanitas Vanitatum! which, of us is happy in this world? Which of us has his desire? or, having it, is satisfied?--Come, children, let us shut the box and the puppets, for our play is played out.'

Yet in reality Thackeray is not a cynic and the permanent impression left by his books is not pessimistic. Beneath his somewhat ostentatious manner of the man of the world were hidden a heart and a human sympathy as warm as ever belonged to any man. However he may ridicule his heroes and his heroines (and there really are a hero and heroine in 'Vanity Fair'), he really feels deeply for them, and he is repeatedly unable to refrain from the expression of his feeling. Nothing is more truly characteristic of him than the famous incident of his rushing in tears from the room in which he had been writing of the death of Colonel Newcome with the exclamation, 'I have killed the Colonel!'

In his books as clearly as in those of the most explicit moralizer the reader finds the lessons that simple courage, honesty, kindliness, and unselfishness are far better than external show, and that in spite of all its brilliant interest a career of unprincipled self-seeking like that of Becky Sharp is morally squalid.

Thackeray steadily refuses to falsify life as he sees it in the interest of any deliberate theory, but he is too genuine an artist not to be true to the moral principles which form so large a part of the substratum of all life.

Thackeray avowedly took Fielding as his model, and though his spirit and manner are decidedly finer than Fielding's, the general resemblance between them is often close. Fielding's influence shows partly in the humorous tone which, in one degree or another, Thackeray preserves wherever it is possible, and in the general refusal to take his art, on the surface, with entire seriousness.

He insists, for instance, on his right to manage his story, and conduct the reader, as he pleases, without deferring to his readers' tastes or prejudices. Fielding's influence shows also in the free-and-easy picaresque structure of his plots; though this results also in part from his desultory method of composition. Thackeray's great fault is prolixity; he sometimes wanders on through rather uninspired page after page where the reader longs for severe compression.

But when the story reaches dramatic moments there is ample compensation; no novelist has more magnificent power in dramatic scenes, such, for instance, as in the climactic series in 'Vanity Fair.' This power is based largely on an absolute knowledge of character: in spite of a delight in somewhat fanciful exaggeration of the ludicrous, Thackeray when he chooses portrays human nature with absolute finality.

'Henry Esmond' should be spoken of by itself as a special and unique achievement. It is a historical novel dealing with the early eighteenth century, and in preparing for it Thackeray read and assimilated most of the literature of the period, with the result that he succeeded in reproducing the 'Augustan' spirit and even its literary style with an approach to perfection that has never been rivaled. On other grounds as well the book ranks almost if not quite beside 'Vanity Pair.' Henry Esmond himself is Thackeray's most thoroughly wise and good character, and Beatrix is as real and complex a woman as even Becky Sharp.

SECONDARY MIDDLE AND LATER VICTORIAN NOVELISTS

Several of the other novelists of the mid-century and later produced work which in a period of less prolific and less highly developed art would have secured them high distinction. Charles Kingsley (1819-1875) spent most of his life, by his own self-renouncing choice, as curate and rector of the little Hampshire parish of Eversley, though for some years he also held the professorship of history at Cambridge. An aggressive Protestant, he drifted in his later years into the controversy with Cardinal Newman which opened the way for Newman's 'Apologia.' From the outset, Kingsley was an enthusiastic worker with F. D. Maurice in the Christian Socialist movement which aimed at the betterment of the conditions of life among the working classes.

'Alton Locke' and 'Yeast,' published in 1849, were powerful but reasonable and very influential expressions of his convictions--fervid arguments in the form of fiction against existing social injustices. His most famous books are 'Hypatia' (1853), a novel dealing with the Church in its conflict with Greek philosophy in fifth-century Alexandria, and 'Westward Ho!' (1855) which presents with sympathetic largeness of manner the adventurous side of Elizabethan life. His brief 'Andromeda' is one of the best English poems in the classical dactylic hexameter.

Charles Reade (1814-1884), a man of dramatic disposition somewhat similar to that of Dickens (though Reade had a University education and was admitted to the bar), divided his interest and fiery energies between the drama and the novel. But while his plays were of such doubtful quality that he generally had to pay for having them acted, his novels were often strong and successful. Personally he was fervently evangelical, and like Dickens he was often inspired to write by indignation at social wrongs.

His 'Hard Cash' (1863), which attacks private insane asylums, is powerful; but his most important work is 'The Cloister and the Hearth' (1861), one of the most informing and vivid of all historical novels, with the father of Erasmus for its hero. No novelist can, be more thrilling and picturesque than Reade, but he lacks restraint and is often highly sensational and melodramatic.

Altogether different is the method of Anthony Trollope (1815-1882) in his fifty novels. Trollope, long a traveling employe in the post-office service, was a man of very assertive and somewhat commonplace nature.

Partly a disciple of Thackeray, he went beyond Thackeray's example in the refusal to take his art altogether seriously as an art; rather, he treated it as a form of business, sneering at the idea of special inspiration, and holding himself rigidly to a mechanical schedule of composition--a definite and unvarying number of pages in a specified number of hours on each of his working days. The result is not so disastrous as might have been expected; his novels have no small degree of truth and interest.

The most notable are the half dozen which deal with ecclesiastical life in his imaginary county of Barsetshire, beginning with 'The Warden' and 'Barchester Towers.' His 'Autobiography' furnishes in some of its chapters one of the noteworthy existing discussions of the writer's art by a member of the profession.

Richard Blackmore (1825-1900), first a lawyer, later manager of a market-garden, was the author of numerous novels, but will be remembered only for 'Lorna Doone' (1869), a charming reproduction of Devonshire country life assigned to the romantic setting of the time of James II. Its simple-minded and gigantic hero John Ridd is certainly one of the permanent figures of English fiction.

Joseph H. Shorthouse (1834-1903), a Birmingham chemical manufacturer, but a man of very fine nature, is likewise to be mentioned for a single book, 'John Inglesant' (1881). Located in the middle of the seventeenth century, when the strife of religious and political parties afforded material especially available for the author's purpose, this is a spiritual romance, a High Churchman's assertion of the supremacy of the inner over the outer life. From this point of view it is one of the most significant of English novels, and though much of it is philosophical and though it is not free from technical faults, parts of it attain the extreme limit of absorbing narrative interest.

Walter Pater (1839-1894), an Oxford Fellow, also represents distinctly the spirit of unworldliness, which in his case led to a personal aloofness from active life. He was the master of a delicately-finished, somewhat over-fastidious, style, which he employed in essays on the Renaissance and other historical and artistic topics and in a spiritual romance, 'Marius the Epicurean' (1885). No less noteworthy than 'John Inglesant,' and better constructed, this latter is placed in the reign of the Roman Emperor Marcus Aurelius, but its atmosphere is only in part historically authentic.

GEORGE MEREDITH (1828-1910)

Except for a lack of the elements which make for popularity, George Meredith would hold an unquestioned place in the highest rank of novelists. In time he is partly contemporary with George Eliot, as he began to publish a little earlier than she. But he long outlived her and continued to write to the end of his life; and his recognition was long delayed; so that he may properly be placed in the group of later Victorian novelists. His long life was devoid of external incident; he was long a newspaper writer and afterward literary reader for a publishing house; he spent his later years quietly in Surrey, enjoying the friendship of Swinburne and other men of letters.

Among novelists he occupies something the same place which Browning, a person of very different temperament and ideas, holds among poets. He writes only for intelligent and thoughtful people and aims to interpret the deeper things of life and character, not disregarding dramatic external incident, but using it as only one of the means to his main purpose. His style is brilliant, epigrammatic, and subtile; and he prefers to imply many things rather than to state them directly. All this makes large, perhaps sometimes too large, demands on the reader's attention, but there is, of course, corresponding stimulation. Meredith's general attitude toward life is the fine one of serene philosophic confidence, the attitude in general of men like Shakspere and Goethe.

He despises sentimentality, admires chiefly the qualities of quiet strength and good breeding which are exemplified among the best members of the English aristocracy; and in all his interpretation is very largely influenced by modern science. His virile courage and optimism are as pronounced as those of Browning; he wrote a noteworthy 'Essay on Comedy' and oftentimes insists on emphasizing the comic rather than the tragic aspect of things, though he can also be powerful in tragedy; and his enthusiasms for the beauty of the world and for the romance of youthful love are delightful. He may perhaps best be approached through 'Evan Harrington' (1861) and 'The Ordeal of Richard Feverel' (1859). 'The Egoist' (1879) and 'Diana of the Crossways' (1885) are among his other strongest books. In his earlier years he wrote a considerable body of verse, which shows much the same qualities as his prose. Some of it is rugged in form, but other parts magnificently dramatic, and some few poems, like the unique and superb 'Love in the Valley,' charmingly beautiful.

RUDYARD KIPLING

The name which naturally closes the list of Victorian writers is that of Rudyard Kipling, though he belongs, perhaps, as much to the twentieth century as to the one preceding. The son of a professor of architecture and sculpture in the University of Bombay, India, he was born in that city in 1865. Educated in England in the United Services College (for officers in the army and navy), he returned at the age of seventeen to India, where he first did strenuous editorial work on newspapers in Lahore, in the extreme northwestern part of the country.

He secured his intimate knowledge of the English army by living, through the permission of the commanding general, with the army on the frontiers. His instinct for story-telling in verse and prose had showed itself from his boyhood, but his first significant appearance in print was in 1886, with a volume of poems later included among the 'Departmental Ditties.' 'Plain Tales from the Hills' in prose, and other works, followed in rapid succession and won him enthusiastic recognition. In 1890 he removed to the United States, where he married and remained for seven years. Since then he has lived in England, with an interval in South Africa. He wrote prolifically during the '90's; since then both the amount of his production and its quality have fallen off.

Kipling is the representative of the vigorous life of action as led by manly and efficient men, and of the spirit of English imperialism. His poem "The White Man's Burden" sums up his imperialism--the creed that it is the duty of the higher races to civilize the lower ones with a strong hand; and he never doubts that the greater part of this obligation rests at present upon England--a theory, certainly, to which history lends much support. Kipling is endowed with the keenest power of observation, with the most genuine and most democratic human sympathies, and with splendid dramatic force.

Consequently he has made a unique contribution to literature in his portrayals, in both prose and verse, of the English common soldier and of English army life on the frontiers of the Empire. On the other hand his verse is generally altogether devoid of the finer qualities of poetry. 'Danny Deever,' 'Pharaoh and the Sergeant,' 'Fuzzy Wuzzy,' 'The Ballad of East and West,' 'The Last Chantey,' 'Mulholland's Contract,' and many others, are splendidly stirring, but their colloquialism and general realism put them on a very different level from the work of the great masters who express the deeper truths in forms of permanent beauty.

At times, however, Kipling too gives voice to religious feelings, of a simple sort, in an impressive fashion, as in 'McAndrews' Hymn,' 'The Recessional,' and 'When earth's last picture is painted.' His sweeping rhythms and his grandiose forms of expression, suggestive of the vast spaces of ocean and plain and of inter-stellar space with which he delights to deal, have been very widely copied by minor verse-writers.

His very vivid and active imagination enables him not only to humanize animal life with remarkable success, as in the prose 'Jungle-Books,' but to range finely in the realms of the mysterious, as in the short stories 'They' and 'The Brushwood Boy.' Of short-stories he is the most powerful recent writer, as witness 'The Man Who Would Be King,' 'The Man Who Was,' 'Without Benefit of Clergy,' and 'Wee Willie Winkie'; though with all the frankness of modern realism he sometimes leads us into scenes of extreme physical horror. With longer stories he is generally less successful; 'Kim,' however, has much power.

THE HISTORIANS

The present book, as a brief sketch of English Literature rather strictly defined, has necessarily disregarded the scientists, economists, and philosophers whose writings did much to mold the course of thought during the Victorian period. Among the numerous prominent historians, however, two must be mentioned for the brilliant literary quality of their work.

James Anthony Froude (1818-1894) was a disciple of Carlyle, from whom he took the idea of making history center around its great men and of giving to it the vivid effectiveness of the drama.

With Froude too this results in exaggeration, and further he is sadly inaccurate, but his books are splendidly fascinating. His great 'History of England from the Fall of Wolsey to the Armada' is his longest work; his 'Sketch' of Julius Casar is certainly one of the most interesting books of biography and history ever written. John Richard Green (1837-1883), who was a devoted clergyman before he became a historian, struggled all his life against the ill-health which finally cut short his career.

His 'History of the English People' is an admirable representative of the modern historical spirit, which treats general social conditions as more important than mere external events; but as a narrative it vies in interest with the very different one of Macaulay. Very honorable mention should be made also of W. E. H. Lecky, who belongs to the conscientiously scientific historical school. His 'History of Rationalism in Europe,' for example, is a very fine monument of the most thorough research and most effective statement; but to a mature mind its interest is equally conspicuous.

THE TWENTIETH CENTURY

Beginning as early as the latter part of the eighteenth century literary production, thanks largely to the tremendous increase of education and of newspapers and magazines, has steadily grown, until now it has reached be wildering volume and complexity, in which the old principles are partly merged together and the new tendencies, for contemporary observers, at least, scarcely stand out with decisive distinctness.

Most significant to-day, perhaps, are the spirit of independence, now carried in some respects beyond the farthest previous Romantic limits, and the realistic impulse, in which the former impulses of democracy and humanitarianism play a large part.

Facts not to be disregarded are the steady advance of the short story, beginning early in the Victorian period or before, to a position of almost chief prominence with the novel; and the rise of American literature to a position approaching equality with that of England. Of single authors none have yet certainly achieved places of the first rank, but two or three may be named.

Mr. William De Morgan, by profession a manufacturer of artistic pottery, has astonished the world by beginning to publish at the age of sixty-five a series of novels which show no small amount of Thackeray's power combined with too large a share of Thackeray's diffuseness. Mr. Alfred Noyes (born 1880) is a refreshingly true lyric poet and balladist, and Mr. John Masefield has daringly enlarged the field of poetry by frank but very sincere treatment of extremely realistic subjects. But none of these authors can yet be termed great. About the future it is useless to prophesy, but the horrible war of 1914 is certain to exert for many years a controlling influence on the thought and literature of both England and the whole world, an influence which, it may be hoped, will ultimately prove stimulating and renovating.

Whatever may be true of the future, the record of the past is complete. No intelligent person can give even hasty study to the fourteen existing centuries of English Literature without being deeply impressed by its range and power, or without coming to realize that it stands conspicuous as one of the noblest and fullest achievements of the human race.

THE POETS OF THE VICTORIAN AGE—ALFRED TENNYSON (1809-1892)

O young Mariner,
You from the haven
Under the sea-cliff,
You that are watching
The gray Magician
With eyes of wonder,
I am Merlin,
And I am dying,
I am Merlin

Who follow The Gleam.

....

O young Mariner,
Down to the haven
Call your companions,
Launch your vessel,
And crowd your canvas,
And, ere it vanishes
Over the margin,
After it, follow it,
Follow The Gleam.

One who reads this haunting poem of "Merlin and The Gleam" finds in it a suggestion of the spirit of the poet's whole life,--his devotion to the ideal as expressed in poetry, his early romantic impressions, his struggles, doubts, triumphs, and his thrilling message to his race.

Throughout the entire Victorian period Tennyson stood at the summit of poetry in England. Not in vain was he appointed laureate at the death of Wordsworth, in 1850; for, almost alone among those who have held the office, he felt the importance of his place, and filled and honored it.

For nearly half a century Tennyson was not only a man and a poet; he was a voice, the voice of a whole people, expressing in exquisite melody their doubts and their faith, their griefs and their triumphs. In the wonderful variety of his verse he suggests all the qualities of England's greatest poets.

The dreaminess of Spenser, the majesty of Milton, the natural simplicity of Wordsworth, the fantasy of Blake and Coleridge, the melody of Keats and Shelley, the narrative vigor of Scott and Byron,--all these striking qualities are evident on successive pages of Tennyson's poetry. The only thing lacking is the dramatic power of the Elizabethans. In reflecting the restless spirit of this progressive age Tennyson is as remarkable as Pope was in voicing the artificiality of the early eighteenth century. As a poet, therefore, who expresses not so much a personal as a national spirit, he is probably the most representative literary man of the Victorian era.

Works

At the outset of our study of Tennyson's works it may be well to record two things, by way of suggestion. First, Tennyson's poetry is not so much to be studied as to be read and appreciated; he is a poet to have open on one's table, and to enjoy as one enjoys his daily exercise. And second, we should by all means begin to get acquainted with Tennyson in the days of our youth. Unlike Browning, who is generally appreciated by more mature minds, Tennyson is for enjoyment, for inspiration, rather than for instruction. Only youth can fully appreciate him; and youth, unfortunately, except in a few rare, beautiful cases, is something which does not dwell with us long after our school days. The secret of poetry, especially of Tennyson's poetry, is to be eternally young, and, like Adam in Paradise, to find every morning a new world, fresh, wonderful, inspiring, as if just from the hands of God.

Except by the student, eager to understand the whoje range of poetry in this age, Tennyson's earlier poems and his later dramas may well be omitted. Opinions vary about both; but the general judgment seems to be that the earlier poems show too much of Byron's influence, and their crudeness suffers by comparison with the exquisitely finished work of Tennyson's middle life. Of dramatic works he wrote seven, his great ambition being to present a large part of the history of England in a series of dramas. Becket was one of the best of these works and met with considerable favor on the stage; but, like all the others, it indicates that Tennyson lacked the dramatic power and the humor necessary for a successful playwright.

Among the remaining poems there is such a wide variety that every reader must be left largely to follow his own delightful choice. Of the Poems of 1842 we have already mentioned those best worth reading. The Princess, a Medley (1847), a long poem of over three thousand lines of blank verse, is Tennyson's answer to the question of woman's rights and woman's sphere, which was then, as in our own day, strongly agitating the public mind. In this poem a baby finally solves the problem which philosophers have pondered ever since men began to think connectedly about human society. A few exquisite songs, like "Tears, Idle Tears," "Bugle Song," and "Sweet and Low," form the most delightful part of this poem, which in general is hardly up to the standard of the poet's later work. Maud (1855) is what is called in literature a monodrama, telling the story of a lover who passes from morbidness to ecstasy, then to anger and murder, followed by insanity and recovery. This was Tennyson's favorite, and among his friends he read aloud from it more than from any other poem. Perhaps if we could hear Tennyson read it, we should appreciate it better; but, on the whole, it seems overwrought and melodramatic. Even its lyrics, like "Come into the Garden, Maud," which make this work a favorite with young lovers, are characterized by "prettiness" rather than by beauty or strength.

Perhaps the most loved of all Tennyson's works is In Memoriam, which, on account of both its theme and its exquisite workmanship, is "one of the few immortal names that were not born to die." The immediate occasion of this remarkable poem was Tennyson's profound personal grief at the death of his friend Hallam. As he wrote lyric after lyric, inspired by this sad subject, the poet's grief became less personal, and the greater grief of humanity mourning for its dead and questioning its immortality took possession of him. Gradually the poem became an expression, first, of universal doubt, and then of universal faith, a faith which rests ultimately not on reason or philosophy but on the soul's instinct for immortality.

The immortality of human love is the theme of the poem, which is made up of over one hundred different lyrics. The movement takes us through three years, rising slowly from poignant sorrow and doubt to a calm peace and hope, and ending with a noble hymn of courage and faith,--a modest courage and a humble faith, love-inspired,--which will be a favorite as long as saddened men turn to literature for consolation. Though Darwin's greatest books had not yet been written, science had already overturned many old conceptions of life; and Tennyson, who lived apart and thought deeply on all the problems of his day, gave this poem to the world as his own answer to the doubts and questionings of men. This universal human interest, together with its exquisite form and melody, makes the poem, in popular favor at least, the supreme threnody, or elegiac poem, of our literature; though Milton's Lycidas is, from the critical view point, undoubtedly a more artistic work.

The Idylls of the King ranks among the greatest of Tennyson's later works. Its general subject is the Celtic legends of King Arthur and his knights of the Round Table, and the chief source of its material is Malory's Morte d'Arthur. Here, in this mass of beautiful legends, is certainly the subject of a great national epic; yet after four hundred years, during which many poets have used the material, the great epic is still unwritten. Milton and Spenser, as we have already noted, considered this material carefully; and Milton alone, of all English writers, had perhaps the power to use it in a great epic. Tennyson began to use these legends in his Morte d'Arthur (1842); but the epic idea probably occurred to him later, in 1856, when he began "Geraint and Enid," and he added the stories of "Vivien," "Elaine," "Guinevere," and other heroes and heroines at intervals, until "Balin," the last of the Idylls, appeared in 1885. Later these works were gathered together and arranged with an attempt at unity. The result is in no sense an epic poem, but rather a series of single poems loosely connected by a thread of interest in Arthur, the central personage, and in his unsuccessful attempt to found an ideal kingdom.

Entirely different in spirit is another collection of poems called English Idyls,[236] which began in the Poems of 1842, and which Tennyson intended should reflect the ideals of widely different types of English life. Of these varied poems, "Dora," "The Gardener's Daughter," "Ulysses," "Locksley Hall" and "Sir Galahad" are the best; but all are worthy of study. One of the most famous of this series is "Enoch Arden" (1864), in which Tennyson turns from mediaeval knights, from lords, heroes, and fair ladies, to find the material for true poetry among the lowly people that make up the bulk of English life. Its rare melody, its sympathy for common life, and its revelation of the beauty and heroism which hide in humble men and women everywhere, made this work an instant favorite. Judged by its sales alone, it was the most popular of his works during the poet's lifetime.

Tennyson's later volumes, like the Ballads (1880) and Demeter (1889), should not be overlooked, since they contain some of his best work. The former contains stirring war songs, like "The Defence of Lucknow," and pictures of wild passionate grief, like "Rizpah"; the latter is notable for "Romney's Remorse," a wonderful piece of work; "Merlin and The Gleam," which expresses the poet's lifelong ideal; and several exquisite little songs, like "The Throstle," and "The Oak," which show how marvelously the aged poet retained his youthful freshness and inspiration. Here certainly is variety enough to give us long years of literary enjoyment; and we need hardly mention miscellaneous poems, like "The Brook" and "The Charge of the Light Brigade," which are known to every schoolboy; and "Wages" and "The Higher Pantheism," which should be read by every man who thinks about the old, old problem of life and death.

Characteristics Of Tennyson's Poetry

If we attempt to sum up the quality of Tennyson, as shown in all these works, the task is a difficult one; but three things stand out more or less plainly. First, Tennyson is essentially the artist. No other in his age studied the art of poetry so constantly or with such singleness of purpose; and only Swinburne rivals him in melody and the perfect finish of his verse. Second, like all the great writers of his age, he is emphatically a teacher, often a leader. In the preceding age, as the result of the turmoil produced by the French Revolution, lawlessness was more or less common, and individuality was the rule in literature. Tennyson's theme, so characteristic of his age, is the reign of order,--of law in the physical world, producing evolution, and of law in the spiritual world, working out the perfect man. In Memoriam, Idylls of the King, The Princess,-here are three widely different poems; yet the theme of each, so far as poetry is a kind of spiritual philosophy and weighs its words before it utters them, is the orderly development of law in the natural and in the spiritual world. This certainly is a new doctrine in poetry, but the message does not end here. Law implies a source, a method, an object. Tennyson, after facing his doubts honestly and manfully, finds law even in the sorrows and losses of humanity. He gives this law an infinite and personal source, and finds the supreme purpose of all law to be a revelation of divine love. All earthly love, therefore, becomes an image of the heavenly. What first perhaps attracted readers to Tennyson, as to Shakespeare, was the character of his women,--pure, gentle, refined beings, whom we must revere as our Anglo- Saxon forefathers revered the women they loved. Like Browning, the poet had loved one good woman supremely, and her love made clear the meaning of all life. The message goes one step farther. Because law and love are in the world, faith is the only reasonable attitude toward life and death, even though we understand them not. Such, in a few words, seems to be Tennyson's whole message and philosophy.

If we attempt now to fix Tennyson's permanent place in literature, as the result of his life and work, we must apply to him the same test that we applied to Milton and Wordsworth, and, indeed, to all our great poets, and ask with the German critics, "What new thing has he said to the world or even to his own country?" The answer is, frankly, that we do not yet know surely; that we are still too near Tennyson to judge him impersonally. This much, however, is clear. In a marvelously complex age, and amid a hundred great men, he was regarded as a leader. For a full half century he was the voice of England, loved and honored as a man and a poet, not simply by a few discerning critics, but by a whole people that do not easily give their allegiance to any one man. And that, for the present, is Tennyson's sufficient eulogy.

ROBERT BROWNING (1812-1889)

How good is man's life, the mere living! how fit to employ
All the heart and the soul and the senses for ever in joy!

In this new song of David, from Browning's Saul, we have a suggestion of the astonishing vigor and hope that characterize all the works of Browning, the one poet of the age who, after thirty years of continuous work, was finally recognized and placed beside Tennyson, and whom future ages may judge to be a greater poet,--perhaps, even, the greatest in our literature since Shakespeare.

The chief difficulty in reading Browning is the obscurity of his style, which the critics of half a century ago held up to ridicule. Their attitude towards the poet's early work may be inferred from Tennyson's humorous criticism of Sordello.

It may be remembered that the first line of this obscure poem is, "Who will may hear Sordello's story told"; and that the last line is, "Who would has heard Sordello's story told." Tennyson remarked that these were the only lines in the whole poem that he understood, and that they were evidently both lies. If we attempt to explain this obscurity, which puzzled Tennyson and many less friendly critics, we find that it has many sources. First, the poet's thought is often obscure, or else so extremely subtle that language expresses it imperfectly,--

Thoughts hardly to be packed
Into a narrow act,
Fancies that broke through language and escaped.

Second, Browning is led from one thing to another by his own mental associations, and forgets that the reader's associations may be of an entirely different kind. Third, Browning is careless in his English, and frequently clips his speech, giving us a series of ejaculations. As we do not quite understand his processes of thought, we must stop between the ejaculations to trace out the connections. Fourth, Browning's, allusions are often far-fetched, referring to some odd scrap of information which he has picked up in his wide reading, and the ordinary reader finds it difficult to trace and understand them. Finally, Browning wrote too much and revised too Little. The time which he should have given to making onc thought clear was used in expressing other thoughts that flitted through his head like a flock of swallows. His field was the individual soul, never exactly alike in any two men, and he sought to express the hidden motives and principles which govern individual action. In this field he is like a miner delving underground, sending up masses of mingled earth and ore; and the reader must sift all this material to separate the gold from the dross.

Here, certainly, are sufficient reasons for Browning's obscurity; and we must add the word that the fault seems unpardonable, for the simple reason that Browning shows himself capable, at times, of writing directly, melodiously, and with noble simplicity.

So much for the faults, which must be faced and overlooked before one finds the treasure that is hidden in Browning's poetry. Of all the poets in our literature, no other is so completely, so consciously, so magnificently a teacher of men. He feels his mission of faith and courage in a world of doubt and timidity. For thirty years he faced indifference or ridicule, working bravely and cheerfully the while, until he made the world recognize and follow him. The spirit of his whole life is well expressed in his Paracelsus, written when he was only twenty-two years old:

I see my way as birds their trackless way.
I shall arrive,--what time, what circuit first,
I ask not; but unless God send his hail
Or blinding fire-balls, sleet or stifling snow,
In some time, his good time, I shall arrive;
He guides me and the bird. In his good time.

He is not, like so many others, an entertaining poet. One cannot read him after dinner, or when settled in a comfortable easy-chair. One must sit up, and think, and be alert when he reads Browning.

If we accept these conditions, we shall probably find that Browning is the most stimulating poet in our language. His influence upon our life is positive and tremendous. His strength, his joy of life, his robust faith, and his invincible optimism enter into us, making us different and better men after reading him. And perhaps the best thing he can say of Browning is that his thought is slowly but surely taking possession of all well-educated men and women.

Life

Browning's father was outwardly a business man, a clerk for fifty years in the Bank of England; inwardly he was an interesting combination of the scholar and the artist, with the best tastes of both. His mother was a sensitive, musical woman, evidently very lovely in character, the daughter of a German shipowner and merchant who had settled in Scotland. She was of Celtic descent, and Carlyle describes her as the true type of a Scottish gentlewoman. From his neck down, Browning was the typical Briton,--short, stocky, large-chested, robust; but even in the lifeless portrait his face changes as we view it from different angles. Now it is like an English business man, now like a German scientist, and now it has a curious suggestion of Uncle Remus,--these being, no doubt, so many different reflections of his mixed and unremembered ancestors.

He was born in Camberwell, on the outskirts of London, in 1812. From his home and from his first school, at Peckham, he could see London; and the city lights by night and the smoky chimneys by day had the same powerful fascination for the child that the woods and fields and the beautiful country had for his friend Tennyson. His schooling was short and desultory, his education being attended to by private tutors and by his father, who left the boy largely to follow his own inclination. Like the young Milton, Browning was fond of music, and in many of his poems, especially in "Abt Vogler" and

"A Toccata of Galuppi's," he interprets the musical temperament better, perhaps, than any other writer in our literature. But unlike Milton, through whose poetry there runs a great melody, music seems to have had no consistent effect upon his verse, which is often so jarring that one must wonder how a musical ear could have endured it.

Like Tennyson, this boy found his work very early, and for fifty years hardly a week passed that he did not write poetry. He began at six to produce verses, in imitation of Byron; but fortunately this early work has been lost. Then he fell under the influence of Shelley, and his first known work, Pauline (1833), must be considered as a tribute to Shelley and his poetry. Tennyson's earliest work, Poems by Two Brothers, had been published and well paid for, five years before; but Browning could find no publisher who would even consider Pauline, and the work was published by means of money furnished by an indulgent relative. This poem received scant notice from the reviewers, who had pounced like hawks on a dovecote upon Tennyson's first two modest volumes.

Two years later appeared Paracelsus, and then his tragedy Strafford was put upon the stage; but not till Sordello was published, in 1840, did he attract attention enough to be denounced for the obscurity and vagaries of his style. Six years later, in 1846, he suddenly became famous, not because he finished in that year his Bells and Pomegranates (which is Browning's symbolic name for "poetry and thought" or "singing and sermonizing"), but because he eloped with the best known literary woman in England, Elizabeth Barrett, whose fame was for many years, both before and after her marriage, much greater than Browning's, and who was at first considered superior to Tennyson. Thereafter, until his own work compelled attention, he was known chiefly as the man who married Elizabeth Barrett. For years this lady had been an almost helpless invalid, and it seemed a quixotic thing when Browning, having failed to gain her family's consent to the marriage, carried her off romantically. Love and Italy proved better than her physicians, and for fifteen years Browning and his wife lived an ideally happy life in Pisa and in Florence. The exquisite romance of their love is preserved in Mrs. Browning's Sonnets from the Portuguese, and in the volume of Letters recently published,--wonderful letters, but so tender and intimate that it seems almost a sacrilege for inquisitive eyes to read them.

Mrs. Browning died in Florence in 1861. The loss seemed at first too much to bear, and Browning fled with his son to England. For the remainder of his life he lived alternately in London and in various parts of Italy, especially at the Palazzo Rezzonico, in Venice, which is now an object of pilgrimage to almost every tourist who visits the beautiful city. Wherever he went he mingled with men and women, sociable, well dressed, courteous, loving crowds and popular applause, the very reverse of his friend Tennyson. His earlier work had been much better appreciated in America than in England; but with the publication of The Ring and the Book, in 1868, he was at last recognized by his countrymen as one of the greatest of English poets. He died in Venice, on December 12, 1889, the same day that saw the publication of his last work, Asolando. Though Italy offered him an honored resting place, England claimed him for her own, and he lies buried beside Tennyson in Westminster Abbey. The spirit of his whole life is magnificently expressed in his own lines, in the Epilogue of his last book:

One who never turned his back, but marched breast forward,
Never doubted clouds would break,
Never dreamed, tho' right were worsted, wrong would triumph,
Held we fall to rise, are baffled to fight better,
Sleep to wake.

Bibliography

Abercrombie, D.: *Elements of General Ponetics*, Edinburgh, Edinburgh University Press, 1967.

Adams, Robert M., *The Land and Literature of England: A Historical Account*. New York: Norton, 1983.

Ailsby, Christopher: *Roll of Infamy*, Osceola, MBI, 1997.

Barter, James: *The Ganges*, San Diego, Lucent Books, 2003.

Bateson, F. W. *A Guide to English Literature.* Chicago: Aldine, 1965.

Baugh, Albert C.: *A Literary History of England.* 1967. 4 vols. London: Routledge, 1977.

Brian, L. : *Uniforms and Insignia of the Luftwaffe*, London, Arms and Armor, 1999.

Burgess, Anthony. *English Literature.* London: Longman, 1958.

Bush, Douglas: *English Literature in the Earlier Seventeenth Century, 1600-1660*, Oxford, Clarendon Press, 1962.

Cahalan, M.: *The Irish Novel: a Critical History*, Boston, Twayne Publishers, 1988.

Coulton, G. G.: *Chaucer and His England.* Kessinger Publishing, 2006.

Courthope, John: *A History of English Poetry*, London, MacMillan and Co., 1903.

Cox, Michael. *The Concise Oxford Chronology of English Literature.* Oxford: Oxford UP, 2004.

Crane, Salmon: *A Census of British Newspapers and Periodicals, 1620-1800*, London, Cambridge University Press, 1927.

Crystal, D.: *Prosodic Systems and Intonation in English*, Cambridge, Cambridge University Press, 1969.

Douglas, B.: *English Literature in the Earlier Seventeenth Century, 1600-1660*, Oxford, Clarendon Press, 1962.

Dupuy, N.: *The Compact History of the Revolutionary War*, New York, Hawthorn Books, 1963.

Eades, B.: *The Jacobean and Caroline Stage*, Oxford, Clarendon Press, 1941.

Eaglestone, Robert. *Doing English: A Guide for Literature Students.* London: Routledge, 1999.

Ferrence, G.: *Deadly Fashion: the Rise and Fall of Cigarette Smoking in North America*, New York, Garland, 1989.

Florette, Henri: *Kings Mountain*, Garden City, Doubleday, 1950.

Garrison, Webb: *Great Stories of the American Revolution*, Nashville, Rutledge Hill Press, 1990.

Gerald, Eades: *The Jacobean and Caroline Stage*, Oxford, Clarendon Press, 1941.

Gilbert, A. J. *Literary Language from Chaucer to Johnson.* London: Macmillan. 1979.

Gilmer, Moss: *The Patriots of Kings Mountain*, Blacksburg, Scotia-Hubernia, 1990.

Hopper, Vincent Foster: *Chaucer's Canterbury Tales (Selected): An Interlinear Translation*, Barron's Educational Series, 1970.

Horsman, E. A.: *The Victorian Novel*, Oxford, Clarendon Press, 1990.

Hudson, William Henry. *An Outline History of English Literature.* London: Bell, 1932.

John, S.: *This Destructive War: The British Campaign in the Carolinas, 1780-1782*, University of Alabama Press, 1985.

Knowles, G.: *Patterns of Spoken English: An Introduction to English Phonetics*, London, Longman, 1987.

Koehl, Lewis: *The Black Corps*, Madison, University of Wisconsin Press, 1983.

Last, R. W.: *Affinities. Essays in German & English Literature [for] Oswald Wolff.* Wolff, 1971.

Laver, J.: *Principles of Phonetics*, Cambridge, Cambridge University Press, 1994.

Moss, B.: *The Patriots of Kings Mountain*, Blacksburg, Scotia-Hubernia, 1990.

Naipaul, V.S. : *A House for Mr. Biswas: With an Introduction by Ian Buruma*, New Delhi, Penguin, 1992.

Nath, Narendra: *Indian Religious Historiography*, New Delhi, Munshiram Manoharlal Publishers, 1996.

Neil Bissoondath: *Indo-Caribbean-Canadian Diaspora*, New Delhi, Rawat, 2005.

Pierre, Turner: *Uniforms and Insignia of the Luftwaffe*, London, Arms and Armor, 1999.

Rahilly, J.: *Phonetics: The Science of Speech*, London, Arnold, 1999.

Raja Rao: *The Fictionist*, Delhi, B.R. Publishing, 2003.

Sage, Lorna, ed. *The Cambridge Guide to Women's Writing in English.* Cambridge: Cambridge UP, 1999.

Saintsbury, George. *A Short History of English Literature.* 1898. New York: Macmillan, 1907.

Salman Rushdie: *New Critical Insights*, New Delhi, Atlantic Pub., 2003.

Sydney, J.: *Brands, Consumers, Symbols and Research*, Thousand Oaks, Sage Publications, 1999.

Terence, P.: *The Later Jacobean and Caroline Dramatists*, Lincoln, University of Nebraska Press, 1978.

Texts, Issues: *Essays on Indian Literature*, Delhi, Pencraft International, 2003.

Vann, J. : *Victorian Novels in Serial*, New York, Modern Language Association of America, 1985.

Walter, Ernst: *The English Novel: a Short Critical History*, London: Phoenix House, 1954.

White, Keogh: *The Kings Mountain Men: The Story of the Battle with Sketches of the American Soldiers Who Took Part*, Baltimore, General Publishing Company, 1966.

Wyatt, A. J. *The Tutorial History of English Literature.* 2nd ed. London: Clive, 1901.

Yeats, W.B. : *Poetry and Plays*, New Delhi, Atlantic, 2002.

Yonah, A.: *Combating Terrorism: Strategies of Ten Countries*, Mich., University of Michigan Press, 2002.

Index

❑❑❑